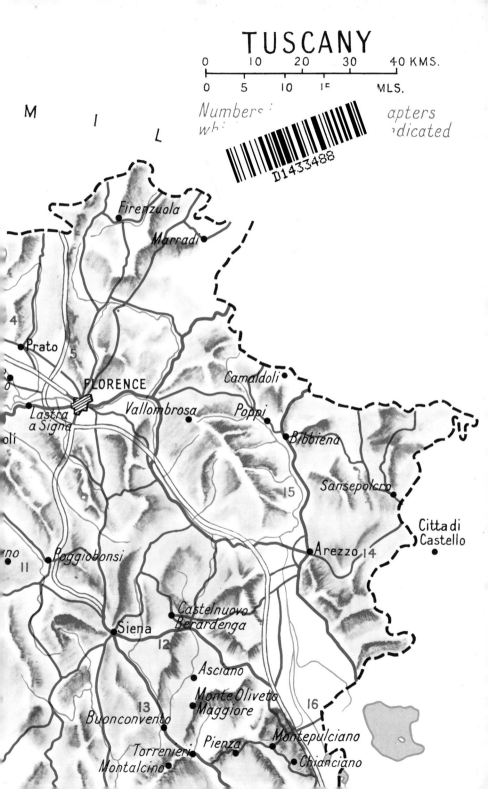

TUSCANY

| 0 | 10 | 20 | 30 | 40 KMS. |
| 0 | 5 | 10 | 1̅5̅ | MLS. |

Numbers ... apters
wh... dicated

M   I   L

Firenzuola

Marradi

4

Prato

5

FLORENCE

Camaldoli

Vallombrosa

Poppi

Lastra
a Signa

Bibbiena

oli

Sansepolcro

15

Poggibonsi

Arezzo 14

Citta di
Castello

no

11

Castelnuovo
Berardenga

Siena

12

Asciano

Monte Oliveto
Maggiore

16

13

Buonconvento

Pienza

Montepulciano

Torrenieri

Montalcino

Chianciano

THE COMPANION GUIDE TO
Tuscany

THE COMPANION GUIDES

GENERAL EDITOR: VINCENT CRONIN

*It is the aim of these Guides to provide a
Companion, in the person of the author,
who knows intimately the places and
people of whom he writes, and is able to
communicate this knowledge and affection
to his readers. It is hoped that the text
and pictures will aid them in their prep-
arations and in their travels, and will help
them to remember on their return*

THE COMPANION GUIDE TO

TUSCANY

ARCHIBALD LYALL

Collins
ST JAMES'S PLACE, LONDON
1973

Maps by Charles Green

© *Archibald Lyall 1973*
ISBN 0 00 211131 4
Printed in Great Britain
Collins Clear-Type Press
London and Glasgow

Contents

Illustrations

CHAPTER 1

Historical Introduction

CHAPTER 1

Historical Introduction

While it might be long debated whether Tuscany or Umbria is the noblest region of Italy, few except some jealous Venetian or Neapolitan would deny the primacy to the two neighbours taken together. In many ways Tuscany, which is roughly heart-shaped itself, is, with Umbria, the real heartland of Italy—a heart as much from the geographical point of view as from the artistic, literary and linguistic. It links the peninsula proper, which is an up-ended oblong, with the northern regions which lie horizontally across it. It is the topmost piece of the upright of the T which symbolises the map of Italy. If one ignores the two peninsulas in the far south, Tuscany and Umbria form the geographical centre of the country. Unless he sticks all the way to the narrow corridor along the Adriatic coast, the traveller between north and south is bound to pass through this area, now as in ancient times.

Tuscany is a 'Region' and is divided into the nine provinces of Florence, Leghorn, Siena, Pisa, Pistoia, Lucca, Arezzo, Massa-Carrara and Grosseto. A Region in Italy is a historical conception, while a Province is a modern administrative unit. Lying in the centre of the Apennine tangle, Tuscany is three-fifths hill-country and one-tenth plain, mostly along the lower valleys of the Arno, the Ombrone and the Chiana. The remainder is officially classed as mountainous, for although the only really high mountain is the extinct volcano of Monte Amiata at nearly six thousand feet Tuscany is enfolded on the

11

north and east by the main chain of the Apennines, which curves round her like a long protecting arm bent to shield her from the Alpine winds. On the west her border is the Tyrrhenian Sea, for many centuries her principal outlet on the world.

Apart from its nearly perfect geographical unity, Tuscany has a historical and racial unity, shared with Western Umbria and Northern Latium, as the homeland of one of the most remarkable races of ancient Europe, **the Etruscans.** We of Western Christendom derive our civilisation, over and above what we have inherited from our own rude forefathers, from three main outside sources, Rome, Greece and Israel. That we all know well enough but what we seldom realise is that 'Roman' culture is very largely Etruscan in origin.[1] Rome was on the edge of Etruscan territory, where it bordered the lands of the Latins and the Sabines and for a century it was ruled by a dynasty of Etruscan kings, the Tarquins. The civilisation of the Etruscans was higher than that of their Latin and Sabine neighbours and it was readily absorbed by the Romans, who passed it on to us.

From the cities of Etruria proper the Etruscans expanded northwards to the Po, founding the cities of Bologna and Modena and the Adriatic port of Spina; southwards they overran Rome and Latium and spread into Campania, where they founded Capua and were only halted by the Greeks of Cumae. The root of their name is Turs, and the Greeks called them Tyrrhenoi, a name which survives in the Tyrrhenian Sea. The Romans called them Etrusci and their land Etruria, which has come down to us, through the medieval form Tuscia, as Toscana or Tuscany.

The origin of the Etruscans is still a matter of dispute among scholars. Some consider them immigrants from north of the Alps because originally they used to cremate their dead, while

[1]When a lady tells you she left her maisonette to go the cinema and was shown to her seat by a charming usherette, she little guesses that she is employing the Etruscan suffix *-ita*, and if she saw a film of the Coronation she would be equally surprised to learn that the crown and the orb were also of Etruscan origin.

others with more reason follow Herodotus in tracing them to Asia Minor. The recent tentative identification of their language with Albania, the ancient Illyrian, which is the oldest surviving tongue in south-eastern Europe, would seem to confirm the view of Dionysus of Halicarnassus that they were the aboriginal inhabitants of the land, the heirs of the Iron Age Villanovian culture of the eighth and ninth centuries BC, which has left many remains in Tuscany and Emilia. (The Villanovians also practised urn burial.) If that is so, the Etruscans attained rapidly to civilisation and soon Etruria was transformed from the scattered hamlets of the Villanovians into a land of flourishing walled cities, formed into a powerful confederation. Their twelve principal cities, which included some of the largest in the ancient Mediterranean, composed the Etruscan League. Each was ruled by a priest-king or 'lucumon.' The head of the league at the time of the wars against Rome in the sixth century BC was Lars Porsenna of Clusium (the modern Chiusi), celebrated by Macaulay in his *Lays of Ancient Rome*. If they could be said to have a capital it was at Volsinii (Bolsena), which was their chief religious centre.

The really intriguing mystery about the Etruscans, however, is less their origin than their language, for if one knew that one would know where they came from. Little is known of it except that it is pre-Indoeuropean, although affinities have been traced with Illyrian and with a Pelasgian dialect of Lemnos. The Etruscans used an adaptation of the Greek alphabet; their language is therefore easy enough to read but to translate it is another matter—until and unless a Rosetta Stone is discovered. Some words and sentences occur so frequently in votive, funerary and similar inscriptions that scholars have been able to compile a vocabulary of several hundred words. Further than that they have not penetrated the code. If the Etruscans had any written literature, it has not come down to us.

The most interesting, perhaps, of the Etruscan works of art which have survived are the vivid and beautiful tomb-paintings of Tarquinia, but there is also some very fine plastic art such as the statues from Veii in the Villa Giulia in Rome and the Winged Horses in the Museum at Tarquinia. The pottery and bronzes tend to be either rather crude if of native inspiration or else very skilful imitations of the Greek. Most of the best 'Etruscan' vases were in fact imported from Greece in exchange for the iron and other mineral exports of Etruria.

In many ways the debt of the Etruscans to the Greeks was at least as great as that of the Romans to the Etruscans. They owed their art and their alphabet to them and they worshipped the twelve great gods of Hellas with a few local additions of their own. They were greatly addicted to omens and divination of all kinds, from the flight of birds to the entrails of sacrifices. They were intensely interested in a life after death and filled vast cemeteries with tombs containing decorated terra-cotta urns bearing portraits of the deceased, vases, jewels, bronzes, furniture, arms, food and anything else which could be of use to the dead man on his long journey. They were, it is hardly too much to say, obsessed with death or, to be more correct, with its absence, the continuance of life as it was on earth which, if the Tarquinia paintings are anything to go by, consisted largely of banqueting, dancing, flute-playing, hunting and fishing. For the Etruscans were a gay people who loved life so much that they could not bear to think of giving it up.

Originally the territory of the Umbrians, an Italic people, extended from the mouth of the Po to the Tyrrhenian coast but the Etruscans drove them east of the Tiber and erected their own cities on their lands. Comparatively little is known of the political, cultural and social development of the Umbrians who, apart from the Eugubine Tablets at Gubbio, have left us few remains.

Before long their Etruscan conquerors were compelled themselves to watch their territories contracting. The Greeks drove them from Campania, Hiero of Syracuse sank their fleet, and Latium revolted, while the Gauls conquered all their possessions north of the Apennines. Long and unsuccessful wars against the Romans finally forced the Etruscans and the

Umbrians to submit in the third century BC; remarkably, they remained loyal to Rome even through the invasion of Hannibal a few decades later. Very soon their cultures and languages disappeared and they became absorbed in the Roman system.

At the end of the third century AD Diocletian annexed Umbria to what he called Tuscia, but in the Dark Ages Tuscia became reduced to the present Tuscany, Umbria became part of the Lombard Duchy of Spoleto, and the southern region became detached when Italy was divided between the Lombards and the Byzantines, to become a part of Latium and later of the Papal States.

Tuscany shared the general misery of Italy in the Dark Ages, when marauding barbarians—Alemanni, Goths, Lombards and Franks—ravaged the countryside and fought continually against the Byzantines, who represented continuity with Rome. Umbria, as we have seen, became a Lombard principality, and Tuscany became another with its capital at Lucca. To the latter succeeded a Frankish County of Lucca, later to become the Marquisate of Tuscany. The period after the death of 'the Great Countess' Matilda in 1115, saw the rise of the Communes or free cities, who gradually threw off the yoke of the nobles and the bishops to establish some measure of popular government.

The quarrels between the communes, the bishops and the nobles were complicated by the centuries-long struggle between the Papacy and the Empire, which claimed northern and central Italy as part of Charlemagne's empire. In the upshot they were torn apart by the wars between the Guelphs, who supported the Pope, and the Ghibellines, who upheld the emperor. Florence was the centre of Guelph power in Tuscany and as a natural result her threatened rivals such as Siena, Arezzo and Pisa were Ghibelline, but nearly all the cities had both factions within their gates ready to rend them with their feuds. One party would win and would exile its opponents, who would lose no time in seeking outside aid to recover their power.

Peace and stability were not possible in such a situation. Inevitably one city after another fell to the expanding power of

15

Florence. Some, like San Gimignano, were so weary of perpetual civil strife that they voluntarily put themselves under the suzerainty of Florence for protection, while others resisted fiercely, such as Siena, which held out until 1555 and was only conquered by the Emperor Charles V. Meanwhile the Arno valley was a vast marsh with a few miserable, serf-tilled islands in it, the Serchio was chronically in flood and the Maremma was a desert on account of the malaria. The streets of the cities were infested with *bravi* and *sbirri* (read 'gunmen') in the pay of one lord (read 'gangster chief') or another, and the countryside with bandits and mercenaries.

The remarkable thing is that amidst all this Tuscany gave rise to a literary and artistic flowering unknown since Periclean Greece and sometimes called 'the Tuscan miracle.' An exiled Ghibelline from Florence, Dante Alighieri, chose the vulgar speech of Tuscany in which to write his great epic poem and it is thanks to *The Divine Comedy* that Tuscan became the literary language of Italy.[1]

In Pisa a striking new local architecture developed out of the Lombardic Romanesque style, while Giovanni Pisano and his son Nicola revolutionised sculpture as a result of their studies of the antique sarcophagi in the Campo Santo. In Florence Cimabue and after him Giotto and his followers breathed new life into the dry bones of Byzantine painting, until it eventually took shape after several generations in the Ghirlandaios, the Pollaiuolos, the Lippis and Sandro Botticelli. In Siena Duccio di Buoninsegna, with his followers, Simone Martini, Lippo Memmi and the Lorenzetti brothers, were doing the same thing along more conservative lines. Florence turned for inspiration to Roman and Greek models, while Siena preferred to develop within the more formalised Gothic-Byzantine tradition.

Simultaneously with the revival of the arts came a revival of

---

[1]The best Italian is considered still to be the Tuscan—'*lingua toscana in bocca romana*,' as the saying goes But beware of copying one very odd peculiarity in the Tuscan dialect, the aspiration of the hard c so that it is pronounced like a guttural h. Your maid will ask you for '*la hiave della hamera*' and you will hear people go into a 'hafé' and order a '*Hoha-Hola.*'

St Martin, patron of the Duomo at Lucca, sharing his cloak with a beggar at Amiens. The saint's expression, his natural seat on the horse, and the head and neck of the horse itself make it one of the finest examples of 13th century Italian sculpture.

Farmland to the North-west of Lucca.

classical learning and Greek philosophy and a new spirit of free thought and free inquiry. Taken as a whole these movements were known as the Renaissance or Rebirth, which spread all over Europe but which originated in and long drew its vital force from Tuscany. Seeing that this great artistic revival was centred on Florence, which is outside the scope of this book, it will be more convenient to deal with the artists of the various cities as we come to them rather than attempt an outline of the movement as a whole—which, without Florence, would be to write *Hamlet* without the Prince of Denmark and, with Florence, would merely duplicate another volume in this series. Suffice it to say that many of the greatest Florentine artists were drawn to the capital from other parts of Tuscany. Thus Masaccio, Paolo Uccello, Sansovino and Michelangelo all came from the neighbourhood of Arezzo.

Volterra, Pistoia and Arezzo had already yielded to Florence and with the conquest of Pisa in 1406 she ruled all Tuscany except Siena and Lucca. Siena was to fall after a stubborn resistance in 1555 and Lucca alone preserved its independence until the nineteenth century. In 1434 the oligarchy which ruled Florence had been forced to give way to the Medici, under whom she reached her greatest heights and who, with two brief interruptions, were to rule Tuscany for another three centuries. In 1570 Cosimo de' Medici was granted by the Pope the title of Grand Duke of Tuscany. He has some right to be called the true founder of the state, who unified the mutually suspicious cities, ruthlessly but without favouritism, and welded them into a Tuscany. After the brief reign of Francesco I, his brother Ferdinando I played a real part in international politics, supporting Henri IV of France in order to prevent the Spaniards from subjugating all Italy. He it was who developed Leghorn as the port of Tuscany. After him the Medici became ever feebler and finally, with Giangastone, became extinct in 1737.

Upon the death of the last of the Medici the Grand Duchy passed to Francis Stephen of Lorraine, husband of the Empress Maria Theresa. The dynasty of Lorraine was active in the improvement of the Tuscan economy and the draining of the malarial marshes of the Maremma. Expelled by Napoleon, it was restored in 1815 and, though mild and liberal in comparison with most of the other Italian rulers, the Grand Duke Leopold II was finally driven out on a wave of nationalism in 1859. The following year Tuscany voted its annexation to Victor Emmanuel's Piedmont. Henceforth its history, like that of Umbria, is merged in the history of the Kingdom of Italy.

CHAPTER 2

Massa and the Versilia

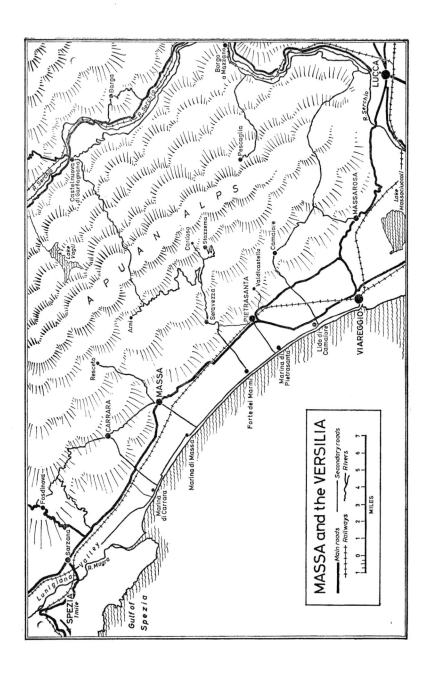

MASSA and the VERSILIA

Main roads — Secondary roads — Railways +++++ Rivers

MILES
1 0 1 2 3 4 5 6 7

LUCCA

Borgo a Mozzano

Barga

R. Serchio

Pescaglia

MASSAROSA

Castelnuovo di Garfagnana

Lake Vagli

Cardoso

Stazzema

A P U A N   A L P S

Camaiore

Valdicastello

Lido di Camaiore

VIAREGGIO

Lake Massaciuccoli

Seravezza

PIETRASANTA

Arni

Marina di Pietrasanta

Reseto

MASSA

Forte del Marmi

Marina di Massa

CARRARA

Fosdinova

Marina di Carrara

Sarzana

SPEZIA

1mile

Lunigiana Valley

R. Magra

Gulf of Spezia

CHAPTER 2

Massa and the Versilia

The natural approach to Tuscany from England or from France is by way of Genoa and the Ligurian coast, which are traversed both by the great modern international expresses and by the ancient Aurelian Way, whose official designation of Strada Statale No. I establishes it beyond dispute as the principal highroad of Italy. When they emerge from the mountains which shut off the Gulf of Spezia on the north, both road and railway penetrate swiftly into the heart of Tuscany by way of the Versilia, the corridor which runs between the sea and the Apennines.[1]

They cross a small river called the Magra, Dante's

> *Macra che, per cammin corto,*
> *Lo genovese parte del toscano*

and enter Tuscany near **Sarzana,** where the humanist Pope Nicholas V was born and where Castruccio Castracani, the warlord of Lucca, built himself a great stronghold in the fourteenth century. In the Middle Ages Sarzana was known as Luna Nuova, not after the new moon but because the site of the ancient city of Luna lay close by near the mouth of the Magra. To-day nothing but a ruined amphitheatre remains of the place which Livy called 'the first city of Etruria' and whose harbour was described by Strabo as one of the finest and largest in the world.

At Sarzana the Via Aurelia is joined by another strategic road,

[1]Administratively, the northern half of the 'panhandle' constitutes the Province of Massa, while the southern, the Versilia itself, is in Lucca.

the Via Francigena which runs over the Cisa Pass from Parma through Pontremoli and down the many-castled Lunigiana Valley. This, one of the great medieval roads of Europe, was so called because it was the highway which brought the Franks and all the other Northern barbarians, from the Lombards down to Charles VIII of France, to the sack of Central Italy. Farther on, it leads through Siena directly down to Rome and usurps the name of the Roman Via Cassia, which used to run some thirty miles east of Siena until eventually it petered out in the swamps of the Val di Chiana when that stretch became waterlogged in the Middle Ages. The new motor road, the Strada del Sole, roughly follows its line to Rome.

The southward-bound traveller will pass first through the little town of **Massa** which, with the neighbouring Carrara, survived as an independent duchy under the dynasty of Cibo Malaspina, right down to the nineteenth century. The Palazzo Malaspina, a long *sang de boeuf* building now the Prefecture, is in the Piazza Aranci, to the east of the Piazza Puccini on the main road, and a little farther on, down the Via Dante, is the Duomo, which is likewise of little interest. The town is dominated by La Rocca,[1] the elegant Renaissance castle of the Dukes, which has been recently restored.

I sometimes feel that this long straight avenue between the blue sea and the white-capped mountains should be lined with stone lions or sphinxes, for it forms the most magnificent imaginable approach to the enchanted land of Tuscany. Inland, like a stark backcloth to the lush green plain, rise the jagged six thousand foot ridges of the **Apuan Alps,** gashed here and there with livid scars, which yield the snow-white Carrara, the most famous marble in the world. Michelangelo came up to Carrara to choose the marble for his sculptures, and in our own day Mr. Betjeman writes of the 'soaked Carrara-covered earth' of Highgate Cemetery, London. The mountains, harsh, precipitous and bare, are truly Alpine in character, quite different from the rounded, wooded Apennines. They derive their name from a

[1] A *rocca* is a ruined castle, while a *castello* is a walled village or hamlet.

local Ligurian tribe, the Apuans. Although on the map they may appear well provided with communications, they are in fact better suited to the walker or the climber than to the motorist, for many of the steep roads were built only to serve the high quarries and are deeply cut up by their heavy loads of marble. The mountains have for many centuries been hollowed out and hacked about by man until they have assumed fantastic Dantesque shapes. An excellent guide to them is published by the Italian Alpine Club (C.I.A.) under the title of *Guida delle Alpe Apuane.*

There is a fourteenth-century arcaded cathedral at Carrara but more rewarding (and on the main road) is the capital of the Versilia, **Pietrasanta**, which is built round a medieval piazza bordered by two Gothic churches and a town hall. The Cathedral is rich in examples of the work of the early sixteenth-century Versilian sculptor Stagio Stagi. The poet Carducci was born at Valdicastello in the Commune of Pietrasanta.

Seaward of the Via Aurelia and parallel to it a dreary road runs for twelve miles between pine-shrouded villas on the one side and sternly wired-off bathing beaches on the other. Depressing as this unbroken line of small seaside resorts may appear to the foreigner, the Riviera della Versilia is crowded with Italians in the short months of summer—Marina di Carrara at the northern extremity, Marina di Massa, the fashionable Forte dei Marmi, Marina di Pietrasanta, Lido di Camaiore. At the southern end **Viareggio,** a town of some forty thousand people, possesses a little river which once served as the port of the otherwise landlocked Republic of Lucca. It is still a considerable fishing port and on account of its mild climate, its shelving sandy beach and very expensive publicity, is frequented by what the local tourist brochure, blandly ignoring the contradiction in terms, calls a *vastissima e distintissima clientela.*

It was on the still desolate shore about a mile north of Viareggio that Shelley's body was washed up on 17th July, 1822. Nine days earlier he had been drowned when his little sailing boat was swamped by a sudden squall in the Gulf of Spezia many miles

23

away to the north. As a precaution against the plague, the law of Tuscany required that all bodies cast up by the sea should be burnt on the spot. Accompanied by Byron and Leigh Hunt, his friend Trelawney therefore built an iron furnace on the sands and solemnly burnt the poet's body to the ancient Greek accompaniment of wine, frankincense, salt and oil. One can only guess at some possible connection with the nine days' immersion in the sea, but whatever the reason Shelley's heart remained unconsumed and Trelawney burnt his hand when he broke the sanitary regulations of the Grand Duchy and snatched it from the flames.

CHAPTER 3

Lucca

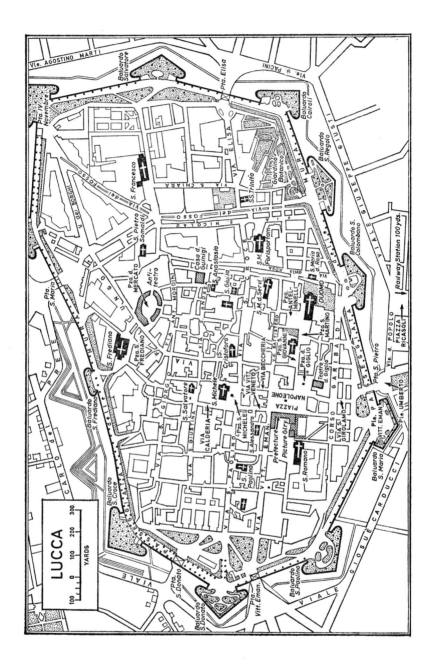

CHAPTER 3

Lucca

From Viareggio the Via Aurelia runs southwards through the forest of Migliarino to Pisa, while another road leads due east to **Lucca.** Apart from the minuscule Duchy of Massa, which was absorbed by Modena, the state of Lucca was the only one in Tuscany to preserve its independence from Florentine aggression until the last century. From 1556 onward it was an oligarchic republic on the lines of Venice and Ragusa but in 1805 Napoleon turned it into a principality and bestowed it upon his sister, Elisa Baciocchi. She ruled it with the efficiency which might be expected from the sister of Napoleon and from the lady whose intelligent face looks at us from Marie Benoist's canvas in what was once her palace. The little state, it is somewhat surprising to learn, was formally annexed to the Grand Duchy of Tuscany only in 1847.

Lucca, although one of the most interesting and delightful cities in Italy, has, in the century and more since Bagni di Lucca fell out of fashion, been relatively little visited and so has remained unspoilt. She owes her good fortune to the fact that she was on neither the main road nor the railway to Florence, Pisa and Rome. Her seclusion, however, may well be considered as ended with the building of the Strada del Mare, which now carries motorists between the Via Aurelia and Florence by way of Lucca, Pistoia and Prato.

Shielded from the sight of her rival, Pisa, by a low range of

27

hills, Lucca lies in a broad and fertile basin on the left bank of the Serchio, which flows down through wooded ravines from the bare heights of the Apennines. The Garfagnana, as its upper valley is known, is ideal for walking and climbing. Barga, with its thirteenth-century cathedral and its magnificent views, is the acknowledged gem of this region. Some fifteen miles up the river from Lucca **Borgo a Mozzano** is now a place of pilgrimage for those interested in technical assistance. This commune of 9000 inhabitants was the scene of an experiment initiated by Shell Italiana to raise the quantity and quality of agricultural production, reduce costs and introduce new activities. In the five years from 1955 the farmers' incomes increased over a hundredfold. The object was to help them to help themselves. Now Borgo is the seat of a technical assistance training centre providing courses for specialists from all over the world.

Just beyond Borgo is the well-known spa of **Bagni di Lucca,** which consists of the three adjoining villages of Ponte a Serraglio, Bagni alla Villa and Bagni Caldi, embowered among chestnut woods. Augustus Hare in the mid-Victorian period could still describe Bagni di Lucca as 'the favourite summer residence of strangers in Italy.' Its more recent foreign visitors had included Byron, Shelley, Heine, Lamartine and Elizabeth Browning. Centuries earlier, Montaigne had said that after he had tried half the watering places of Europe Bagni di Lucca alone had given him back his health. Readers of Webster will recall several references to 'the baths of Lucca' in *The Duchess of Malfi.* It possessed a theatre and an elegant club. In Hare's day there was still an English church with a resident chaplain at La Villa. Now the Bagni have a rather faded air, although there are some handsome Empire buildings and beautiful public gardens.

If foreigners no longer flock to the elegant spa, known for its waters since the Middle Ages but in its present form largely the creation of Elisa Baciocchi, they have nevertheless begun to discover the beauties of the countryside round Lucca (where

they can live so much cheaper than in Florence) and more
English families will doubtless follow those who have recently
settled in the Lucchesia. In the neighbourhood, too, are a
number of beautiful villas, the country houses of the Lucchese
'patricians,' the only title which the nobles of the oligarchy
would permit themselves, such as the Villa at Marlia, restored
and embellished by Elisa Baciocchi, and the sixteenth-century
Villa Mansi at Segromigno, which was transformed in the
eighteenth-century by Filippo Juvara, the great architect who
created Turin.

After the fall of Rome Lucca was first the Gothic and later
the Lombard capital of Tuscany, *caput Tusciae*, and even if she
lost the primacy later to Florence, her flourishing silk and woollen
industries, her banking and her mint, ensured her continuance
as a powerful and prosperous city. Her walls were three times
expanded and those of the sixteenth century (begun in the fifteenth) survive intact to this day. Their broad top forms a sort of
hanging garden, a shaded two-way car or coach-and-four promenade four kilometres round. The views therefrom are equally
fine whether one looks outwards over the rich countryside to the
mountains or inwards over the churches, belfries, palaces and
piazzas. The best of all, I think, is from the Baluardo di San
Frediano, which overlooks the seventeenth-century Villa Pfan-
ner, formerly Controni, with its pool, its flowering shrubs and
its rows of statues, opening onto a handsome outside staircase.[1]

Lucca has also kept her four great gates through which alone
she can be entered. Passing under the menacing teeth of the
portcullis of the Porta S. Pietro from the Viareggio-Florence
road or from the railway station and following the Via S.

[1]The eighteenth-century poet, Fra Puccini da Casoli, wrote of Lucca:

> *Nella Toscana in mezzo a una pianura*
> *Cinta da spalti, e fosse di bell'arte*
> *Con intorno colline di verdura*
> *Ed amene montagne da ogni parte*
> *Giace vaga città con forti mura,*
> *Ch'Ercole, o Polifemo, o il fiero Marte*
> *Minacciar non potrebbono e si appella*
> *Lucca gentile popolata e bella.*

Girolamo one soon arrives at the Piazza Puccini,[1] better known as the **Piazza del Giglio,** the Square of the Lily, from the neo-classical theatre on one side of it. On the corner facing one is the Hotel Universo which still, after eighty years, lives up to Augustus Hare's description of it as 'most excellent and reasonable.' The Piazza del Giglio is the obvious base from which to explore Lucca. It is central, there are shady sidewalk cafés, and the Universo has an excellent restaurant itself, while the Ristorante del Giglio next door is another.

On the west side of the Piazza del Giglio opens the vast Piazza Napoleone and on the east, running into one another, are the Piazza S. Giovanni, the Piazza S. Martino and the Piazza Antelminelli, which is called after the noble family whose palace once stood there. Its most famous scion was Castruccio Castracani, who in a short time extended the dominion of Lucca over Pistoia, Volterra and Sarzana. In 1325 he was confronted by the combined armies of the Guelph coalition at Altopascio. In the ensuing victory he took fifteen thousand prisoners and captured the *carroccio*, the war chariot which bore the standard of Florence and which he brought back in triumph to Lucca. It is typical of his flamboyant character that the captives were loaded with silver chains and given a banquet in the Piazza before being sent off to prison. As a military genius Macchiavelli rated him higher than Scipio or Philip of Macedon and had he not died of malaria three years later he would probably have conquered and unified all Tuscany. So dependent, however, were these city-states upon Carlyle's 'Hero' and so little concerned with the economic forces later to be formulated by Karl Marx that within fourteen years of Castruccio's death Lucca had lost her independence and fallen under the rule of Pisa.

As one walks into the Piazzas, one's eye, first caught by S. Giovanni on the left (with a fine west portal and some traces of the original Roman building), is very swiftly diverted and dazzled by the fantastic façade of **the Duomo** directly ahead of one.

[1]The musicians Puccini, Catalani and Boccherini were all natives of Lucca. The fourth Tuscan composer, Mascagni, was a Leghorn man.

The original church is said to have been founded by S. Frediano or Frigidianus, a far-wandering Galway man who became Bishop of Lucca in the sixth century, but the oldest part of the existing cathedral is this façade, the work of one Guidectus or Guidetto da Como, whose signature, with the date 1204, is to be seen near the base of the last column on the right of the first of the three rows of arcades. It is in a Romanesque style peculiar to Lucca— and only to two or three churches in Lucca. On a more or less conventional Pisan-Lombardic arcaded façade Guidetto has superimposed wild fantasies which might have come out of the medieval bestiaries.

The lower part of the white marble front consists of three round arches opening on to a deep porch, atrium, narthex or pronaos. The group on the pillar to the right of the central arch, which shows St Martin, the patron of the Cathedral, sharing his cloak with a beggar at Amiens, is a copy of the original which, for protection against the weather, has been removed to the interior entrance wall. Noting the expression of the saint, his natural seat on his horse, and the head and neck of the horse itself (while tactfully ignoring the legs) one cannot but rank it among the finest examples of thirteenth-century Italian sculpture. It is thought by some to be the work of Guidetto himself. The three upper tiers of arcades are the medium for some of the gayest and most irresponsible fancies in stone to be found in Western Europe. Of the zigzagged, curlicued and inlaid columns of the arcades themselves there are hardly two alike. In the spandrels are scenes of combat and the chase, produced by inlaying a dark green stone into the white marble. Huntsmen with their horns, their hawks and their hounds chase stags and hares, bears and boars. There are fights between lions and dragons. In the corbel beneath the feet of St Martin's horse two dragons gambol and David wrestles with a bear.

These sculptures were not simply ornamentation nor yet mere reflections of the medieval passion for war and the chase. Like the paintings of Hieronymus Bosch or the illustrations in the bestiaries they were intended to symbolise the eternal struggle

31

between good and evil, between God and the Devil. They were a pictorial language evolved by men who believed that every created thing which surrounded a Christian, perpetually beset by temptations as he was on his hazardous journey from the cradle to the grave, was intended to help him to save, or to trap him into losing, his immortal soul. In a word, the whole material world was an allegory of the spiritual one. Thus the huntsman symbolises the preacher, and the spoils of the chase are the souls which he saves. The horn is his voice, which summons men to virtue. The baying hounds are his lesser clergy. The lion and the stag alike symbolise the proud man, the hare the voluptuary, the bear the cruel and avaricious man and the boar the glutton. Since the lion stands also for the faithful guardian of the Church, he is often shown fighting the dragon, who represents the powers of evil.

On the right is a handsome campanile, its lower stories of brownish stone and the upper ones of white marble. It antedates the façade and accounts for the latter's slight asymmetry. Notice how, as was usual with these high, square Romanesque belfries, the tower is lightened by the openings which increase in number from one in the lowest story, through two and three to four in the topmost.[1] Beside it, built of white marble below and red brick above, is the Casa dell' Opera del Duomo, the little museum which houses the Cathedral Treasury. It is worth a visit if only to see the masterpiece of fifteenth-century goldsmith's work which is known as the Cross of the Pisans because it was stolen by a trick from the people of the neighbouring city. The Micheletti Garden opposite lies behind a wall, the work of the Florentine Bartolomeo Ammannati which, crowned with greenery as it is and revealing the garden through grilled windows, Charles Morgan considered the most beautiful in Italy. Behind the garden rises the tiled cupola of the thirteenth-century Baptistery, which is reached through the north transept of S. Giovanni.

Entering the porch of the Duomo, we are confronted with some admirable sculpture, probably the work of Lombard

[1]Known in Italian as *monofore, bifore, trifore* and *quadrifore* respectively.

A figure from the pulpit in S. Andrea at Pistoia by Giovanni Pisano, c. 1300.

Salome dancing before Herod. Filippo Lippi's great fresco, painted between 1456 and 1466, decorates the chancel of the Duomo in Prato.

masters. In the tympanum over the central door is the Ascension of Christ, watched from below by the Madonna and Apostles. Over the right door is the African bishop Regulus preaching to the Arians and above it is the sequel, very simply and powerfully composed, his martyrdom at the hands of the soldiers of Totila. Over the left door is a Descent from The Cross. This is by Nicola Pisano (or certainly from his workshop), who is said to have learned the technique of carving in deep relief by studying the Roman sarcophagus which served as the coffin of the Countess Beatrice in the Campo Santo at Pisa.

On the walls between the doors are four scenes from the life of St Martin, and beneath them the figures of the twelve months which appear on so many of these medieval church doors. The scenes on the left-hand wall represent, above, Martin restoring to life one of his disciples in order that he might return to this world long enough to receive baptism and be saved, and, below, the saint being consecrated Bishop of Tours. On the right wall Martin, having given his tunic to a beggar on the way to church, reveals his bare arms when celebrating mass. Below, he drives out an evil spirit. The series of the months, with the twelve signs of the zodiac, runs from right to left and represents: January, a man seated before the fire; February, fishing with a rod and line; March, pruning the vines; April, gathering flowers; May, a young horseman bearing a rose to his love; June, reaping the corn; July, threshing; August, picking the fruit; September, treading the grapes; October, coopering the wine-barrels; November, ploughing the fields; December, killing a pig for Christmas.

The interior of the Cathedral, which was reconstructed in the fourteenth century and is thus much later than the façade, is noteworthy for one world-famous object of adoration and a number of excellent works of art. To take the pictures first, there is Tintoretto's Last Supper over the third altar in the right aisle, a good Virgin with Saints by Domenico Ghirlandaio in the Sacristy Chapel of S. Apollinare, just off the right aisle, and a very serene and lovely Madonna with SS. Stephen and John the Baptist by Fra Bartolomeo in the Chapel of the Sanctuary. Two cherubs hold a crown over her head while a third sits at her feet playing a lute. In the north aisle is a Presentation of Mary in the Temple by Bronzino.

Jacopo della Quercia, the sculptor who shortly afterwards was to create the Fonte Gaia in his native city of Siena, came to Lucca and has left his masterpiece here in the left transept of the Duomo. It is the cenotaph of Ilaria del Carretto, whom Gabriele d'Annunzio celebrated as 'the white fleur-de-lys.' She was the daughter of the Lord of Finalem and the young wife of Paolo Guinigi, who ruled Lucca as an enlightened despot from 1400 to 1430. On the top of her sarcophagus, which is surrounded by plump *putti* supporting swags of flowers, Ilaria lies in her long robe as though she were asleep with a lapdog at her feet, the symbol of fidelity. Many later Renaissance tombs were to be produced in this style, but it may well be wondered where, in 1408, Jacopo had seen such a work upon which to base his own, for there is nothing among Roman or Etruscan sarcophagi which might have served him as a model. It remains a wonderfully fresh, simple and sincere work of the very early Renaissance.

Lucca produced only two important artists in the course of her long history, the eighteenth-century painter Pompeo Batoni and the fifteenth-century sculptor Matteo Civitali. The Berlinghieri family, it is true, constituted a brilliant school of painting in the early thirteenth century but only the sons, Marco Bonaventura and Barone, were born in Lucca. Berlinghiero Berlinghieri, their father, came from Milan. He was a Lombard like Guidetto da Como, Guido Bigarelli, Biduino and others who worked in Lucca. Matteo Civitali, a pupil of Rossellino and Desiderio da Settignano, can only be studied here in his native city. There are single works by him in the Bargello at Florence and the Victoria and Albert Museum in London and several more in Genoa Cathedral, but that is almost all. The Duomo at Lucca, however, is full of examples of his work, all dating from the last thirty years of the fifteenth century; the pulpit; the majestic altar which forms the tomb of St Regulus in the chapel of that name; the monuments of Pietro da Noceto and Domenico Bertini in the south transept; and the two adoring angels which flank the altar in the Chapel of the Sacrament (and only very narrowly miss being sugary).

His most important work here, probably, is the *tempietto* of Carrara marble which he constructed to house the Holy Face and with which the donor, who had already paid him the stipulated 750 gold ducats, was so delighted that he gave him also a house with a garden. Of the eight sides three are closed and outside one of these Matteo has placed a rather ineffective statue of St Sebastian. The other sides, separated by marble columns, give access to the interior, which contains the greatest treasure of Lucca, originally known as La Santa Croce and miscalled **Il Volto Santo.** It is not in fact the Holy Face printed on St Veronica's handkerchief, of which there are a number in Europe, but a Byzantine crucifix brought from the Levant in the eighth century. It owes its peculiar sanctity to the legend that it was carved by Nicodemus at the command of an angel. Nicodemus had completed all but the head when he fell asleep and awoke to find that the angel had carved it for him while he slept. The fame of the miraculous image became such that even in distant England the favourite oath of King William Rufus was '*Per vultum de Luca!*'

The figure, larger than lifesize, is of cedar wood. It is now blackened with age but at one time the face and hands were flesh-coloured and the tunic was red. The long face with its prominent nose and high cheekbones is distinctly Semitic in character. The eyes of vitreous paste stare rather wildly. On those rare days in the year when the image is uncovered and shown to the public, it is embellished with a great gold crown weighing five kilograms and crusted with jewels, a gold pectoral and a skirt of black velvet embroidered with gold. The feet are encased with silver to prevent them being kissed away by the faithful. Such is the Volto Santo which has rendered Lucca famous as a place of pilgrimage for a thousand years.

We return to the Piazza del Giglio and the great plane-shaded

Piazza Napoleone which was created by Elisa Baciocchi. It is not, however, her statue which adorns it but that of her successor, Maria Louisa of Bourbon-Parma, who was installed as Duchess of Lucca after the Congress of Vienna. Now divided between the Prefecture and the Picture Gallery, the enormous **Palazzo del Governo** which occupies all one side of the square was 'restored' by the Florentine architect Ammannati in 1578. It was acquired by the Anziani, as the rulers of Lucca were called, and used as their Palace by them and their successors, the Princess and the Duchess. The entrance, near the south-west corner of the square, leads into the Cortile degli Svizzeri, called after the Swiss Guards of the oligarchs.

The door and staircase on the right of the Cortile lead up to **the Picture Gallery.**[1] The two unlabelled portraits at the entrance represent Felice and Elisa Baciocchi. In the Sala degli Svizzeri are two or three extremely interesting thirteenth-century crucifixes signed by Berlinghiero Berlinghieri and Deodato Orlandi, but, alas, earmarked for transfer as soon as the Villa Guinigi is opened as an archæological museum. In the characteristic style of Lucca, Christ is represented not in agony but in triumph, not dead, with eyes closed, head drooping and body sagging with its weight, but with head erect and eyes wide open. After that, the general level of the Pinacoteca is not high, for Carlo Ludovico, the last Duke, sold his pictures to the highest bidder and the collection had to be restarted almost from scratch. But there are two great Fra Bartolomeos, brought here from the church of S. Romano, a *Madonna della Misericordia* and a God the Father between SS. Catherine and Mary Magdalene, together with a Holy Family by Andrea del Sarto. One of the most attractive pictures in the gallery, to my thinking, is a lady, modelling apparently as St Catherine, by Ventura Salimbeni the Sienese. There are some interesting Medici portraits by Bronzino and Pontormo, and a very effective portrait of Arch-

[1] Unless otherwise stated, Italian museums close on the afternoons of Sundays and other *giorni festivi.*

bishop Giovanni Domenico Mansi by the Lucchese master Batoni.

From the Piazza Napoleone the Via Beccheria and the Via Vittorio Veneto both lead to the square in which stands the church of **S. Michele del Foro,** so called because this was the ancient Roman forum. S. Michele, begun in 1143, was clearly modelled on the Duomo at Pisa, with blind arcading all round the bottom and *loggette* above. At a later date it was planned to increase the height of the building but in fact only the west front was so raised before funds ran out. The result is a disproportionately high façade with blue sky behind the upper part, like that of a cathedral on a film set or the ornate, isolated front of the old burnt-out church of S. Paulo at Macao. The work was entrusted to that inspired lunatic, Guidetto da Como, a Gaudi before his time, who produced something even more exuberant than the front of the Cathedral. The three dozen or so columns of the four upper rows of arcades are of various coloured marbles and each of a different design from the others. Some are twisted, some carved in zigzags and some in spirals; some are inlaid with coloured marbles to form mosaics; some are so deeply carved with human, animal and monstrous forms that they look like totem poles. There are scores of sculptured capitals also and in a late nineteenth-century restoration some of them were carved with portraits of such heroes of the Risorgimento as Garibaldi, Victor Emmanuel, Cavour and Napoleon III but, rather fortunately perhaps, they are too high up to be seen well without opera glasses. Of them all, one feels that the fisherman of Nice alone could bear comparison with the dignified heads of the earlier centuries.

The spandrels are filled with the same green and white intarsia as those on the façade of S. Martino. They are richly inlaid with hunting and fishing scenes. The key to the symbolism in both churches is here made clear for all to see at the extreme right end of the first arcade, where a seated personage presents an episcopal staff to a smaller figure, who hands a tall cross to a yet smaller one. This signifies the transmission of power to

37

the preacher. In the next division the preacher is seen 'in the field' blowing his hunting horn, while his dogs pursue a boar.

Surmounting the whole extravagant structure, which rises like the gaily decorated poop of an enormous galleon, is a colossal statue of St Michael, holding the imperial orb surmounted by a cross to symbolise power over the Devil. The great bronze wings are detached in order to lessen wind-resistance in a storm. On the right-hand corner of the façade is a Madonna and Child by Matteo Civitali which, weatherworn though it may be, is still a thing of haunting beauty. In the corner of the square opposite it is Nicola Civitali's loggiaed Palazzo Pretorio. The interior of the church contains a good Filippino Lippi, SS. Jerome, Sebastian, Roch and Helena, a crucifix on wood of the Berlinghieri period and an enamelled terracotta Virgin and Child by Luca della Robbia.

From the front of S. Michele the Via Calderai runs up to **S. Frediano,** the third of the great churches of Lucca, which was built in the first half of the twelfth century on the remains of an earlier basilica founded, according to legend, by the Irishman Frigidianus. The apse consists of a semicircle of blind arcades in the Lombardic style. Crowning the façade is an enormous mosaic of Christ enthroned, surrounded by a rainbow mandorla and flanked by two angels. Below, the twelve apostles gesticulate in amazement, for despite the inclusion of the throne the scene apparently represents the Ascension. The mosaic dates from the early thirteenth century and may be the work of the Berlinghieri but it was very much restored in 1829 and it is perhaps for that reason that it seems to lack the direct impact of the contemporary mosaics of Rome and Florence. Frankly, it is wooden and uninspired.

On the right, as you go into the unadorned, austere interior, is an enormous thirteenth-century font designed by Master Roberto. Carved all round it are scenes, crude enough maybe but vigorous and sincere, of the story of Moses. The connection with the redemption by baptism is that, as Christ brought the

Second Law, so Moses brought the First Law; as Jesus delivered mankind from the bondage of sin, so Moses delivered his people from the bondage of Egypt. In the centre of the large basin, intended for total immersion, rises a smaller one, crowned by a little *tempietto*. The font now in actual use is the work of Matteo Civitali. The second chapel on the right is dedicated to the little St Zita, the patron saint of maidservants, who for forty-eight years served the Fatinelli family. In time of famine she fed the poor from her master's stocks and the deficiency was miraculously replaced. (There is a somewhat similar legend attaching to S. Verdiana of Castelfiorentino.) Her half-mummified body is displayed every year on 27th April when all the maidservants of Lucca bring bunches of flowers to her. Some of them no doubt are praying for a similar miracle to happen before their mistress's next stocktaking.

In the Chapel of the Sacrament is a marble polyptych which is attributed to Jacopo della Quercia but is more probably the work of his pupils. Beneath the altar is the tomb of an Anglo-Saxon king, Richard, the brother-in-law of St Boniface. He died here in 722 on his way to the Holy Land. The donors of the chapel, the Trenta couple, lie beneath two stone slabs by Jacopo della Quercia. The frescoes in the Chapel of St Augustine are the work of Amico Aspertini, the follower of Francesco Francia, who himself painted the Immaculate Conception in this church, showing the Virgin being touched with a rod by God the Father. The figures below are David, Solomon, St Augustine and St Anselm, while the kneeling figure is believed to be the schoolman Duns Scotus.

Crossing the Piazza S. Frediano and the Via Fillungo, a busy shopping street which offers the most direct way (turn right) of returning to the Piazza del Giglio, we come to the picturesque market-place of the city. It is an oval space which was once the Roman amphitheatre. The circle of houses surrounding it is built on the ruins of the seats while the narrow approaches to it were once the entrance corridors. From the amphitheatre it is a short step to the **Case dei Guinigi,** the medieval house,

39

still in good preservation, of that important family. It has almost the last of the many towers which caused the poet Fazio degli Uberti to liken the city to a grove of trees.

Andando noi vedemmo in piccol cerchio
Torreggiar Lucca a guisa di boschetto.

(Another medieval writer compares Siena with a cane-brake.) On the top of the Guinigi tower, like a shock of green hair, grow several sturdy holm-oak trees. Not far away the narrow Chiasso Barletti runs between high brick Gothic houses from the Torre dell' Ore to the apse of S. Michele.

The visitor with a few days to spare can spend them well exploring the lanes and squares of this old city and visiting the numerous smaller churches which survive from the Middle Ages; Gothic **S. Romano of the Dominicans,** where in a rather attractive baroque interior St Romanus lies behind the high altar under a tomb by Matteo Civitali; twelfth-century **S. Pietro Somaldi** near the market with its arcaded façade of grey and white marble and its red-brick campanile; eleventh-century **S. Maria Forisportam,** also with an arcaded Pisan façade, which gets its curious name 'Without the Gate' because the walls of the city were only expanded to include it a hundred and fifty years after it was built; twelfth-century **S. Salvatore,** distinguished for its curiously carved lintels by Biduino showing the baptism and a miracle of St Nicholas; white marble-fronted **S. Francesco** where the monument of Castruccio Castracani may be seen on the wall between the third and fourth altars on the right; **S. Giulia** and **S. Maria dei Servi,** which both contain 13th century crucifixes; rose-red **S. Anastasio** with a Circumcision by Jacopo Ligozzi; **S. Trinità,** which boasts a somewhat insipid Madonna and Child by Matteo Civitali; eleventh-century **S. Cristoforo** where, near the first pilaster on the right, are the epigraphs of the uneven, and too often saccharine, sculptor who so narrowly missed greatness; little **S. Alessandro** which was built in the eleventh century by Pope Alexander II, who had been Bishop of Lucca, and has come down to us almost intact to-day; the white Gothic **Oratory of S.**

Maria della Rosa, which contains a statue of a Madonna and Child from the Pisan School of the 14th century; all these and others are mute witnesses to the wealth of Lucca, called *La Industriosa*, in the Middle Ages, when she took second place to Florence alone for wealth and population in all Tuscany.

CHAPTER 4

Pistoia

CHAPTER 4

Pistoia

The road from Lucca to Pistoia (the old road, not the new motorway) is beset by signs urging one to visit the Giardino di Pinocchio. Do not be deterred by this. It is the gimmick to attract people to the beautiful gardens of the **Villa Garzoni** at Collodi, a 'stately home' which is open to visitors from eight in the morning until eight at night. The gardens, laid out in the seventeenth century by the Marchese Romano Garzoni, are particularly celebrated for their fountains. Marble statues stand out pale against the dark hedges of myrtle, while flights of stairs lead up to the villa itself. To the left, beyond the stream, a mosaic and an obelisk constitute a monument to the puppet Pinocchio, hero of the famous children's book of that name. It is a production in somewhat dubious taste, erected in 1954 out of contributions from children all over the world, and it costs an extra fee to visit it. It was erected here because the author, Carlo Lorenzini, was born in Collodi in 1826 and took his pseudonym from his native village.

A little farther on, the road passes through **Pescia**. The cultivation of flowers, especially carnations, has been greatly developed recently in this sheltered neighbourhood and if you pass through in the summer it is worth while pausing to visit the new flower market in the Via Amendola. On the eastern side of the river which bisects the little city (for such it is entitled to call itself although it has fewer than 10,000 inhabitants) the

45

Church of S. Francesco—not the Cathedral, which contains little of interest—has, over the third altar on the right, a famous portrait of St Francis by Bonaventura Berlinghieri. It was painted in 1235; that is to say, only nine years after the death of the saint, who had himself stayed in Pescia in 1211 and whose features must have been familiar to many of Berlinghieri's friends.

Some five miles farther on is **Montecatini Terme** (see front endpaper map), one of the most popular watering places in Italy. It consists of a number of right-angled streets, lined for the most part with hotels and *pensioni*. (The inclusion of Montecatini within its boundaries gives the little province of Pistoia the second highest figure for the number of hotels in all Tuscany after Florence itself.) At the northern end of the town is the attractive park which contains no fewer than five different thermal establishments, each dispensing a different kind of water. There are counters just on the left as you go in, marked Tamerici and Torretta, which are classed as 'strong', Regina, classed as 'medium', and Tettuccio and Rinfresco 'weak', where pretty barmaids dispense your chosen beverage free—but you have already paid quite a stiff entrance fee to get into the park. You have to bring your own glass or else hire one for fifty lire from the *bicchieraia* next door to the bars. I drank two glasses of water belonging to different brands. They tasted like warm brine and gave me a pain in the stomach. They are supposed, however, to be very good for the liver. Eleven months of rich food and one month at Montecatini make up the annual regimen of many a well-to-do Italian.

Northwards, out of Pistoia Province, roads lead over the Apennines by the Abetone and Porretta Passes. Both of these are summer resorts and also winter sports centres. The provincial capital itself has long been famous for its gunsmiths, and the pistol is said to have been invented here and named after the city. **Pistoia** was notorious beyond any city in Tuscany, even Siena, for the bitterness and ferocity of its internecine feuds and family vendettas, Guelphs against Ghibellines, Blacks against Whites, and Cancellieri against Panciatichi. For this fatal fratricidal

46

habit its valiant inhabitants were to pay with many misfortunes and finally with their independence.

The centre of the city is the great **Piazza del Duomo.** The twelfth-century Romanesque Cathedral is of black and white marble. Beside it is a campanile and opposite in the same style is the octagonal baptistery. The sacristan will open it if required, but there is little to see in the interior. The entrance to **the Duomo** is through a large portico with Andrea della Robbia reliefs in the central vault and in the lunette over the main door. The three-aisled, much restored, interior contains several objects of interest. On the right-hand wall is the monument of Cino da Pistoia, the fourteenth-century poet, jurist and friend of Dante to whom Petrarch addressed the lovely sonnet which begins '*Piangete, donne, e con voi pianga l'amore.*' A bas-relief shows him lecturing to a class of pupils, seated at their desks with their books for all the world as though they were in a modern schoolroom. One of the pupils is traditionally believed to be Petrarch and another the lady to whom Cino wrote his vernacular love poems, Selvaggia de' Vergiolesi, daughter of the Pistoian commander during the terrible eleven months' siege of 1305.

A little farther up the right aisle is the Chapel of St James, some relics of whom were brought to Pistoia in 1145. It contains the great silver altar known as the *dossale di S. Jacopo.* (The 100-lire ticket covers also the Diocesan Museum which is entered through the sacristy on the right of the high altar.) The *dossale* was made over a period of nearly two hundred years, between 1287 and the early fifteenth century. The reliefs on the front illustrate fifteen stories from the New Testament by Andrea and Jacopo d'Ognabene. At the sides are nine stories from the Old Testament and nine from the life of St James. The whole is crowned by a statue of the Redeemer surrounded by twenty-four angelic musicians. Apostles, saints and prophets are scattered about for good measure and bring the total number of figures up to six hundred and twenty-eight. In the chapel on the left of the choir is a Madonna and Child with Saints John the Baptist and Zeno, which was probably designed

47

and begun by Verrocchio but finished by his pupil, Lorenzo di Credi in 1485.

Two things strike one about the great Piazza. Firstly, it really is in a complete sense the centre of a medieval self-governing city, where the twin authorities were Church and State even though they might be in conflict. It is 'The Little World of Don Camillo.' Next door to the Baptistery is the **Pretorio,** the old Palazzo del Podestà, the seat of the executive, and opposite it, beside the Cathedral, is the **Palazzo del Comune,** the seat of the legislature. Both branches of the civil power thus share the Piazza with the spiritual power. The other thing which strikes one is the unambitious simplicity of these handsome buildings, designed with unerring taste but designed strictly for use. It is interesting to compare the austerity of a piazza such as this with the riot of ornamentation, statuary, pinnacles and finials, which marks the city centres of the same period in Germany and Flanders. What the moral is I do not pretend to know. One finds oneself talking easily of the persisting tradition of classical restraint running through Italian architecture and then one thinks of Venice and Milan, of the façades of Lucca, Siena and Orvieto.

The Pretorio, now the Tribunal, is known beyond the boundaries of the city for the Latin inscription over the judges' bench:

Hic locus odit, amat, punit, conservat, honorat Nequitiam, Leges, Crimina, Jura, Probos.[1]

According to local tradition the curious black marble head on the wall to the left of the central window in the fourteenth-century Palazzo del Comune represents Filippo Tedici, the traitor who sold Pistoia to Castruccio Castracani in 1315, but it is more probably Musetto, the vanquished Moorish King of Majorca. The Palazzo del Comune has a handsome inner courtyard and staircase. On the top floor is a small picture gallery, but Pistoia was not an important art centre, and the

[1] 'This place hates, loves, punishes, preserves, honours injustice, laws, crimes, rights, honest men.'

collection contains little of interest to any but the specialist, unless it be the fine Deposition of the School of Giotto. The city, nevertheless, can boast of one of the most remarkable works of the della Robbia in the shape of the great polychrome frieze which runs round the top of the **Ospedale del Ceppo** in the square at the end of the Via Pacini behind the Palazzo del Comune. The work, executed by pupils under the personal direction of Giovanni della Robbia, represents the Seven Works of Mercy: on the left wall, clothing the naked and, across the façade, harbouring pilgrims, caring for the sick, visiting prisoners, burying the dead, feeding the hungry, giving drink to the thirsty. All are in enamel except the last, which is of coloured terracotta. The colours are very fresh and the meticulously observed figures (there are about eighty of them) are a great pageant of all the types of the Renaissance from knights to Negroes, from princes to paupers.

By way of the Via Pappe, on the left of the Hospital, the Via del Carmine and the Via S. Andrea we come to the lovely arcaded façade of **S. Andrea,** with a carved pulpit by Giovanni Pisano, dating from about 1300, which is entitled to rank beside his masterpiece in Pisa. Less simple than Nicola Pisano's pulpit in the Pisa Baptistery, on which it is based, it is not so elaborate as his own slightly later pulpit carved for the Duomo of that city. The panels represent the Nativity, the Adoration of the Magi, the Massacre of the Innocents, the Crucifixion and the Last Judgment. There is another fine pulpit, dating from about 1250, by Guido Bigarelli da Como, who made the font in the Baptistery at Pisa, in **S. Bartolomeo in Pantano** on the other side of the Via Pacini.

A little beyond S. Andrea in the much modernised church of **S. Francesco** are a number of interesting fourteenth-century frescoes of undetermined authorship. The twelfth-century church of **S. Giovanni Fuorcivitas,** so called because it was originally outside the city walls, contains a Visitation by Andrea della Robbia, a polypytch over the high altar by Taddeo Gaddi and a thirteenth-century pulpit by the Dominican Fra Guglielmo of Pisa, a disciple of Nicola Pisano. The façade is in the typical style of the Tuscan twelfth century, with three rows of arcading and alternate courses of white marble and that green marble of Prato, which is so dark as to give the impression of being black. **S. Pietro** is another church in the same style, but for me its principal interest is not æsthetic but *folcloristico*, for it was only in 1595 that the authorities abolished the mystic marriage of the Abbess of S. Pietro with the Bishop of Pistoia. In the presence of the congregation assembled in S. Pietro the Bishop gave the Abbess a ring and she in turn presented him with a richly furnished bed. I have seen some curious local ceremonies in Italian churches, such as the Mass of the Sword which takes place every year in the Cathedral at Cividale, but this must surely have been one of the most remarkable which ever survived from the Middle Ages up to the threshold of the seventeenth century

CHAPTER 5

Prato

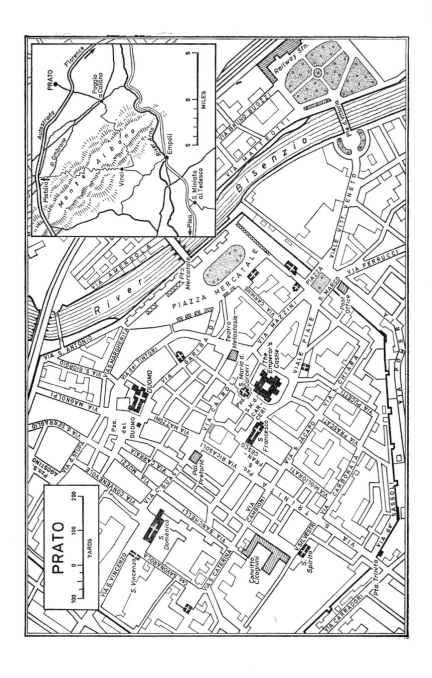

CHAPTER 5

Prato

Prato, long accustomed to leading a double life, is now having to adapt itself to a triple one. The small and ancient centre of the city, safely enclosed in its medieval walls, is a rich museum of architecture, painting and sculpture, while the rapid growth of its woollen industry has earned the place the nickname of 'the Tuscan Manchester' (although 'Bradford' would perhaps be more apt). In the 1960's it has become also a very important road centre, the meeting place of two of the great new motorways which are revolutionising the Italian system of communications. Just outside the town the Strada del Sole from Milan to Rome debouches into the plain from the Apennines and crosses the Strada del Mare which runs from Florence to the sea and on to Genoa and Nice.

The unhurried traveller arriving in the afternoon or evening might do far worse than stay the night in Prato and potter round its art treasures instead of pushing on to hunt for a room in the hurly burly of Florence or going over the Apennines to Bologna. There is a comfortable, air-conditioned Category II hotel, the Flora, in the Via Cairoli. It has no dining-room but sends its guests to the Stella d'Italia restaurant in the nearby Piazza del Duomo opposite the south flank of the Cathedral.

To take one step back through the three lives of Prato, the textile factories (most of them very small, it is true) have increased in ten years from three thousand odd to over five thousand. (Its

Arte di Lane, or woolworkers' guild, existed in the tenth century.) In the same period the population has grown by 30,000. Prato is one of the outstanding manifestations of 'the Italian miracle.' Outside the centre, which fortunately is untouchable under the laws for the preservation of the artistic patrimony of Italy, Prato is speading (entirely unplanned and undirected) like an inkblob on a tablecloth, and immigrants keep pouring in to work in the expanding industries. Already Prato, formerly a typical 'small town,' is the third most populous city in Tuscany.

The lovely little **Duomo** houses a very precious relic, the Holy Girdle of the Virgin. The legend goes that, always in character, the Apostle Thomas, who had not been an eyewitness of the Assumption, expressed some doubts as to its occurrence, whereupon the Madonna leaned out of Heaven and handed him down her girdle to assure his faith. According to the same legend, he entrusted it to a friend before leaving on his missionary journey to India. For a thousand years and more it remained in the same family until a knight of Prato called Michele Dagomari, who had fared to Jerusalem on the First Crusade, married the daughter of a Greek priest, the lineal descendant of St Thomas's friend. He gave the girdle to his daughter as her dowry and Michele brought it home with him, in a box packed with rushes, to Prato in 1141. It should be mentioned just for the record that there is a rival girdle at Tortosa in Spain, which was brought down from Heaven in 1178.

The Duomo, set in a spacious paved square, is striped horizontally in bands of white and of the dark local marble which seems, when one examines it very closely, to be a kind of green porphyry. The white stripes are admirably relieved here and there by blocks of pinkish marble. While the arcaded south side has retained its original twelfth-century Romanesque character, the Gothic façade is mainly fourteenth-century work. It is difficult to try and hang a date on to a building such as this where work was going on almost continuously from the eleventh to the mid-fifteenth century but the architects have, as so often in Italy, succeeded admirably in fusing the various styles into a harmonious whole and avoiding any abrupt transitions. To no one is more credit due for this than to Giovanni Pisano, who in the fourteenth century was entrusted with the difficult task of enlarging the Romanesque cathedral in the then fashionable Gothic style and changing a Greek cross into a Latin one.

The terra-cotta lunette of the Madonna and Child over the west door is by Andrea della Robbia and on the corner to the right of the door is the famous open-air pulpit known as the **Pulpit of the Holy Girdle.** Two of the greatest artists of the age, Donatello and Michelozzo, were commissioned to build it in collaboration expressly for the public exhibition, on ceremonial occasions, of the Holy Girdle. Completed in 1439, it is one of the loveliest of the minor masterpieces of Italy. It is decorated in the manner, rich and yet at the same time fresh and unworried, which one associates with the early Renaissance. The pulpit is shaped like a chalice, with a circular baldaquin above. While the exact division of labour is not, I think, known, it is reasonable to suppose that Michelozzo was responsible for the general design, which is of a singular harmony, and Donatello for the sculptures. Outstanding among these are the seven panels round the parapet, which bear exquisite bas-reliefs of laughing children, dancing and playing musical instruments. It is the very spirit of the Rebirth which was taking place in Florence in the early fifteenth century.

The girdle is kept in the Cappella del Santo Cingolo on the left of the west door. The frescoes, depicting the story of the girdle, are the work of Agnolo Gaddi and date from the end of the fourteenth century. They are difficult to see, however, since the whole chapel is shut off by a heavy bronze grille, the work of that same Maso di Bartolomeo who designed the great bronze candlesticks in front of the high altar both in this cathedral and in that of Pistoia. Giovanni Pisano himself carved the statue of the Madonna and Child. Between the fourth and fifth pillars on the left of the nave is the beautiful pulpit of 1473, the work of Mino da Fiesole, assisted by Antonio Rossellino.

It is adorned with reliefs of the lives of the Virgin, St Stephen and St John the Baptist.

The tempestuous life of Fra Filippo Lippo reached its climax here in this city of Prato, when, while confessor to the Convent of S. Margherita in the Mercatale, he seduced a young nun, one of his penitents, ran away with her and soon produced a son, later to be known in the world of art as Filippino Lippi. Even in the tolerant moral climate of the fifteenth century the affair caused a considerable scandal but Pope Pius II solved the problem in a liberal and practical manner by absolving the renegade monk from his vows so that he was free to marry the mother of his child. Lucrezia Buti, as this frail, ethereal blonde was called, served Filippo as the model for dozens of Madonnas. Here in the Cathedral of Prato the versatile ex-nun modelled as Salome dancing before Herod, in the great fresco with which Filippo decorated the chancel between 1452 and 1466. The sacristan will turn on the electric light, but the best, indeed the only, time to see the frescoes by natural light is in the morning.

The window above was made in 1459 by Lorenzo da Pelago to a design by Filippo Lippi. The two cycles of frescoes, with three horizontal tiers apiece, work of the painter's maturity, are typically Florentine in their grace, their gaiety and their narrative power. In Filippo's hands the grim stories of fanaticism, cruelty and martyrdom do not seem to differ so very much from the light tales of Boccaccio. It is something one may like or not, but there it is. On the right wall are depicted scenes from the life of St John the Baptist. There is a wonderful picture of the banquet of a rich Florentine gentleman with lords and ladies in contemporary costumes, which passes for the fatal banquet of Herod. The identical twin of Filippo's Madonnas does duty for Salome, still looking as though butter would not melt in her mouth. On the left wall are scenes from the life of St Stephen. Of special interest is the last one of all, where the saint is being buried in just such a Renaissance chapel as Filippo Brunelleschi had built thirty years earlier for the Pazzi in Florence, for the four mourners at the foot of the bier are traditionally supposed to represent Fra Filippo himself, his assistant Fra Diamante, Carlo de' Medici in ecclesiastical robes, the donor of the fresco (whose monument is over the sacristy door in the north transept)—and the long-dead Giovanni Pisano, builder of the wall on which the paintings stand.

The late fourteenth-century frescoes in the first chapel to the left of the choir are attributed to Agnolo Gaddi; on the right wall is the story of St James and on the left that of St Margaret of Cortona, a sort of medieval Mary Magdalene who after a lurid past died in the odour of sanctity. The frescoes in the chapel to the right of the high altar are by two fifteenth-century painters. One, Andrea di Giusto, painted the Martyrdom and burial of St Stephen and the Betrothal of the Virgin. The other (unknown) was responsible for the other scenes from the life of the Virgin and the funeral of St Stephen. The picture under glass near the door at the end of the south transept is the Death of St Jerome by Filippo Lippi. The tabernacle of the Madonna and Child nearby is the work of Benedetto da Maiano.

From the south flank of the Duomo the busy Via Mazzoni, more commonly known as the Corso, leads to the Piazza del Comune. In the centre is the statue of Francesco di Marco Datini, the fourteenth-century merchant and banker of Prato, who on his death left his great wealth to the poor of his native city. (Other sons of this little city include the painter Filippino Lippi, as we have mentioned, the dramatist Sem Benelli, and the author of *Kaputt* and *La Pelle*, Curzio Malaparte, who was the son of a German settled in Prato in the textile business.) The gay, many-spouted little bronze fountain, called the Fontana di Bacchino because it represents the Infant Bacchus, is a copy of the 1665 original by Ferdinando Tacca, which has now been removed for better preservation to the Galleria Comunale in the Palazzo Pretorio next door.

The **Palazzo Pretorio** itself is an imposing Gothic building, the result of the fusion of a brick house of the thirteenth century with another in white limestone, which was added in the fourteenth. An outside staircase leads up to the first floor entrance

57

and since 1953 the Municipal Picture Gallery has been installed here. The collection is not one to be missed. It includes two works by Filippino Lippi. He painted the lovely 'Tabernacle' which is in the first room, in 1498 for the house he had just bought for his widowed mother, Lucrezia Buti. It was just in front of S. Margherita, the convent where he had been so lawlessly begotten. Long kept covered and locked up for protection, it was completely shattered in an air raid in 1944 but has been skilfully and painstakingly restored from hundreds of small fragments like a super-jigsaw puzzle. On the next floor is the other Filippino Lippi (no. 14)—the Madonna with the Baptist and St Stephen. There are also some good Florentine primitives, notably a Madonna with Angels and Saints—a triptych from the studio of Lorenzo Monaco, Bernardo Daddi's Madonna and Child with Saints, and a predella attributed to the same master showing seven scenes of the story of the Girdle from its presentation of St Thomas to its bequest to the Cathedral of Prato by the dying Michele Dagomari. The sixth scene illustrates the curious incident of Michele being admonished by angels for sleeping with the girdle under his head. In the version in the Cathedral he kept it under his bed for safety.

From the Piazza del Comune the Via Ricasoli leads to the thirteenth-century **S. Francesco,** with its handsome green and white striped façade. At the foot of the chancel steps is the tombstone of the banker Datini, whose late fourteenth-century palace still stands on the corner of the Via Ser Lapo Mazzei on the other side of the Piazza S. Francesco. It now contains a wealth of medieval mercantile archives invaluable to the economic historian of the Middle Ages. The walls of the chapterhouse opening off the cloister of S. Francesco are covered with a number of frescoes by Niccolò Gerini, which date from the last decade of the fourteenth century.

Behind S. Francesco is Giuliano da Sangallo's handsome Renaissance church of **S. Maria delle Carceri,** built in the shape of a Greek cross. It dates from the end of the fifteenth century and is considered to be his masterpiece. The interior is marked

58

by its harmonious proportions, while its white plaster and brown sandstone are lightened by an enamelled frieze and medallions of the Evangelists in white on blue by Andrea della Robbia. The church is in the style of, and invites comparison with, Brunelleschi's Cappella dei Pazzi at Florence, Antonio Sangallo the Elder's S. Biagio at Montepulciano and Bramante's S. Maria della Consolazione at Todi. At the side of S. Maria delle Carceri rise the white walls, square towers and Ghibelline battlements of the **Emperor's Castle,** as it is called. It was built in the first half of the thirteenth century by the Emperor Frederick II in the style of the great Hohenstaufen castles of the south and is probably the work of Apulian architects. It is the only castle of this type in North or Central Italy. The outer walls have been well restored but hardly anything is left of the internal structure.

In the Via Silvestri (the fifth street on the right down the Via S. Trinità, leading out of the Piazza S. Francesco) is the church of the **Santo Spirito** which, should the side door be closed, may be entered through the cloister with the permission of the Prior. Among the works of art which it contains is a fine Presentation in the Temple, which used to be attributed to Filippo Lippi but is now believed to have been designed by him and executed by Fra Diamante, the pupil who collaborated with him in the Cathedral. The hanasome early eighteenth-century palace in the piazza adjoining, the Convitto Cicognini, houses one of the most famous boarding schools in Italy. Gabriele d'Annunzio was a pupil there for seven years.

A few miles south of Prato, where the foothills of the Monte Albano ridge rise on the far bank of the Ombrone, are two well-known Medici villas. The villa at **Poggio a Caiano** was originally bought by Lorenzo the Magnificent, who had it transformed by Giuliano da Sangallo in 1484. The loggia which runs along the façade has a rich della Robbia ceiling, and the *salone* is frescoed by Andrea del Sarto, Pontormo and Francia-bigio. This beautiful villa, in the middle of a large park, subsequently became the favourite residence of the Grand Dukes of

Tuscany. It was here that Francesco I and Bianca Cappello died in mysterious circumstances in 1587. In the hills behind Poggio, at a height of some six hundred feet, is the equally lovely villa of Artimino, built in 1594 by Bernardo Buontalenti for the Grand Duke Ferdinando I.

To the south of Monte Albano is the valley of the Arno and on the far bank of the river runs the highway from Florence to Pisa by way of **Empoli,** the junction where one changes trains for Siena. The Collegiata at Empoli, whose beautiful Romanesque front of 1032 faces on to the Piazza, was largely rebuilt after the War, in which Empoli was badly damaged. In the Piazzetta S. Giovanni on the right is the Museo della Collegiata, of which the Baptistery forms one of the two ground floor rooms. It contains an Adoration by Cosimo Rosselli and a marble font sculptured with *putti* of the school of Donatello. On the first floor are a number of good pictures, notably a frescoed *Pietà* by the Umbrian Masolino da Panicale which used to be in the Baptistery; another fresco of St Andrew and St John the Baptist, one of the rare documented works by Starnina, detached from S. Stefano; a triptych, Madonna with Saints, by Lorenzo Monaco; several works by the two Botticinis, Lorenzo di Bicci and his confusingly named contemporary, Bicci di Lorenzo; an Adoration by Jacopo del Sellaio. On the plastic side are a Madonna and Child by Mino da Fiesole and a number of della Robbias. Although several works have been brought here from Santo Stefano, that church still contains, in the lunette over the sacristy door, a delicate fresco of the Madonna and Child with Angels by Masolino.

Eleven miles from Empoli, on the southern slopes of Monte Albano, is the village of **Vinci,** which has given its name to Leonardo da Vinci. (Ser Piero, his father, came from Vinci, although the painter himself was probably born in the next village.) Four rooms of the castle have been turned into a museum. In addition to models of the various machines designed by Leonardo, it houses the Biblioteca Leonardiana, a library which serves as a centre of study and research for those interested in the multilateral master. Not far away, just outside Lamporecchio, is the Villa Rospigliosi, which Bernini designed for Pope Clement IX. You ask the way to '*Lo Spicchio*.'

Some six or seven miles west of Empoli and two or three miles off the Pisa road is **S. Miniato al Tedesco**[1] once the centre of the Imperial power in Tuscany and one of the thickest concentrations of German population. In the tenth century Otto I established here the Head Office of the Imperial Ministers with jurisdiction throughout Tuscany, and an Imperial Vicar of German nationality is mentioned in 1113. S. Miniato was the birthplace of the great Countess Matilda of Tuscany, who caused endless trouble by bequeathing her dominions to the Church. It is also one of several Italian towns (Sarzana is another) which claim to be the cradle of Napoleon's family before it migrated to Corsica, and in 1796 Napoleon came here to visit Canon Filippo Buonaparte, the last survivor of the S. Miniato branch of the family.

There are a number of frescoes in S. Domenico (whose proper title is SS. Jacopo e Lucia), in the twelfth-century Duomo, in S. Francesco and in the Municipio but they are all by unknown or unimportant artists. Over the second altar to the right in S. Caterina is a powerful and moving Gothic crucifix in wood by an unknown carver of the early fourteenth century.

The dominating feature of the city is the high tower, a reconstruction of the thirteenth-century tower, destroyed during the War, in which the Emperor Frederick II, misled by slanderers, imprisoned and blinded his great chancellor, Piero della Vigna; the latter dashed his brains out in despair against the wall of his cell. It is one of the saddest stories of the Middle Ages, of the ingratitude of princes and the malevolence of courtiers. The tower is built at the highest point of the ridge on which the city stands, and the view embraces wide stretches of the Arno valley and extends in the other direction as far as Leghorn, Volterra and S. Gimignano.

[1] 'Tedesco' is Italian for 'German.'

61

CHAPTER 6

Pisa

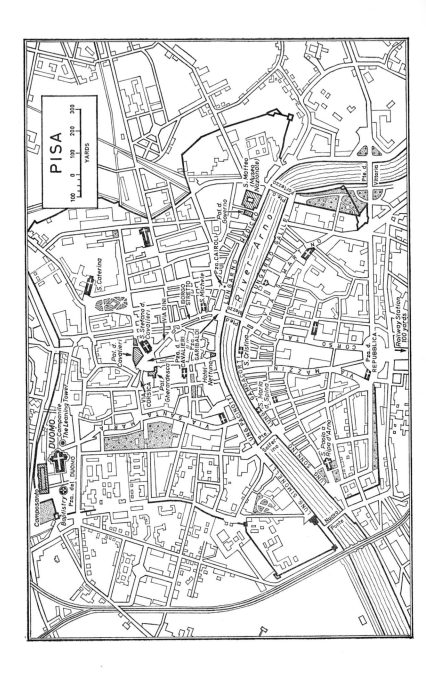

PISA

YARDS

100 0 100 200 300

River Arno

DUOMO
Companile
The Leaning Tower
Camposanto
Baptistry
Pza. del DUOMO

S. Caterina

S. Stefano d. Cavalieri
S. n. n.
Pal. d. Cavalieri
Pza. d. CAVALIERI
VIA DINI
BORGO STRETTO
S. Michele
Pza. GARIBALDI
Hotel Nettuno
VIA CORSICA
Pal. Gherardesca

VIA SANTA MARIA
LUNG PACINOTTI
S. Maria d. Spina
Ponte Solferino
LUNG SIMONELLI
Ponte Nuovo

Pza. CAIROLI
Pal. d. Governo
S. Matteo (Museo Nazionale)
LUNGARNO MEDICEO
LUNGARNO GAMBACORTI
S. Cristina
LUNGARNO GALILEI
Pte. d. Vittoria
Pte. d.
VIA MAZZINI
CORSO
Pza. d. REPUBBLICA
S. Paolo a Ripa d'Arno

Railway Station 100 yards

CHAPTER 6

Pisa

> *La Torre di Pisa*
> *Che pende, che pende,*
> *La Torre di Pisa*
> *Che mai non cadrà!*

runs a song familiar to every Italian child, and it is the Leaning Tower 'which leans and leans and never shall fall,' which has made the name of Pisa familiar also to millions who could not tell you where or what Pisa is.

For the historian Pisa is an ancient city, formerly a Greek colony, an Etruscan city, a Roman settlement, and afterwards one of the four great maritime republics of Italy; for the scholar it is the seat of one of the oldest and most illustrious universities in Italy; for its inhabitants it is a sleepy town (what the Italians call *'una città morta'*[1]) with a good climate and an easy, agreeable tempo of life; but for the traveller it is the Piazza del Duomo or Campo dei Miracoli, the Field of Miracles, which is a broad meadow on the northern edge of the city with four superb and perfectly harmonised buildings rising white from the green lawns. Besides the Campanile or Leaning Tower itself, there are the Cathedral or Duomo, the Baptistery and the Camposanto or Cemetery. It is bounded on two sides by the crenellated red walls of the city.

The great buildings of the Campo were built when Pisa was

[1]Pisa had over 120,000 inhabitants in the thirteenth century, under 10,000 in the sixteenth, and has about 100,000 to-day.

at the height of her fame and prosperity, the conqueror of Amalfi and the rival of Genoa and Venice. She had taken Sardinia and Corsica from the Arabs. She had played a prominent part in the First Crusade and as a result established colonies and trading posts all over the Levant. In 1063, three years before Duke William conquered England, her fleet burst the chain of the Saracen port of Palermo and captured six richly laden ships. She decided to devote the booty carried off from the infidel to building the magnificent cathedral which we see to-day.

The greatness of Pisa came to an end when the Genoese destroyed her fleet off the island of Meloria in 1284. Her sea power lost, she was further weakened by internecine strife and external warfare until in 1406 the Visconti of Milan, who were at that time her overlords, ceded the city to her arch-enemy Florence. The political history of Pisa was finished, although she continued to shine in the world of scholarship. Her university contained one of the most famous law schools in Italy, with the earliest known manuscript of the Pandects in its library, and it produced such famous scientists as Galileo, who was forced by the Inquisition on pain of death to recant his heretical theory that the earth goes round the sun but who was allowed to contribute to the laws which govern gravity and the pendulum; and Pacinotti, the inventor of the electro-magnetic ring.

The Arno runs through the centre of Pisa in a long, slow arc from east to west and divides the city into two nearly equal parts, of which the northern half is much the more ancient and interesting. At the southern extremity of the town is the railway station. Thence the Corso Italia runs down into the city and crosses the Arno by the **Ponte di Mezzo,** the Middle Bridge, at the northern end of which is the Piazza Garibaldi, generally considered the centre of the town. It is on the Ponte di Mezzo that the ancient Bridge Game, the Gioco del Ponte, is played on the first Sunday in June between the north bank, the Tramontana, and the south bank, the Mezzogiorno. The game was revived in 1935 after an interruption of 150 years and consists in pushing a sort of wheeled trolley over from the middle of

66

the bridge to your opponents' bank. Each of the eight hundred players is dressed in twelfth-century costume.

On either bank of the broad, slow river stretch promenades called the Lungarni. The houses which line them were mostly built at the beginning of the nineteenth century and display a most satisfying unity of colour and style. Pisa was among the worst damaged of all the Italian cities during the War (forty-eight per cent), for in 1944 the Arno here marked the front line for forty days, with the Germans on the north bank facing the Americans on the south; but even where the houses of the Lungarno have been destroyed they have been skilfully rebuilt in the old colour scheme of ochre walls and green shutters. Shelley lived from 1821-22 in the Palazzo Scott at the eastern end of the Lungarno Galilei when it was still new, while Byron wrote six books of *Don Juan* in the sixteenth-century Palazzo Toscanelli on the Lungarno Mediceo opposite. It is now No. 11 and houses the state archives. In June the *lumineria* takes place along the Lungarni - a kind of *son et lumière*.

Just to the west of the Piazza Garibaldi is the Lungarno Pacinotti, where there are two pleasant old-style hotels, the Nettuno and the Victoria. Other hotels in Pisa are the luxury Albergo dei Cavalieri close to the station (but a long way from the architectural monuments), the new Albergo Duomo near the Cathedral, with a roof-garden bar from which there is a good view of the buildings of the Campo, and, also near the Duomo, the second category Villa Kinzica[1] (where I once saw Botticelli's Venus calmly lunching with her husband at the next table to mine—the same grave, pale, triangular face, the same spun gold hair and the same infinitely sad grey eyes. Greatly intrigued to find out whether the Tuscan strain could be so persistent, I talked to them, only to find that they were Danes from Copenhagen.) For myself, when I go to Pisa, I ask for a front room at the Nettuno, for the sake of the lovely view in both directions of the sweep of the Arno—'*il bello di Pisa.*' And

[1]This curious word is Arabic for 'warehouses' and was the name of the quarter where the Moslem merchants were allowed to establish their *fonduks*.

one can look across the river to the little church of S. Cristina, where St Catherine of Siena received the stigmata, and on a windless day watch the ochre and green houses riding upside down in the water. Between the Nettuno and the Victoria is the Hussar, the Caffè dell' Ussero, which in the time of the Risorgimento was a great resort of students and patriots and political exiles, as the newspaper cuttings round the walls of the red-plush inner sanctum recall. The Ussero has built out an open air terrace and bar over the river and it is a very pleasant place to sit in the cool of the evening and look up and down the Arno, surveying a prospect which has changed little since the days of Byron and Shelley, for '*questo Lung'Arno è uno spettacolo così bello, così ampio, così magnifico,*' in the words of Leopardi.

Down river on the southern bank the spires and pinnacles of the remarkable little church of **S. Maria della Spina** are silhouetted against the sunset. S. Maria della Spina is like a Gothic reliquary, built of pure marble and breathtakingly rich in decoration, statues and pinnacles. Inside are some very fine statues; of the Madonna by Andrea Pisano, of Christ and of St Peter by Nino Pisano and of John the Baptist by Tommaso Pisano, although the loveliest of all, Nino's nursing *Madonna del Latte*, seems to have stuck to the fingers c { the Museum (upstairs in Room 21), whither it was removed during the restoration of the war-damaged church. In the presbytery there are bas-reliefs of the Cardinal Virtues by Andrea Guardi. The church was originally built as an oratory in the fourteenth century on the banks of the river to protect the new bridge, but in 1871 it was removed to its actual site because of the percolation of the water. Its present name dates from the time when it was presented by a Pisan merchant with a thorn from the Crown of Christ. It is built of white, blue-grey and pink marbles. On the front facing the street are thirteen statues of Christ and the Apostles from the workshop of Giovanni Pisano, and above are other statues by Nino Pisano and his assistants. The whole resembles an elaborately decorated jewel box.

On the other side of the Piazza Garibaldi the Lungarno

68

The open-air Pulpit of the Holy Girdle from the Duomo in Prato, with bas-reliefs of children dancing and playing musical instruments. Completed in 1439 by Donatello and Michelozzo, it is one of the loveliest minor masterpieces in Italy.

The Field of Miracles, Pisa, with its four famous buildings: the Cathedral, the Baptistery, the Cemetery and the Leaning Tower.

Mediceo leads to the Piazza Cairoli, to the thirteenth-century Gothic Palace of the Medici, in which Charles VIII of France stayed in 1494 and here received the Florentine ambassador Savonarola. It is now the **Palazzo del Governo,** and next to the **Museo Nazionale**[1] in the old Benedictine convent of **S. Matteo.** The first four rooms on the ground floor are devoted to Pisan Romanesque sculpture from the tenth to the thirteenth century, which formerly adorned the Cathedral façade. The next two rooms contain a number of very weather-worn but still deeply moving sculptures by Giovanni Pisano and his school taken mostly from the outside of the Baptistery, where the rains of centuries have ground them down to blocks which might almost be the work of a modern impressionist. In addition to a number of gradules—human and animal heads which formed a frieze under the cornice of the Cathedral—there are many impressive saints, sibyls and prophets. Look in particular at the lovely figure of a dancing woman in Room 5, believed to be the work of Giovanni himself, and the two female saints in Room 6. Room 8 contains a striking collection of polychrome statues in wood, which are very obviously speaking likenesses of living models. Particularly beautiful are the Angel of the Annunciation and the Virgin *Annunziata*, attributed to Andrea Pisano. Farther on are some fine Florentine sculptures, including a curious dandified bust of Christ, some rare *exultets* (for illustrating the Easter hymns) dating back to the eleventh century, and some good examples of goldsmith's work. In the middle of the jewellery room is an interesting rock crystal cross with thirteenth-century illuminations. From the last rooms, containing examples of later painters such as Guido Reni, one goes out into the cloister and then immediately to the right up the stairs to the first floor, which is almost entirely devoted to painting.

Whenever I pass through Pisa and have half an hour to spare, I go to the first room, No. 20, on account of the Christ on the Cross which hangs in the middle of the right-hand wall. It is by an unknown Pisan artist of the thirteenth century, strongly

[1]Closed on Mondays.

under Byzantine influence, painted in tempera on parchment backed on wood, and for me at least the little scenes of the Passion, the mourning women and the angels which surround it are the loveliest things in the Museum. All are painted in black and very subdued reds and purples on a gold background. Notice how curiously the golden haloes, which are the same colour as the background, occlude the buildings behind them. The same room contains a very interesting *Christus Triumphans* of the twelfth century, surrounded by scenes of the Passion.

Pisa was not a great school of painting. Giunta Pisano and Enrico di Tedice left few heirs, and in the course of the four-teenth century it lost nearly all its creative impulse, pressed on the one side by Florentine and on the other by Sienese influ-ences. There are, however, some good pictures here from other schools, notably the great polyptych by Simone Martini of Siena, which should by rights be returned to the church of S. Caterina. Look out for a Madonna and Child by Gentile da Fabriano; Masaccio's St Paul, a fragment of the polyptych he painted for the church of the Carmine; a couple of Benozzo Gozzolis; a fine St Francis Preaching to the Fishes by Magnasco; and Jacques Callot's very individual conception of the Martyrdom of St Sebastian. The foreign room at the end finishes on an unexpec-tedly monarchist note with two small Winterhalters of Napoleon III and the Empress Eugénie, and a George IV by Sir Thomas Lawrence.

From the Piazza Garibaldi the arcaded **Borgo Stretto** (The Street Called Strait), which is the main shopping centre of the town, runs due north, prolonging the Corso Italia. On the right is the church of **S. Michele in Borgo,** one of three Pisan churches with very handsome façades, whose interiors have been badly bombed and, although restored, have practically nothing left of their original art treasures. S. Michele and S. Caterina are noteworthy for the way in which ogival forms have been grafted on to an architecture still fundamentally Romanesque, while the west front of **S. Paolo a Ripa d'Arno,** beyond the river and past S. Maria della Spina, is pure Romanesque, a smaller but even richer version of that of the Duomo. It has a Madonna painted on wood by Turino Vanni.

From the Borgo Stretto the Via Dini leads off to the great **Piazza dei Cavalieri,** which was the centre of the city in the days of the Republic it used to be called 'the Square of the Seven Streets.' It is almost entirely surrounded by dignified sixteenth-century buildings and is dominated by the handsome Palazzo dei Cavalieri, which was designed by Vasari in 1562 to be the headquarters of the Knights of St Stephen, an Order recently founded by the Grand Duke Cosimo I to fight against the Turks. It has a projecting roof and a slightly concave façade entirely covered with graffiti of coats of arms, warriors and flowers, white on a brown background, from the industrious hand of Vasari. It is now the seat of the famous Scuola Normale Superiore, a sort of parallel but higher university, entry to which is only possible by winning a scholarship. Professor Fermi, who won the Nobel Prize for Physics, was one of its alumni.

Next to the palace is the church of **Santo Stefano dei Cavalieri,** built in 1565, also to the plans of Vasari. Inside, it has a fine carved and gilded ceiling, depicting scenes from the exploits of the Order. On the walls are scores of captured Turkish banners and rich carvings from the poops of the galleys of the Order. Under the bronze and porphyry altar are the relics of Pope St Stephen and above it is a chair believed to have been his. Behind the altar is a gilded bronze bust of St. Lussorio by Donatello.

On the far side of the square is the **Palazzo Gherardesca,** also by Vasari, really twin palaces joined across a covered passageway. This occupies the site of the famous Hunger Tower, where the traitor Count Ugolino della Gherardesca, his sons and his nephews, were locked up to die of starvation and the key thrown into the Arno. The tale is recounted in the thirty-third canto of the 'Inferno.' To get to the **Piazza del Duomo,** take the street on the left, the Via Corsica, and then turn right down Via S. Maria.

71

At the end of the Via S. Maria is the Piazza, which in addition to being the setting for one of the most famous groups of buildings in Europe is the public park of Pisa. Side by side with the tourists, with their guides and their cameras, are the Pisan children romping on the grass, tugging at coloured balloons and sucking ice-creams off barrows, and the local lovers walking hand in hand or taking photographs of each other. It gives the Campo an air of being still lived in and not just a tourist show. The newcomer's eye will instantly be drawn from the Cathedral in front of him to the famous **Leaning Tower** on the right of it and, if he is young, he will very likely want to climb it before tackling the other buildings.

The campanile would be a very remarkable building in itself apart from the curious angle at which it rises. There has long been a theory that the architect built the tower on a slant to demonstrate his virtuosity, but there is little doubt that the inclination is due to a slip in the foundations, where every square centimetre of ground has to bear a pressure of five kilograms. The tower, a hundred and eighty feet high, was begun in 1173 in the Pisan-Romanesque style, perhaps by that same Bonanno who made the bronze doors of the Cathedral. Probably it was a subsidence of the subsoil which brought the work to a halt when the builders were half-way up. It was only a hundred years later that the remaining three stories and the bell-chamber were added by Giovanni di Simone and an attempt made to correct the inclination. (The top stories are almost vertical.) At present it is 13.8 feet out of the true and the inclination is increasing by eight-tenths of a millimetre every year. Work has been done to strengthen the foundations by pumping in quantities of cement and the campanile seems safe for a few centuries to come.

The tower is an enormous cylinder, surrounded by six galleries one above the other, as on the façade of the Cathedral. (Try and banish the irreverent comparison with the baskets on the head of a Covent Garden porter.) It is hollow and a spiral staircase of 292 steps in the thickness of the wall leads to the belfry at the top. There is access to each gallery through a door which lights the dark, steep stairway. The overhanging side of the Tower seems to have a peculiar fascination for those who go up it and one can sit outside the Kinzica and watch the stout-hearted, but less strong-headed, people who have reached the top, sidling along and clinging to the inside wall to resist that invisible hand in the small of their backs, which is pressing them towards the outside edge. It was here that Galileo carried out his famous experiments concerning the speed of falling bodies.

The **Cathedral,** begun in 1063 to the designs of Buscheto, initiated the Pisan style of architecture. Hitherto the Romanesque architecture of Tuscany had been the work of masters from Lombardy, but now the Pisans, fresh from their contacts with the world of the Arabs and the Greeks, introduced Oriental motifs to create a new Pisan-Romanesque style, which soon spread to Lucca, Pistoia and the other neighbouring cities.

The great church, entirely of marble, is a basilica with a nave, a transept, a Gothic cupola and an apse. The prevailing colour is white, but it is relieved by dark grey bands, by rose-coloured blocks here and there and by lozenges and rosettes inlaid with coloured stones like Oriental rugs hanging on the walls.

The lower level of Rainaldo's façade includes three doors and four blind arches, while the upper consists of four galleries, one above the other, diminishing in size towards the summit. They impart a wonderful air of lightness to the whole west front and carry the eye upwards to the Madonna at the apex. The three great bronze doors were originally by Bonanno, but were damaged when the Cathedral caught fire in 1595. The present panels are the work of followers of Giambologna. The central door is covered with scenes in bas-relief of the life of Christ and the two outer ones of the life of the Virgin. They are exquisitely fashioned and are covered with a rich green patina except where they have been polished to a golden colour by thousands of questing forefingers, such as the occasional heads which project temptingly from the prevailing low relief and such piquant objects as the lizards and snakes which peer from the foliage of the borders. Above the doors are lozenges and rosettes inlaid with coloured marbles. At either end of the first gallery are gargoyles and statues of evangelists. The flanks of the nave are ornamented with blind arches in the same way as the west front.

The right transept terminates in a small apse, in which the Door of St Ranieri (the Patron Saint of Pisa), on the side facing the Campanile, is the normal entrance to the Cathedral. It still has Bonanno's original bronze panels depicting the life of Christ in twenty-five enchanting, naïve and yet powerful scenes. They are perhaps the most fascinating (I do not say the greatest) single work of art in the whole Cathedral. Notice on the wall of the apse to the right of the door a curious relief, standing on end, of two ships passing a lighthouse.

The interior gives an impression of great height and majesty. It consists of a nave with four side-aisles, north and south transepts with two, and a large apse. The long vistas of round arches, striped white and black, recall the Great Mosque of Cordoba, especially in the smaller arches of the triforium. The original works of art in the nave were destroyed by the fire of 1595, as was the ceiling, and the walls are now covered with paintings by various seventeenth- and eighteenth-century artists of no very outstanding merit. From the ceiling hangs a great bronze lamp by Battista Lorenzi known as Galileo's Lamp, because Galileo was said to have noticed the oscillation of the lamp after the sacristan lit it, and worked out from it his theory of pendulums. Alas for the legend, it is now held that the theory antedates the lamp by six years. In the left aisle of the right transept is the tomb by Tino di Camaino of Dante's hero, the Emperor Henry VII. The lifesize figures of the emperor and his counsellors which formerly surrounded it have unfortunately been removed to the Camposanto.

The **chancel** is closed by a balustrade which makes it very difficult to see Sogliani's Madonna and Child and the five beautiful Saints by Andrea del Sarto within it. The two bronze angels bearing candelabra are the work of Giambologna, who also made the lovely bronze crucifix on the high altar. Above in the apse is a great mosaic of Christ Enthroned between the Madonna and St John the Baptist. It is generally described as the last work of Cimabue but it is not certain how much of it is actually by him. He was apparently called in to finish the work begun by lesser artists. It is not as impressive as one, were it all Cimabue's own work, would have a right to hope for. Below it are pictures by Beccafumi, Sodoma and Sogliani.

At the top end of the left aisle is the famous Gothic **pulpit** by Giovanni Pisano. It is hexagonal and has eleven supports, the central one of which is richly decorated with allegorical figures of the Seven Liberal Arts[1] on the base and the Four Theological Virtues on the shaft. The lions killing horses at the base of the outer columns symbolise the victory of Christianity over paganism. On the architraves at the top of the columns are Sibyls. The surfaces of the pulpit above represent, from left to right: 1, the Annunciation, the Visitation and the Birth of the Baptist; 2, the Birth of Christ; 3, the Adoration of the Magi; 4, the Presentation in the Temple and the Flight into Egypt; 5, the Massacre of the Innocents; 6, the Arrest and the Flagellation of Christ; 7, the Crucifixion; 8, the Saved; 9, the Damned. It is very interesting to go from these exciting sculptures directly to the Baptistery to compare them with his father's work there.

The **Baptistery** is the circular building opposite the west front of the Cathedral. The lower two stories are Romanesque but the superstructure is rich in Gothic decoration. Many of the carved figures are copies of originals by Giovanni and his school which are now in the Museum. The cupola is crowned by a figure of St John the Baptist. On the right jamb of the main door are the Apostles and on the left the Months of the Year. In the lunette is a copy of Giovanni Pisano's Madonna now in the Museum.

[1]These were grammar, dialectic, rhetoric, arithmetic, geometry, music and astronomy.

The two principal features of the spacious interior are the font and the pulpit. The great font by Guido Bigarelli of Como is like an octagonal room sawn off waist-high and was intended for total immersion. It has four small fonts for infants, and is richly decorated with coloured marbles and intricately carved rosettes. Nicola Pisano's pulpit, which revolutionised the sculptor's art in Italy, is hexagonal, like his son's in the Cathedral, and stands on seven columns. At the top of the pillars stand allegorical figures of the Virtues. Reading from left to right, the five panels of the parapet carry: 1, the Nativity, with the Annunciation to Mary and the Annunciation to the Shepherds. This panel is of particular interest in that the Mary of the Nativity is clearly taken from the Hippolyta on the Roman sarcophagus of Countess Beatrice of Canossa in the Camposanto, which Nicola had studied. 2, the Adoration of the Magi; 3, the Presentation in the Temple; 4, the Crucifixion; 5, the Last Judgment.

The sculptures display a classic sense of gravity and form. Particularly noteworthy is the lovely composition of the figures at the right of the Adoration. In marked contrast is the Gothic impetuosity and the strong dramatic feeling of Giovanni's pulpit in the Cathedral, which reveals a much greater capacity for conveying emotion, for example in the Crucifixion and the Massacre of the Innocents, although it is sometimes at the expense of the formal beauty which distinguishes his father's work.

The Baptistery has most remarkable acoustic properties, which the guardian will demonstrate by carolling away on different notes which echo away into the cupola and blend together like organ music. He will not be averse to one's showing appreciation of his virtuosity as one goes out.

From the main door the path to the left leads to the entrance to the **Camposanto,** the long white building with the blind arches which bounds the Campo on the north. It was built in 1278 by Giovanni di Simone and according to the chroniclers it contains the fifty-three cartloads of earth from Golgotha which the Crusader Archbishop Ubaldo dei Lanfranchi had imported

The Last Judgment. Frescoes at the Camposanto in Pisa by an unknown master of the 13th century.

Crucifixion by a 13th century Pisan artist, heavily under Byzantine influence, in the Museo Nazionale di S. Matteo in Pisa. Painted in tempera on parchment backed on wood, it is one of the finest works in the Museum.

for illustrious Pisans to be buried in. The dimensions are said to be those of Noah's Ark, 415 feet long by 137 wide.

The interior consists of an oblong gallery, surrounding the grassed-over burial ground, which is open to the sky. Before the War the galleries were lined with sarcophagi and paved with hundreds of tombstones, while the walls were covered with frescoes by famous Renaissance painters, but on 27th July, 1944, the building was hit by an American shell and set on fire. The lead of the roof melted in the heat and ran down the walls, destroying or badly damaging the frescoes. The remains were taken down and after years of patient restoration all those which could be made anything of were replaced on the walls in 1962. One interesting result of their removal was to reveal the sinopias or red chalk cartoons beneath them, upon which they were based. Since frescoes must be painted on wet plaster and cannot be altered once it is dry, speed in working is essential and it is necessary to make these outline drawings. Many of them are now to be seen on the walls beside their originals.

The entrance wall on the right of the door contains frescoes by Benozzo Gozzoli of Old Testament subjects; of the Life of St Ranieri by Antonio Veneziano and Andrea da Firenze; and of the Life of St Ephisus by Spinello Aretino. On the left of the door are badly damaged scenes from the Life of Job attributed to Taddeo Gaddi. On the west wall hang the medieval chains of the port of Pisa, carried off as trophies after her defeat at Meloria. One set was returned by Florence in 1848 and the other by Genoa in 1860 in token of fraternity. After the chains are frescoes of the Story of Judith by Guidotti and of Cain by Piero di Puccio of Orvieto. Notice his curious Theological Cosmography, looking rather like an archery target, with its sinopia beside it in the corner. His work continues on the north wall with Adam and Eve and the Building of the Ark. The rest of the north gallery was once devoted to Benozzo Gozzoli's twenty-three frescoes of the Old Testament but, alas, these are even more ruined than most of the other paintings. The best preserved depicts the Building of the Tower of Babel. A little way along the north gallery is the Ammannati Chapel, which leads into a hall which serves as a museum and picture gallery. One of its treasures is a famous Arabo-Coptic bronze griffin brought from the East. On the left wall is Benozzo Gozzoli's Grapè Harvest and The Drunkenness of Noah. On the right wall is the famous fresco of the Triumph of Death, whose authorship, though uncertain, is now usually ascribed to Francesco Traini, the last important Pisan painter, and The Last Judgment by the same master. In the middle of the north gallery is the famous Roman sarcophagus of Hippolytus and Phaedra which inspired Nicola Pisano.

The fortunate Pisans have hills, sea and forest at their doors. Mercifully shielding the old rivals Pisa and Lucca from the sight of each other like the sheets of cardboard which mollify fighting fish in Siam, the Monti Pisani rise to three thousand feet and shelter the seventeenth-century **Certosa di Pisa**, the largest Charterhouse in Italy after Pavia, with works by Franceschini, Ciarrè, Vanni, followers of Giambologna. Another ecclesiastical building, the eleventh-century basilica of S. Piero in Grado, rises in the solitudes of the mouth of the Arno on the spot where St Peter is said to have landed in Italy on his voyage from Antioch and where apparently the old Roman harbour was. North of the river mouth stretches the great pine forest of S. Rossore, formerly a royal property and now a presidential hunting reserve. Special permission is required to visit it, except on public holidays, but the Macchia di Migliarino beyond it is partly open to the public and is equally rich in game. On the south bank of the Arno are the growing seaside resorts of Marina di Pisa and Tyrrhenia, where there are now large film studios. Beyond, past the miles of sand and the dark pinewoods of the Tombolo behind is the old Portus Pisanus, where the modern port of Leghorn now stands.

CHAPTER 7

Leghorn

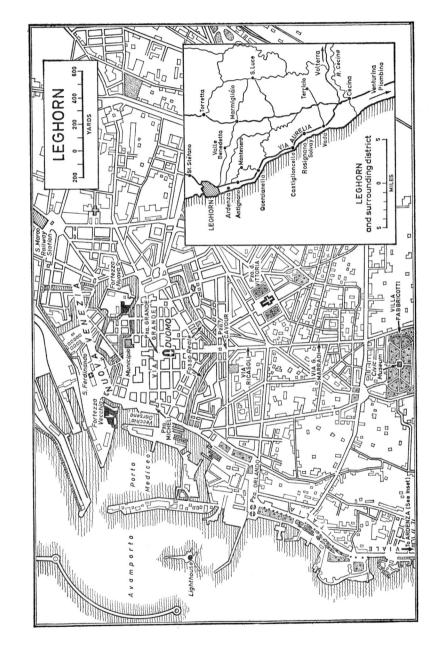

LEGHORN

YARDS

200   0   200   400   600

LEGHORN
and surrounding district

MILES

5   0   5

S. Luce
Torretta
Valle
Benedetta
Marmigliaio
Montenero
St. Stefano
Terícío
Volterra
R. Cécina
Cécina
Venturina
Piombino
VIA AURELIA
Castiglioncello
Quercianella
Rosignano
Solvay
Vada
LEGHORN
Ardenza
Antignano

S. Marco
Railway
Station

Fortezza
Nuova

Fortezza
Vecchia

S. Ferdinando

VENEZIA
NUOVA

Municipio

Pza. GRANDE

VIA GRANDE

DUOMO

Fosso Reale

Pza.
CAVOUR

Pza. d.
VITTORIA

VIA
RICASOLI

VIA G.
MARRADI

Civic
Museum

VILLA
FABBRICOTTI

Fortezza
Vecchia

Vecchia
Darsena

Pza.
MICHEL

Pza.
ORLANDO

VIALE

To ARDENZA (See inset)

Porto
Medíceo

Avamporto

Lighthouse

CHAPTER 7

Leghorn

Livorno is a busy maritime city better known to many generations of Englishmen as Leghorn. Nowadays the British and Americans in Italy talk indifferently of 'Leghorn' and 'Livorno.' And indeed few places are more often on their lips, for after the War the city rose like a phœnix from the ashes of its ninety bombings to become the biggest American military concentration in the Mediterranean, the port and supply base for the U.S. forces not only in North Italy but in Germany as well. The dumps, hutments, engineering shops and vehicle depots crowd the pinewoods of Tombolo[1] between the high road and the sea almost continuously from Leghorn to Pisa.

Leghorn is not only the second largest town in Tuscany but the fourth largest port in Italy. It is, in fact, a Tyrrhenian Trieste, the artificial creation of a monarch who needed an outlet to the sea. It was Cosimo I of Tuscany who first conceived the plan of building a port for his duchy at Livorno, a fortified village immediately to the south of Porto Pisano, the old port of Florence which had become silted up. The construction of the new harbour was begun in 1571 and took over forty years to complete. In 1591 and 1593, Ferdinando I promulgated the so-called

---

[1] 'Tombolo' is a word frequently met with along the Tyrrhenian coast, or it means 'sand dunes' and from Marina di Massa down to Monte Circeo the coast, except where the hills come down to the sea in rocky bluffs, is composed of sand dunes backed by pinewoods.

costituzione livornina conceding a number of rights and privileges to immigrants, who now began to flow in from other parts of Italy and from abroad. The liberty to practise their religion brought Jews, Moors, Greeks and 'New Christians.' (Maria Theresa was later to take very similar measures to populate her new port of Trieste.) There is even now a very large Israelite colony in Leghorn. Their famous sixteenth-century synagogue in the Piazza Elia Benamozegh was destroyed in the War but the new one built on its site and completed in 1962 is among the more exciting modern buildings in Italy.

The construction of the Porto Mediceo was completed in 1618 and commerce increased steadily after the institution of a free port. When that was abolished in 1860, its loss was made good by the foundation of new industries and in particular of the Orlando shipbuilding yards. With eighty per cent of the centre of the city destroyed or badly damaged by Allied bombing and what was left of the port installations systematically wrecked by the departing Germans, Leghorn was prostrate in 1944. Now the damage has nearly all been repaired and partly thanks to 'U.S. Forces in Germany' the city has recovered its old prosperity.

The old centre of Leghorn was the Piazza Grande, with the Cathedral at one end of it. North of it is the *municipio* and, beyond, a quarter cut up by waterways called Nuova Venezia, where the church of S. Ferdinando still has fine stucco decorations in the interior and, of all odd things, a statue of St Edward, King of England. West from the Piazza the Via Grande runs straight down to the **Piazza Micheli** on the harbour, where in several small restaurants, bars and cafés one can sit, eat and drink by the waterfront and watch the ships in the Vecchia Darsena. Close by and fortunately undamaged is the solitary artistic monument of the city, Bandini's marble statue of Ferdinando I in his robes as Grand Master of the Knights of St Stephen. It is commonly known as *I Quattro Mori*, for below, at the foot of the Grand Duke's pedestal, are four chained bronze blackamoors added in 1624-6 by Pietro Tacca, who is said to have gone for his models to the prisoners in the neighbouring hulks. Away to the right, just across the water, are the red-brick ruins of Antonio da Sangallo's Fortezza Vecchia.

Before the War this quarter consisted of tall, grave, handsome houses dating from the seventeenth and eighteenth centuries but they have all been destroyed and the centre of the town is now entirely modern. The Duomo, built at the end of the *Cinquecento* to the design of Alessandro Pieroni, and most of the other churches have been restored, more or less in their original baroque style, but there is practically nothing left of the spirit of Medicean Leghorn. Even the centre of gravity of the city has now shifted to the newer quarter south of the Fosso Reale, with the Piazza Cavour replacing the Piazza Grande. The main axis of this district is the Via Ricasoli, which runs due south from the Piazza Cavour to the **Villa Fabbricotti.** This is a public park marked by fine trees and in the middle of it is the eighteenth-century *palazzina* which houses the Labronica Library and the Civic Museum named after the nineteenth-century Livornese painter Giovanni Fattori, the leader of the *macchiaioli.* This impressionist school has always been popular in Italy but is only now becoming better known and appreciated abroad. The first three rooms are dedicated to the works of Fattori himself. The succeeding rooms are mainly devoted to Livornese painters of the nineteenth and twentieth centuries. They include a landscape by Amadeo Modigliani, the most famous son of the Jewish colony of Leghorn. In Room viii is a small collection of Old Masters: a Madonna and Child attributed to Botticelli; another by Cima da Conegliano, a battle scene by Borgognone and a Crucifixion by Neri di Bicci. The archæological section includes some of the finds from Roselle, which was the Etruscan city of Rusellae, but is not normally open to the public.

From the harbour the broad **Viale Italia,** the showpiece of Leghorn, runs due south along the seafront. On the one side are luxury flats and villas, while on the other gardens of palm, pine and tamarisk separate it from the sea. The *viale* passes a number of bathing establishments, the Aquarium, the Naval

Academy and the racecourse in the mile or two before it arrives at Ardenza, a suburb of villas and bathing beaches. A little farther on is another bathing resort, Antignano. On a height just inland from Ardenza and Antignano, about 750 feet above the sea, the **Sanctuary of Montenero** houses the miraculous *Madonna delle Grazie*, proclaimed by Pius XII as the Patron Saint of Tuscany. It has belonged to the Vallombrosans since 1792 and is a popular place of pilgrimage. It can be reached directly from Leghorn Central Station by trolleybus No. 2 and a funicular, but there is little to see except the fine view and an interesting gallery of those modern primitives known as ex-votos. Byron and Shelley, Napoleon III and Lamartine, and the poet Ugo Foscolo at one time or another stayed in villas at Montenero.

Southwards stretch a number of small seaside resorts— Quercianella, Castiglioncello (the most popular, with a number of hotels, pensions, and villas) and Rosignano, where Solvay have a big chemical factory, down to Cecina, the only town between Livorno and Piombino. From here a road runs inland to gaunt Volterra and over the mountains to Siena, while the Via Aurelia continues Romeward. At Venturina a road turns right handed to Piombino, and nearby is the railway junction of Campiglia Marittima, where the expresses to Rome stop and are met by a local train which takes passengers in a quarter of an hour to Piombino and the Elba boat.

CHAPTER 8
Elba

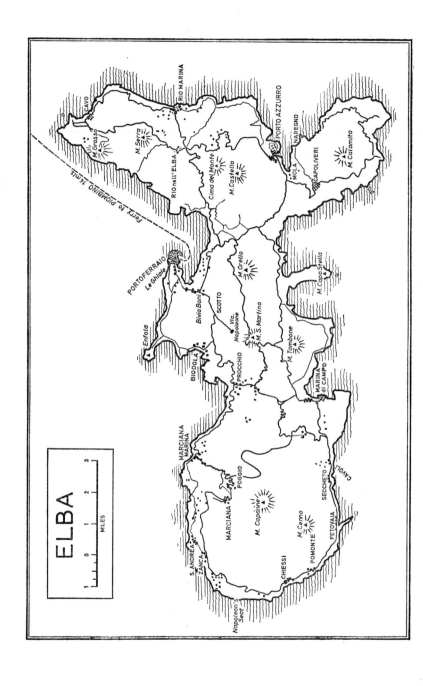

CHAPTER 8

Elba

The first reaction of most English people to the name of Elba will be the subject of the best known and most ingenious palindrome in the language: 'Able was I ere I saw Elba.' The 'I' is, of course, the Emperor Napoleon, who was banished there in 1814 after his defeat by the Allies at Leipzig and allowed to play at ruling the little island as an independent monarch. Putting the best face he could on things, he wrote ahead to General Dalesme in Elba: 'General, I have sacrificed my rights to the interests of the Country, and have reserved to myself the Sovereignty and ownership of the Island of Elba, to which all the Powers have consented. Be so good as to acquaint the Inhabitants with the new state of Affairs, and the choice which I have made of their Island as my residence in consideration of the agreeable character of their customs and of their climate. Tell them that they will be the object of my liveliest interest.' Nevertheless, the caged eagle stayed in the island less than three hundred days before taking off again for France. After Waterloo it was to be not Elba but St Helena for him.

In the last few years Elba has become known also as a holiday resort. It has no art, no architecture and no antiquities but it has almost everything else required for a peaceful summer holiday—mountain, plain and especially sea. Rocky bluffs drop down to deep, clear blue waters where the skin-diver and the underwater fisherman will find nearly every kind of Mediter-

87

ranean fish. (While sharks have appeared in the waters off Ostia and Monte Circeo, they have not as yet been reported from Elba.) The headlands are separated by small, unspoilt bays, where a handful of bathers lie in the sun, swim in the warm shallow sea or sip cool drinks under coloured umbrellas. The amenities of these bays range from complete solitude, through nothing but a very primitive little bar-kiosk or perhaps a small *trattoria*, to a luxury hotel, so that the visitor can choose to a nicety his own degree of sophistication. Shaped as it is like a crumpled napkin, the island is so small and so deeply indented (with 147 kilometres of coastline to a mere 224 square kilometres of land) that distances are very short and the visitor with a car can stay *en pension* or *demi-pension* in the hotel of his choice and drive to a different beach every day.

A network of asphalt roads already links the more interesting places on the island and is being extended every year. There are local bus services, so that it is not essential to take a car with one, but all the same it gives one a feeling of independence and most people seem to do so—other than those, of course, who fly out by way of Pisa airport. Besides taxis, there are car hire services, both self-drive and chauffeur-driven, but these are nowhere cheap and in the season there may be a run on them. The first time I went to Elba it was only for a preliminary reconnaissance of a day or two and I left my car in the garage on Piombino dock. I was surprised to find that my suitcase was the solitary one in the luggage cubbyhole on the *Æthalia*[1]; eventually I realised that I was the only passenger who had not got a car somewhere in the bowels of the ship with all their things stowed in it. Next time I came with a car myself.

The car-ferry plies almost hourly during daylight between April and September (and less frequently during the winter) to and from Piombino, which is fourteen miles from the island capital of Portoferraio. During the peak months of summer it is wise to book a passage for a car some weeks in advance but outside July and August there is seldom any difficulty. If one boat is

[1] This was the old Greek name for Elba.

full up you are sure of getting on to the next. There is a café-bar and restaurant on the port in which to while away an hour or two of waiting. The *Æthalia*, the largest of the drive-on car-ferries, has a dining-saloon but it is apt to be crowded and there is only time for one service, since the passage takes little more than an hour. Personally I prefer either to eat in the restaurant at the port before I leave or to have sandwiches and beer in the lounge, which leaves me free to enjoy the view. If you miss the last boat and have to stay the night in Piombino, make for the Albergo Centrale in the Piazza Verdi.

Car tickets vary in price with the size of the vehicle. A single ticket for a medium-sized saloon costs two or three thousand lire. Do not cut things too fine, for the booking arrangements are made as difficult as possible and involve three separate queueings where one would do. You get your personal ticket at the *biglietteria* of the Compagnia di Navigazione Toscana next door to the restaurant, but they do not sell car tickets there. You have to go across to another office of the same company to reserve a place for your car, but for some equally odd reason you cannot buy your ticket then but have to return about half an hour before the boat sails.

Some of the sailings go direct to Portoferraio, and others to one of the little ports on the east coast of the island. If you have a car, it does not matter much which boat you take, but if you have not you should make certain beforehand where you are going to be landed. In addition, there is a packet which sails from Leghorn on Fridays and returns on Mondays, calling at the two small islands of Capraia and Gorgona. A weekly boat from Piombino and Marina di Campo serves Pianosa to the south, but permission to go ashore has to be obtained from the judicial authorities, since the island is a penal settlement. Its neighbour, Montecristo, is uninhabited, unless by the swarthy, curlyheaded ghost of Dumas, and has no regular service.

Elba is by far the largest of the seven islands known as the Tuscan Archipelago. All are mountain peaks rising out of the sea except for flat Pianosa, and a glance at an orographical map will show that Elba itself is really composed of half a dozen mountainous islands connected by stretches of flat plain. They are the western, central, north-eastern and south-eastern massifs and the two small peninsulas of Capo Stella and Enfola.

There is no time like the present for visiting Elba. As late as the nineteen-fifties it was still largely undeveloped and possessed few of the comforts which the ordinary holidaymaker demands. This has all been changed. There are good roads, hotels to suit every purse and even, in the high season, one or two night clubs. In a few years the island will no doubt be spoilt, but it is not yet crowded out like the Riviera. There is still room to move around. In addition to Italian cars I saw plenty of German, British and French ones in that order of frequency, one Swedish and even a Venezuelan. Oddly enough, I did not see a single American car or hear an American voice. Even the Americans in Leghorn do not seem to have discovered Elba yet, but the Germans are there in force and, here as elsewhere in Southern Europe, are reported to be buying up land all over the island. In some places, such as Biodola and Sant' Andrea, one hears little except German spoken and in others, such as Marciana Marina, nothing but English. This segregation is due, of course, to the tie-ups and connections between the hotels and the different foreign tourist agencies. One of the factors, besides the lack of any space for a commercial airport and the limited accommodation on the car-ferries, which may yet, one hopes, keep the crowds out of Elba, is its distance from any large city. It is just too far for the weekenders from Rome, who can get to Ansedonia and Porto Santo Stefano in a couple of hours and so prefer to build their villas and keep their yachts there. But the pace of development is rapid and Elba may yet go the way of Majorca.

I had been prejudiced against the island ever since my childhood when I read Macaulay's *Lays of Ancient Rome* and felt so sorry for the eight hundred slaves who sickened in Ilva's mines. I knew Elba was a considerable producer of iron ore, that the Ilva was the most important steel works in Italy and that Portoferraio meant Iron Port, so that I imagined Elba to be a miniature Black Country. Nothing could be further from the truth. The mines are all opencast workings (so that Seius's slaves could not have sickened *in* them, at any rate) and are confined to two small and remote districts, the Rio nell'Elba, Rio Marina and Cavo triangle on the east coast and Capo Calamita in the far south. All the ore is shipped to the great Ilva works on the mainland, where Piombino belches smoke night and day to the clear Italian sky. The country near Rio Marina is a rather attractive red and ochre colour from the workings, but the rest of the island is green except for a few high bare peaks such as Monte Capanne at the western end of the island. Below, the mountains are ringed, first with sweet-scented maquis, then with woodlands of umbrella pine, chestnut, ilex and cork-oak and below them again terraced vineyards, grey, fluttering olive groves and tawny cornfields. The whole is surrounded by the sea, which is generally a shimmering blue sheet edged by a narrow border of white lace.

Portoferraio is an attractive little town, surrounded by thick walls and dominated by two castles, the five-pointed Stella on the east, and the gigantic Falcone on the west, built by Cosimo I de' Medici in the sixteenth century, when the little island was divided between three masters. Portoferraio and two miles round it belonged to the Duke of Tuscany, who magniloquently renamed it after himself, Cosmopoli; Portolongone, as Porto Azzurro was then called, was one of the Spanish *presidios*[1] scattered along the Tuscan coast; while the country districts were still ruled by the Appiani, Lords of Piombino.

Steaming into Portoferraio, the *Æthalia* passes the bomb-shattered ruins of Fort Linguella on the point protecting the Darsena and then continues to the pier. The Darsena is the sheltered harbour, facing southwards and inwards, where the summer yachts and the gaily painted fishing boats moor. Shaped like a horseshoe, it is lined with yellow stucco houses unobtrusively rebuilt to replace those destroyed in the Allied bombings. The

[1]The others were Orbetello, Porto Santo Stefano, Porto Ercole and Talamone.

terrace of the new Hotel Darsena overlooks the quay, and the Porta a Mare leads into the Piazza Cavour, where the cafés and newspaper kiosks are to be found. To the right is the covered market, once the arsenal of the Grand Duke's fleet, and up a short street ahead is the wide, plane-shaded Piazza della Repubblica. Between them, these two big squares occupy most of the level ground in the little town. At the back of them the streets turn into long flights of stone steps and climb steeply to the upper part of the city.

On the summit, near Fort Stella, is the **Palazzino dei Mulini,** where Napoleon lived during his short reign. It is a two-storied pink villa which consisted originally of two connected windmills. The upper story of the central section was added by the emperor. The Little Palace of the Mills is now a museum. The monarch's study, his reception-room, his bathrooms, his bedroom with a green bedspread spangled with golden bees, and his library are all much as he left them in 1815, with their Empire furniture and decorations intact. Among the curiosities is the great flag which he designed for his realm of Elba. On a white ground is a diagonal red stripe adorned with three golden bees—'bees which will one day sting,' wrote one of the faithful *grognards* who had followed him to Elba. Upstairs is a small museum of Napoleoniana, personal relics, uniforms, swords and autograph letters to Marshal Bertrand, who acted as his chief minister. Behind the villa is a neat garden with a view over the sea to the forbidden mainland of Piombino and Populonia. Napoleon's death mask and a cast of his hand, brought here from St Helena, are in the church of the Misericordia, where a requiem mass for him is celebrated every year on 5th May.

The road out of Portoferraio skirts the great bastions of Falcone and leads to the Piazza del Popolo, whence the Viale Manzoni runs right to Le Ghiaie, the bathing beach of the town. (*Ghiaia* means 'gravel' and the beach is of pebbles.) The jetty from which one takes the Piombino packet lies farther on to the left and about a mile beyond it on the right is a signpost marked 'Enfola.' The road is abominable but worthwhile for skindivers and for others in search of seclusion. A low, narrow spit of land just saves the little pyramidal peninsula of **Enfola** from being an island. Until recently this isthmus was the main centre of the tunny-fishing industry but the processing factory now stands idle and empty. Half a dozen of the big wooden tunny boats, solid as ever although they are said to be older than Napoleon, lie in a shed and about sixty iron anchors, rusting on the shore, mark the place where once the nets hauled the great fish inshore to be massacred. Despite the good deepwater bathing and the beauty of its situation Enfola can never become a resort because it has no fresh water.

Returning to the metalled highway, we come to the main crossroads of the island, the Bivio Boni, where one road turns sharp left to Porto Azzurro and the eastern communes, and the other continues straight ahead to Procchio and the west. Soon after, a road goes off to the left at a hamlet called Scotto and leads to Napoleon's summer villa of S. Martino. There is little enough there to see. The yellow classical building with the N's, the eagles and the bees, which faces one at the end of the long avenue of yew trees, was built in 1852 by Prince Anatole Demidoff (who through his marriage to Mathilde, the daughter of Jerome Bonaparte, was entitled to consider himself Napoleon's nephew) to house his collection of Napoleonic relics. He could hardly have chosen a more inaccessible spot for a museum and the exhibits were dispersed in 1880. Napoleon's cottage, (for it is nothing more) is behind the Demidoff villa and reached by a steep path and steps which lead straight into the upper story. There is nothing inside but the original Empire furniture, and Napoleon seldom visited it. From it a staircase leads down to the more pretentious rooms of the Villa Demidoff, which now houses a collection of mainly nineteenth-century pictures. Their interest is largely historical—some views of old Porto-ferraio and some portraits of men who were famous in their day.

Farther on are **Biodola,** with the luxury Hermitage Hotel, on a wide sandy bay, and **Procchio,** also on a wide sandy bay with

93

a luxury hotel, this time the Hotel del Golfo. The Pensione La Pergola here is very highly spoken of. After Bivio Boni, Procchio is the second cross-roads of the island, whence one highway leads south to Marina di Campo and the south coast and the other to Marciana. **Marciana Marina** is a large fishing village on a crescent bay. It has a seafaring tradition and many of the young men become sailors on the *lungo corso* ships. An agreeable promenade runs along the bay with several open-air cafés just opposite the Albergo della Pace, the historic inn of the township. There is also a good new hotel just behind, La Primula, which has a swimming pool in the garden—and this is just as well, for the bathing beach at the other end of the town, beyond the fishing harbour and the old Pisan watchtower miscalled the Torre Medicea, is composed of extremely daunting boulders. If you are travelling on your own, it is as well to make sure of your room, for the Primula tends to fill up with package tours sent out by London agencies.

Inland the ground rises gradually at first through the fields and vineyards to the two hill-top villages of Poggio and Marciana, and then more steeply to the granite peaks of three-thousand-foot Monte Capanne. The two picturesque villages (in the case of Marciana you can walk one way and take a bus the other) are surrounded by thick chestnut woods and in the heat of summer many people like to stay up there, a thousand feet above the sea. Their narrow alleys and stepped streets are photogenic and they afford magnificent views over the miles of vineyards down to Marciana Marina, the sea and across to the mainland. The best known *Aussichtspunkt* is the Belvedere on a hill-top just beyond Marciana, where the asphalt comes to an end and the road continues round the bleak, bull-headed west end of the island.

From Zanca a track runs down to S. Andrea, which has a charming little inn, the Cernia. The drawback is that the sun disappears behind a mountain and leaves the little bathing beach early in the afternoon. From Zanca the road continues along the steep granite screes of Monte Capanne high above the sea. There is a hill here called Napoleon's Seat, where the illustrious exile is supposed to have sat and gazed across the water at his native Corsica, but there is no evidence that he ever got farther than the Sanctuary of the Madonna del Monte near Poggio, where he was staying when the Countess Walewska came to visit him and was sent home with a flea in her ear. Corsica is visible from many points on the island although it is hard to believe (as I was solemnly assured) that on a clear night one can even see the headlights of the cars on the island. The road passes Chiessi and Pomonte, two forgotten fishing villages which, before it was built, were almost completely cut off by the mountain from the rest of the island, not to mention the world beyond. Past Pomonte, on the south coast of the island, are the hamlets of Fetovaia, Secchetto and Cavoli, whose little sandy beaches, not too easy of access from the road, have been discovered by enterprising bathers and campers.

On the other side of a rocky headland lies **Marina di Campo.** Like Marciana Marina and in contrast to Procchio and Biodola it is a genuine little fishing port where there are little unexpected taverns, embowered in oleanders and bougainvilleas, where fishing nets are spread out to dry on the stone quay and where you find people messing about in boats. In the tiny fish market the fresh-caught wares range from sardines to swordfish and from speckled lampreys to big spider crabs, which have a habit of escaping from their trays and baskets and walking about looking for ankles to nip. The principal hotel in the little town is called the Miramare and there is a restaurant and dance place called the Kon-Tiki at the end of the quay, which closes at the beginning of October like so many other places in Elba. Beyond the town a couple of miles of sandy beach back on to pinewoods and nestling among them are a few hotels, including a good one called the Iselba.

There is no good road along the coast eastwards from Marina di Campo and it is best to go back to Procchio and Bivio Boni to get anywhere. The road from Bivio Boni runs across a low neck of land to the south coast and the wide, sandy beach of

Lacona. On the right, near Mola, a road goes up to Capolíveri, a large village on the top of a bare hill. The population is half farming and half mining, and, true to its ancient name of Caput Liberum, it was the only place on the island which refused to accept Napoleon as ruler. From Capolíveri a steep track runs down to the beach of Naregno, which consists of three small hotels in a row. The middle one is called, rather unexpectedly, Frank's Pension. Many Elbans go to Australia to work in the sugar plantations of Queensland but Frank, an Elban, was a bank guard in Melbourne and speaks excellent English. Naregno is a good place to go if you have no transport of your own, for anyone with a car will not want to use it very often on the precipitous and deeply rutted track which connects the beach with Capoliveri. Frank has, however, a launch which goes several times a day to Porto Azzurro just across the Gulf of Mola, which boasts cafés, newspapers and places where one can leave one's car.

Porto Azzurro is the second town of the island. (Some friends of mine stayed at the Hotel Belmare and liked it.) The waterfront is mostly taken up by a big piazza spread with café tables and gay parasols. There are a few restaurants built out over the sea and near them a small bathing beach. Looming above is a great castle built in 1603 by Philip III of Spain, which is now used as a prison. From Porto Azzurro the road runs north past terraces which have been laboriously terraced for vineyards but abandoned since the phylloxera epidemic of a century ago, which killed the vines and drove the vine dressers to leave the land and seek work in the mines of Rio nell' Elba and Rio Marina.

If I have dealt with Elba in some detail, it is on account of the increasing number of foreigners who visit it every year and because, at the time of writing, no English guide exists. Little remains to be said of it except to list its six excellent wines: Sangioveto, a dry red table wine; Procanico, a dry white table wine, excellent with fish; Roselba, a *vin rosé*; the champagne-type Elba Spumante, which comes in three kinds, dry, semi-dry and sweet ('*al moscato*'); the dark red dessert wine, Aleatico, and the sweet white dessert Moscato, which is the especial pride of Capoliveri. The last two serve well as apéritifs or as a short drink in a bar. Napoleon himself told his court at Versailles: 'The inhabitants of Elba are strong and healthy because the wine of their island gives strength and health.'

CHAPTER 9

The Maremma

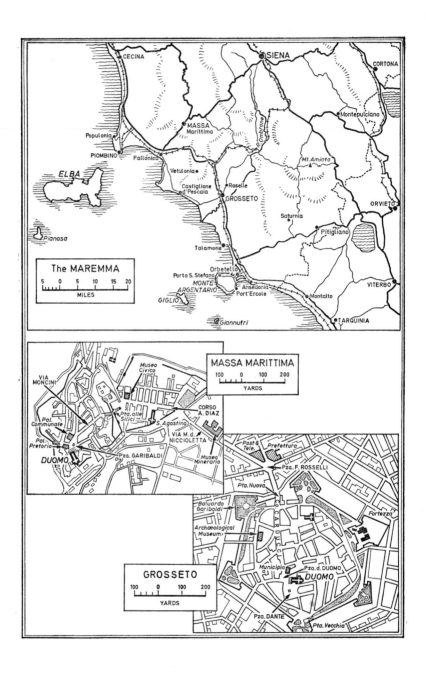

The MAREMMA

5 0 5 10 15 20
MILES

CECINA
SIENA
CORTONA
Montepulciano
Populonia
PIOMBINO Fallónica
ELBA
MASSA Marittima
Ombrone
Mt. Amiata
Vetulonia
Castiglione d'Pescaia Roselle
GROSSETO
ORVIETO
Pianosa
Saturnia
Pitigliano
Talamone
Orbetello
Porto S. Stefano
MONTE ARGENTARIO
Ansedonia
Port'Ercole
Montalto
VITERBO
GIGLIO
Giannutri
TARQUINIA

MASSA MARITTIMA

100 0 100 200
YARDS

Museo Civico
VIA MONCINI
Pta. alle Silici
S. Agostino
CORSO A. DIAZ
VIA M.d. NICCIOLETTA
Pal. Communale
Pal. Pretorio
DUOMO
Pza. GARIBALDI
Museo Minerario

Post & Tele. Prefettura
Pza. F. ROSSELLI
Pta. Nuova.
Fortezza
Baluardo Garibaldi
Archaeological Museum
Municipio
Pza. d. DUOMO
DUOMO
Pza. DANTE
Pta. Vecchia

GROSSETO

100 0 100 200
YARDS

CHAPTER 9

The Maremma

The Maremma, properly speaking, is the name of the coastal plain which extends from Cecina down to Civitavecchia in Latium. Alternatively, the Province of Grosseto is often called the Maremma, since the greater part of that region falls within its boundaries; but in addition to the plain itself, it includes also Monte Amiata, the highest mountain in Tuscany, with the massif and the foothills rising to it, as well as three small, high, blue-girdled islands. Two of them, Giglio and Giannutri, are recognised as part of the Tuscan Archipelago while the third, Monte Argentario, is a sort of sporran loosely dangling by precarious sandspits from the mainland.

In prehistoric times, it seems, this fertile territory belonged to the Umbrians, who are said (on little or no evidence) to have given their name to the Ombrone, the longest river of the Maremma. Then it became one of the principal centres of the Etruscans and contained such important cities as Macaulay's 'sea-girt Populonia' near Piombino, Rusellae, now Roselle, Vetulonia, whose site, generally recognised to be on a hill behind Castiglione delle Pescaia, is still disputed by the stubborn people of Massa Marittima, Statonia (Poggio Buco) near Pitigliano, and Vulci, which lies inland from Montalto and was one of the earliest Etruscan sites to be excavated.

There are ruins to be visited on all these sites, but they are to be recommended to the archæologist and to the walker who fancies a ramble over the hills among the sweet-smelling myrtle, rosemary and thyme, not to mention the thorn-bushes, rather than to the ordinary tourist. The Etruscans built their houses and temples of wood and in few cases do the ruins of their cities amount to more than the walls, impressive rather for their wide circuit than for what is left of their height, perhaps even a gate, a few empty tombs and possibly one or two paved stone streets running through the *macchia* of the hill-top. Those in search of interesting tombs must go to Tarquinia, just over the Latin border, to Chiusi or to Cerveteri, and those in search of works of art must seek them in the museums of the Tuscan cities or in the Villa Giulia and the Vatican Museum in Rome.

The soil of the Maremma has hardly been scratched by the picks of the archæologists and it may yet yield rich secrets and treasures of the Etruscans. But directors of museums and 'digs' sometimes come near to despair when farmers unearth vases and bronzes, sell them to private collectors and then destroy valuable evidence by ploughing up the sites. Not long ago at a Maremman village called Puntone a stubborn peasant found a strip of lead, fifteen centimetres wide by a hundred and fifty long, thickly covered with Etruscan script, and refused to part with it because he wanted to make it into smallshot to shoot thrushes with.

In the Middle Ages the Maremma became depopulated on account of the perpetual wars and the consequent malaria. Any irrigation or drainage system requires a strong central government if it is to operate, and the drainage system of this ravaged land broke down so that the blocked rivers turned into mosquito-ridden swamps behind the banked up coastal dunes. The inhabitants sickened and died, while the more virile saved their lives by going away to become bandits or mercenaries in one or other of the free companies. (The luckless Lady Pia who told Dante in Purgatory: '*Siena me fe, disfece mi Maremma*'[1] did not, however, die of malaria as is widely supposed, but for the simple reason that her husband, Nello dei Pannochieschi, being

[1]Siena made me; Maremma unmade me.

desirous of taking a new wife, threw her head first out of the window of his castle in the Maremma. Something which might have happened anywhere). There exists a curious report to the Sienese governor blaming the malaria on the poisonous breath of serpents which was wafted to the Maremma from Africa by the scirocco and on the lack of Christian breath to counteract it and purge the air—a theory hardly more far-fetched than some of those which prevailed among the learned, equally baffled by the problem of malaria, in the late nineteenth century before the discovery of the anopheles mosquito. The peasants who came down every year to work in the plain took the disease home with them, and even the rather inaptly named Massa Marittima, thirteen hundred feet up on the first spur of the Colline Metallifere, had an evil reputation for malaria, which it did not lose until the Grand Duke Leopold II drained the Scarlino swamp in the nineteenth century.

Massa Marittima where Bernardino Albizzeschi, better known as S. Bernardino of Siena, was born, lies on the road from Follonica which leads up over the hills to Siena. A mining town, it has always lived on the surrounding mineral deposits—principally pyrites, alum, iron, lead, copper and lignite—which were exploited first by the Etruscans and then by the Romans. Massa was responsible for the first mining code or, as we should say, miners' charter, in Europe. It dates from the fourteenth century and is still preserved in the Biblioteca Comunale. It is therefore the measure of the havoc caused by Sienese mis-government, wars, bandits, plagues and malaria that these ancient mines ceased production at the end of the fourteenth century, to resume it only in 1830. To-day the Società Monte-catini employs about three thousand five hundred men to work them, but there was a time when the population of Massa sank to four hundred people, creeping like ague-stricken ghosts round the empty, echoing travertine palaces and churches.

Massa is divided into two parts, the walled Old Town or Città Vecchia (rather unexpectedly the lower half), which was the original Romanesque town of the burghers and the

Commune and, above it, the Gothic Città Nuova, the New Town of the Bishops and later of the Sienese governors, which is about the same age as New College, Oxford. In the Middle Ages the Lower Town was inhabited by the partisans of Pisa, led by the Todini family, and the Upper by the partisans of Siena, led by their rivals, the Pannochieschi. Such, as though mere Guelphs and Ghibellines were not enough, were the murderous divisions in these little cities which gave rise to perpetual feuding—gang warfare dignified by the name of civic strife—and innumerable temptations for the weaker party to call in an outside power to restore its fortunes.

The centre of **Massa** is the triangular Piazza Garibaldi in the Lower Town, which is worthy to rank with any of the city centres surviving from medieval Italy. On the one side is the Duomo, set at a slight, rather coquettish, angle which reveals not only the façade but the left flank and the campanile. The rest of the square is surrounded by medieval palaces which Massa has very fortunately never had the money to demolish and rebuild (just as many a bachelor owes his liberty entirely to his poverty). It therefore remains one of the least spoilt, as it is the least visited, of all the medieval cities of Tuscany.

The handsome Duomo, built of a local stone which has weathered to a golden patina, with blind arcades across the façade and round the sides, is in the Pisan style of the early thirteenth century and was probably designed by the Lombard architect, Enrico da Campione. At the side of the Duomo is a tall campanile, recently restored, with the number of lights increasing, as was usual, towards the top—*monofore, bifore, trifore, quadrifore*, until the ultimate *pentafore* seem to make the two uppermost stories into great windows.

The façade with its seven blind arches rises on a platform at the top of an imposing flight of steps. In the architrave is carved the legend of its patron, S. Cerbone, one time Bishop of Populonia and a disciple of that S. Regulus whom we have already met at Lucca. Lovers of stone menageries (and they flourish especially in the Far East) will like to note that the sculptures feature

104

the bears which disobeyed King Totila's orders to devour the saint, the wild does with whose milk he assuaged the thirst of the papal messengers sent to summon him to Rome on a heresy charge, and the flock of pious geese who accompanied him thither. Similar scenes are repeated in the crypt, carved in bas-relief on the marble *arca* or reliquary of the saint. Unusually for a medieval work of art, it is signed and dated 1324 by Gori di Gregorio of Siena. The spacious interior of the Cathedral contains, immediately on the right of the entrance, a font with fine bas-reliefs by Giraldo da Lugano[1] of 1267, and also two works by the Sienese painter, Segna di Bonaventura, a painted wooden crucifix in the Chapel of the Sacrament and a *Madonna delle Grazie* in the Lady Chapel in the left transept. The latter, badly damaged, has been attributed also to Simone Martini.

In front of the Cathedral on the west side of the Piazza Garibaldi is the Palazzo Pretorio of 1230, formerly the seat of the Podestà and now of the prefect. It is a square block of travertine with steps and *bifore*, still imposing despite the loss of its crenellations. The small three-storied house on its left was the mansion of the Gherardesca Counts of Biserno. Beyond it is the fourteenth-century Palazzo Comunale, which contains the principal treasure of the city, the great, though damaged, *Maestà* of Ambrogio Lorenzetti, which is on the right wall of the mayor's office on the first floor. (The usher will take you to it.) The blue-robed Madonna presses her cheek to the Child's. Her throne is set upon three steps representing the Cardinal Virtues. The top one is inscribed *Caritas*, and Charity, crowned and dressed in red, is seated upon it, holding in one hand a pointed shaft and in the other a flaming heart. On the second step, *Spes*, sits Hope, in dark blue. She holds a high tower and gazes at the jewelled crown which floats above it. The bottom step, *Fides*, is the seat of Faith, clad in emerald green, who looks into a mirror reflecting two faces, the Old Law and the New. On either side

[1]As at Lucca, most of the thirteenth-century sculptors and architects of Massa Maríttima seem to have migrated from the shores of Lake Como and Lake Lugano.

of the Madonna are angels holding lutes, viols and censers, and behind them stands a great company of saints, including S. Cerbone with his geese.

On the right of the Piazza Garibaldi the steep Via Moncini leads to the Upper Town, through the fourteenth-century Porta alle Silici. The castles of the Fortezza dei Senesi and the Fortezza dei Massetani are linked by an audacious flying arch. The nearby Museo Civico in the Palazzo delle Armi contains a Sassetta. Half-way along the Corso Armando Diaz on the right the Romanesque Gothic church of S. Agostino (*circa* 1300) has an impressive interior, and at the end, No. 1 Via Martiri della Niccioleta, is the Museo Minerario, where geologists may study a collection of the various minerals of the Massetano.

Until a hundred and fifty years ago **Grosseto,** the capital of the Maremma, was a small walled city almost synonymous with malaria. Now, since the draining of the marshes, it is the prosperous capital of a rich agricultural zone. Its population has expanded five-fold in the last thirty years and has spread, particularly to the north and west, so far that the present centre of the city is now outside the walls altogether at the Piazza Fratelli Rosselli. Grosseto, on the Via Aurelia, makes an excellent halting place for the motorist driving to or from Rome. The subterranean Buca di S. Lorenzo, beneath the Baluardo Garibaldi and on the main road, with ample parking space, just by the turn at the Porta Nuova, is a cool and pleasant place in which to lunch if you do not mind being grinned at by the autographed photographs of the black-eyed film stars who have preceded you, while you can stay the night in comfort at the Lorena, the Bastiani or the S. Giorgio—Category I, II and III hotels respectively.

The Municipio in the Piazza del Duomo is a modern construction and beside it is the much restored Cathedral. The façade was rebuilt in 1845 but the doors and most of the south side are fourteenth-century. The pink and white marble gives a pleasing effect, however, and if one were not told one would hardly guess what a great part of the building is restoration. On the altar of the Madonna delle Grazie in the left transept is a striking Assumption by Matteo di Giovanni. Just to the left of the Cathedral, over the Sacristy, is the Museum of Sacred Art, which contains some good Sienese pictures and notably Sassetta's exquisite Madonna of the Cherries, so called because the Infant is carrying a cherry to his mouth. Look well at the very Byzantine Last Judgment, of the School of Guido da Siena, and at the Virgin and Child attributed to Simone Martini.

The Archæological Museum houses an Etruscan collection gathered from Rusellae, some five or six miles away, and the other ancient cities of the Maremma. It contains a number of cinerary urns, mostly depicting stock subjects like the Death of Hippolytus and the Fratricide of the Theban Brethren, Eteocles and Polynices, such as one grows to recognise in all the Etruscan Museums. There are also a number of good vases, the black *bucchero* ware which was the typical Etruscan pottery. It may be added that the enterprising Ente Provinciale per Il Turismo has produced a fully annotated and well illustrated guide to the Museum, so that it is quite a good place in which to take one's first tottering steps into the strange world of Etruscan antiquities.

The so long deserted coast of the Maremma is now blossoming into a little scattered kind of a lido, between the pinewoods and the sands, but it is not yet so crowded as the Versilia, the coast near Rome or the built up shores of the Northern Adriatic. Nevertheless, the local guide-book already applies the ominous adjective *'frequentatissima'* to Follonica, the first resort south of the Leghorn border. Farther south, the picturesque old fishing port of Castiglione delle Pescaia has likewise developed a bathing beach beneath the walled and towered *castello*. The principal hotel bears the odd name of Alleluiah and not far away a new luxury hotel, the Riva del Sole, has been carved out among the umbrella pines which border the beach. On the promontory to the north of it, a new resort is being built up at Punta Ala.

Marina di Grosseto, eight miles from the capital, has grown up where a few years ago the long miles of sandy beach were interrupted only by an old Spanish fort, the Torre San Rocco. Talamone, farther south and at the foot of a rocky promontory, has less than five hundred inhabitants but a history which dates from the wars of Marius and Sulla. The Sienese once tried to make it into the port of their ill-fated Republic.

Farther south again is **Ansedonia,** where rich Romans are building week-end villas. It is only a hundred miles from the capital—which, for a Roman driving a fast car along the Via Aurelia, means less than a couple of hours. There is a new luxury hotel, the Villa Dany, while the medieval watch-tower of S. Biagio has been turned into a pension and restaurant. On the hill above are the ruins of the Roman city of Cosa, founded in 273 BC, and for centuries one of the principal commercial centres of the region. (According to Rutilius, its inhabitants were driven out by an army of mice.) It has recently been excavated by the American Academy in Rome. The walls, which rise from twelve to thirty feet in places, are reinforced by eighteen towers and pierced by three main gates and a postern. They enclose a quadrangle nearly a mile in circumference. Below, just at the north end of the bathing beach, are some ruined walls and a curious man-made channel cut in the rock and known as the *Tagliata Etrusca*. This was the ancient port which served the city of Vulci.

Near Ansedonia a road turns off to **Orbetello,** It was the chief of the Spanish *presidios* in the Tyrrhenian and you enter the walled town through a triple-arched gate which still bears the arms of Philip III. The Duomo of S. Maria Assunta in the main square has a handsome Gothic façade but, inside, the only object of interest, if not exactly of reverence, is a rather odd fresco showing Pius XII, surrounded by angels, proclaiming the dogma of the Assumption. Orbetello is built on a tongue of land stretching out in the middle of a lagoon towards Monte Argentario. On either side the lagoon is bounded by two long low sandspits, the Tombolo della Giannella and the Tombolo di Feniglia, both with good bathing beaches. In 1842 a causeway was built to join Orbetello to Monte Argentario, thus dividing the lagoon into two halves. The road to the peninsula runs along this dyke.

Arrived on **Monte Argentario,** you turn left for Port' Ercole, which lies in a sheltered roadstead between two towering Spanish fortresses. In fact, it is two villages in one, for the old walled town, the Port of Hercules, badly shattered by bombing, lies on the slopes of the southern fortress while the newer fishing and yachting port is at the other end of the bay. The market is here and several *trattorie*, of which I can recommend the Bucaniere. The inhabitants are mainly descended from immigrant Neapolitan fishermen. Just behind the Old Town a *strada panoramica* runs up the hill and along the top of the cliffs, but I do not drive up it myself, for I find that if you keep your eyes on the road you cannot see the panorama and if you look at the landscape instead of the road you can very easily become a part of it for good and all.

Porto Santo Stefano on the north coast of Monte Argentario has in the last few years become very fashionable and crowded. Rich Romans keep their yachts there and film stars come up from Cinecittà for much publicised and sometimes rather controversial week-ends. The town itself is situated on a small headland separating two bays, one devoted mainly to yachts and the other to fishing boats, of which there are about a hundred and fifty based on Porto Santo Stefano. It is a very attractive little place despite the summer crowds and the queues of smart cars they bring in their train. There are a number of newish hotels but anyone thinking of staying there in the season would be wise to book well in advance. (The local information office in the Palazzo del Comune grandiloquently calls itself the Associazione Turistica La Perla dell' Argentario.) For luncheon I generally go to the Pace because in addition to fresh sea-food it has an outside dining-room on a terrace overlooking the cobalt-blue waters of the Tyrrhenian. Porto Santo Stefano is the port from which the packetboats take off to rocky, mountainous **Giglio,**

the second largest island of the Tuscan Archipelago, which is now becoming a fashionable resort for summer visitors, under-water fishermen and Romans who want somewhere—but for how long now anywhere on the Mediterranean?—off the beaten track.

CHAPTER 10

Volterra

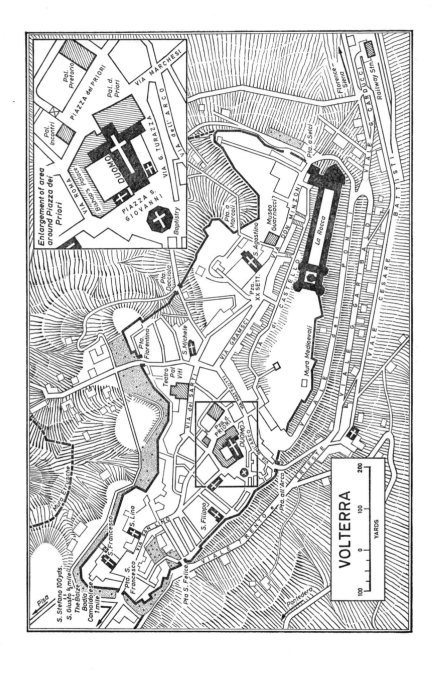

VOLTERRA

Enlargement of area around Piazza dei Priori

PIAZZA dei PRIORI
Pal. Pretorio
Pal. d. Priori
Pal. Incontri
VIA MARCHESI
VIA ROMA
Bishop's palace
DUOMO
VIA G. TURAZZA
VIA DELL' ARCO
PIAZZA S. GIOVANNI
Baptistry

Railway Stn.
Florence Siena
VIALE CARDUCCI
Pta. a Selci
VIALE CESARE BATTISTI
Pta. Diaccia
Pta. a Marcoli
Museo Guarnacci
VIA DON MINZONI
La Rocca
C
CASTELLO
Pza. XX SETT.
S. Agostino
VIA GRAMSCI
Muro Medioevale
VIA DI CASTELLO
S. Michele
Pta. Florentina
Teatro Pal. Viti
VIA DEI SARTI
Pza. d. PRIORI
DUOMO
VIALE PEPOLI
VIALE GARIBALDI

Pisa
S. Stefano 100yds.
S. Giusto ¼mile
The Balze
Badia Camaldolese 1mile
Muro Etrusche
S. Francesco
Pza. S. Francesco
VIA S. LINO
S. Lino
S. Filippo
Pta. S. Felice
VIA FELICE
Pta. all'Arco
Portedera

VOLTERRA

100   0   100   200
YARDS

CHAPTER 10

Volterra

All readers of Macaulay's *Lays*, and of *Puck of Pook's Hill* too for that matter, will remember

> *lordly Volaterra,*
> *Where scowls the far-famed hold*
> *Piled by the hands of giants*
> *For godlike kings of old.*

Still girdled by Etruscan walls over four miles round, Volterra crowns the topmost ridge of the mountains which separate the Val d'Elsa from the Val Cecina. 'It lies back some thirty miles from the sea, on a towering great bluff of rock that gets all the winds and sees all the world,' wrote D. H. Lawrence, who complained bitterly of the icy blasts which blew through this bleak city one blustery April day when he was there. Indeed, I have shivered there myself on a July noon. But one must expect these things in return for a view which extends from the Apennines to (on a very clear day) Corsica and Elba.

Nowadays Volterra, enclosed within medieval walls, occupies little more than a third of the space of the Etruscan city, whose walls ramble across the countryside far outside the town. Volterra was one of the most powerful cities of the Etruscan League, and her territories extended from the banks of the Arno in the far north through Pisa down to Populonia, which was near Piombino. She controlled not only a rich agricultural country, at a time when the Maremma was still drained and healthy, but the whole seacoast of Northern Etruria.

So strong was the situation of the city that it was able to withstand a two-year siege by Sulla and even put up a successful resistance to the Vandals. Little is known of its history in the Dark Ages. It emerged from obscurity in the time of the Othos, shrunken almost to a village nestling in a corner of the Etruscan walls and governed by its bishops. Then it became a commune, fighting alike against the bishops, the feudal nobles of the surrounding country and its neighbour, San Gimignano. Later the Belforti became lords of Volterra until the citizens drove them out. After several transitory Florentine occupations, the city was finally besieged, taken and sacked by the Florentines in 1472 and reduced to full subjection.

Volterra may be reached from Poggibonsi, Pontedera and Cecina. All the approaches are impressive, but I think the most striking is that from Pontedera, for then one sees the Balze from below and climbs up to the city beside them. The Balze, literally the Cliffs, are perhaps the most striking feature of Volterra. They are an enormous abyss, where landslides have carried away an ancient necropoli, a suburb with a church and a stretch of the Etruscan wall. The deserted Badia Camaldolese, a Romanesque monastery dating from the eleventh century, stands isolated on the edge of the precipice, gloomily waiting to be engulfed in its turn. The lower strata of the Balze are of grey clay and the upper of soft yellow sandstone. The clay below is the first to be eroded by the rains and it brings down the sands above it. 'It is a horrible scene, looking down into the rifts and precipices of an arid and ghastly desert, and with the feeling that the flowery surface on which you are standing may be hurled into destruction to-morrow,' was Augustus Hare's reaction to the Balze.

It will be a long time yet, however, before the city itself is 'hurled into destruction,' for the Balze are still nibbling away at the outer circuit of the Etruscan walls, nearly a mile from the centre. That centre is the Piazza dei Priori, surrounded by medieval palaces of a brownish local stone called *panchina*. For, if Volterra contains few works of art of much interest except to Etruscologists, it has preserved almost intact its aspect of a medieval Italian hill town.

On the south-west side of **the Piazza** is the Palazzo dei Priori, now the Town Hall, with the coats of arms of the Florentine governors strung across its façade. It is the oldest Palazzo Comunale in Tuscany and on a smaller scale resembles the Palazzo della Signoria at Florence. Facing it is the Palazzo Pretorio, formerly the seat of the Captain of the People and now of the Questura. It is surmounted by an old tower officially called the Torre del Podestà but popularly known as the Torre del Porcellino or the Piglet's Tower because it is adorned with an indeterminate-looking animal which may possibly be a wild boar. Near the tower, in the east corner of the square, is a passable restaurant called the Etruria. (The best hotel is the Nazionale in the Via dei Marchesi, which in Hare's day was 'a clean and good country inn with very moderate charges.') On the north-west side of the Piazza is the Palazzo Incontri, once a seminary and now the Cassa di Risparmio di Volterra. The present Bishop's Palace stands beside the Palazzo dei Priori with its main front on the Via Roma. Sandwiched between the two palaces is a door which leads into the north transept of the Cathedral.

In the Council Hall on the first floor of the **Palazzo dei Priori** an entire wall is devoted to a fresco of the Annunciation with SS. Giusto, Ottaviano, Cosmas and Damian, believed by some authorities to be the work of Jacopo Orcagna. It was restored in 1958 and 1962 after being damaged in the ten-day Battle of Volterra in 1944, and traces of an earlier fresco were found beneath it. On another wall is the Marriage at Cana and in the adjoining Sala della Giunta is Job, both by Donato Mascagni, a sixteenth-century Camaldolese monk from the Badia.

On the second floor is the Picture Gallery, which consists of two rooms. It contains a particularly attractive Annunciation by Luca Signorelli and a Madonna and Child with Saints by the same master. There are also three paintings by Taddeo di Bartolo of Siena, notably a polyptych with a predella of the

Madonna and Child with Saints. There is a Nativity by Benvenuto di Giovanni dated 1470; a curious swan-like Madonna by Stefano Vanni of Florence called The Madonna with the Long Neck; a Redeemer in Glory with Four Saints by Domenico Ghirlandaio with a delightful landscape in the background; and a powerfully composed Deposition, which is the acknowledged masterpiece of Rosso Fiorentino the Mannerist. From the tower of the Palazzo there is a magnificent panorama over the hills and the sea as far as the islands.

Round the corner in the Via Roma the Bishop's Palace contains a six-roomed **Museum of Sacred Art,** opened in 1936. It is a particularly rich one for so small a town, for it has been able to draw upon the local churches and it is also the haven of the works of art rescued from the church engulfed by the Balze. Do not miss Andrea della Robbia's benevolent and dignified half-length figure of St Linus, the successor of St Peter as second Pope, who was perhaps Volterra's most famous son; Antonio Pollaiuolo's beaten silver bust of S. Ottaviano; nor Giambologna's crucifix in gilded bronze. There used to be a good collection of vestments here, but it was badly damaged when a shell hit it in 1944.

Round the corner from the Museum and directly behind the Piazza dei Priori is the **Piazza S. Giovanni,** across which the Cathedral and the Baptistery face each other. The latter is said to have been built on the ruins of a pagan temple and bears the date 1283 over its door. (The sacristan of the Cathedral will open it for you.) It is an octagonal building with a façade of black and white marble and a cupola in the style of Brunelleschi. The decorated arch over the high altar is said to be by Mino da Fiesole and the octagonal white marble font is the work of Andrea Sansovino. The five panels round it represent Faith, Hope, Charity, Justice and the Baptism of Jesus.

The plain façade of the Cathedral of the Assumption (the **Duomo**) is attributed by Vasari to Nicola Pisano and is said to have been finished in 1254. Immediately on the left, as you go in, is the Oratory of the Addolorata, in which, half hidden

116

One of the 600 Etruscan funerary urns from the Museo Guarnacci in Volterra, one of the most important Etruscan museums in Tuscany. This urn dates from the third century BC.

Harvest time in Tuscany – a scene near Volterra.

behind iron grilles, are two notable works in polychrome terra-
cotta by Zaccaria Zacchi, an Epiphany on the right and a Crib
on the left. The latter has a background painted by Benozzo
Gozzoli who has given us a portrait of himself in the person of
the leading shepherd. (The sacristan will light them up for
you if you can find him.) On the right of the oratory is the
Chapel of the Santissimo Nome di Gesù, and over the altar is
the monogram of Christ painted by St Bernardino of Siena and
presented by him to Volterra when he came on a preaching trip
to the city.

Over the second altar on the left wall of the nave is a good
Annunciation by Mariotto Albertinelli. Nearby is the pulpit
constructed in the sixteenth century with thirteenth-century
Pisan panels representing the Last Supper, the Annunciation and
the Sacrifice of Isaac. The Last Supper quaintly shows Judas
receiving the sop kneeling at the feet of Christ and behind him
the Devil lying under the table and snarling like a dog. Over the
altar in the north transept is Domenichino's Conversion of
St Paul in very bad condition. The High Altar bears a marble
tabernacle of 1470 by Mino da Fiesole and beside it, near the
sacristy door, is a painted wooden Madonna sometimes attributed
to Jacopo della Quercia. In the second chapel of the south
transept is a very famous thirteenth-century Deposition in polychrome wood with five figures lavishly dressed in blue and gold.
Even Christ has a golden loincloth. The Raising of Lazarus on
the altar of the Cappella Serguidi is considered to be the masterpiece of Santi di Tito of Sansepolcro.

From the Via dei Marchesi, running off the Piazza dei Priori,
the steep Via dell' Arco runs down to an Etruscan city gate, the
famous **Porta all' Arco.** (It is not to be recommended to
motorists, for it is a cul-de-sac and there is nowhere to turn at
the bottom of what is almost a cliff.) Half-way down on the left
you can look into a little home-workshop turning out the
alabaster ornaments for which Volterra is famous. They may
be seen and purchased at the Co-operative of the Alabaster
Workers (*Artieri d' Alabastro*) at 2 Via Roma, and elsewhere. There

are many quarries in the Val d'Era and it is one of the leading industries of Volterra. The alabaster is white, of a rather revolting waxen appearance and very easy to work. The little Leaning Towers on sale in Pisa come from here.

The arch itself is Etruscan but the superstructure is Roman and medieval. Nobody knows the significance of the three weatherworn black heads on the outer side of the gate. On 1st of July, 1944, the Germans decided to blow up the gate in a futile attempt to retard the Allied advance but the inhabitants went to the German commander and volunteered to block it themselves. He agreed on condition that the blocking should be completed within twenty-four hours. Men, women and children set to work, regardless of the falling American shells, and in a few hours blocked the whole road leading to the arch. Hence the inscription outside the gate recording proudly that it was saved by 'us Volterrans.'

Follow the Via Matteotti to the left out of the Via dei Marchesi, and the Via Gramsci on the right will take you into the Piazza XX Settembre. On the far side of it is the **Church of S. Agostino** with a thirteenth-century crucifix of carved wood in the Byzantine style and other works of art. A few yards beyond it, on the left in the Via Don Minzoni, is the **Museo Guarnacci,** one of the most important Etruscan museums in Tuscany. It was founded in the eighteenth century by a wealthy connoisseur of Volterra, Monsignor Mario Guarnacci, who initiated extensive excavations in the subsoil round the town. (A unique feature of this museum is that all the exhibits were found within the commune.) On the ground floor are prehistoric, Etruscan and Roman collections, while the first floor is entirely Etruscan. The Museum contains over six hundred funerary urns in alabaster, terra-cotta and tufa, mostly dating from the last period of Etruscan art, from the fourth to the first century BC. (The oldest Italic and Etruscan necropoli were swallowed by the Balze.) As well as mythological scenes on the side, most of them bear a portrait bust of the deceased on the lid, with a single flower for a young person, two for a middle-aged one and three for an old one. The often reproduced carving of the elderly man reclining on his elbow and gazing at his old wife is here on the first floor of the Guarnacci.

On the left of the ground floor is the prehistoric section, which contains rich documentation of the Villanovian Age. The Etruscan section in the main hall contains a number of portrait urns adorned with the stock mythological figures of Tritons, Gorgons, Nereids, Griffins, Furies and various deities, of the Rape of Proserpine, of cavaliers riding down to the underworld or of fights between Gauls and Etruscans. On the right of the atrium is the Roman section with two noble heads of Augustus from the Roman theatre, and at the end you may walk out into a garden celebrated by D'Annunzio in his novel *Forse che si, forse che no*, with a good view at the end of it over Val d'Era.

On the first floor are more urns with mass-produced mythological subjects, such as Hippodamia, Hippolytus and Phaedra, the Theban Brothers, Eteocles and Polynices, the Rape of Helen, Ulysses and the Sirens, Philoctetes on Lemnos and dozens of other old favourites. The urns are succeeded by collections of vases and amphoræ, mostly from the first century BC and mostly of local manufacture. Then follow weapons, furniture, jewellery, domestic utensils, coins and anything else that might have been thought to be of use to a man in the world beyond the tomb. Among the bronzes the most curious is a pencil-thin, immensely elongated figure of a boy known as 'The Evening Shadow.' It reminds one curiously of a Giacometti.

Of the lesser churches of Volterra, **S. Girolamo**, built in the fifteenth century (possibly to a design by Michelozzo), contains two very good works by Giovanni della Robbia in the chapels on either side of the portico, St Francis Delivering the Rule to St Louis of Toulouse and St Elizabeth of Hungary on the right, and the Last Judgment on the left. In the interior is an Annunciation with SS. Michael and Catherine by Benvenuto di Giovanni dated 1466. **S. Francesco**, just beyond S. Lino which stands on the reputed site of the house of the second pontiff, is worth a visit for the Cappella della Croce di Giorno of 1315, which is entered by a door on the right of the façade. It was entirely covered with frescoes in 1410 by Cenni di Francesco Cenni, depicting the Legend of the True Cross and the Life of Christ. Going out of the medieval walls by the imposing **Porta S. Francesco,** you pass the ruined church of Santo Stefano, a section of the Etruscan walls, seventeenth-century S. Giusto and so on to the Balze and the ruins of the Badia abandoned by its monks over a century ago in 1861.

Dominating Volterra is the enormous Medicean fortress known as **La Rocca,** its machicolated walls and towers frowning across the Maremma from the highest crest of the ridge. It is one of the most formidable Renaissance fortresses in Italy. Here the famous bandit Count Felicini spent forty-three years in solitary confinement so cramped that the marks of his feet and elbows are said to be still visible in the naked rock. The fortress cannot, however, be seen without special permission from the Ministry of Grace and Justice, for it is now a penitentiary, housing mainly 'lifers' and long sentence men. Below the Rocca is the Viale dei Ponti, the bench-lined promenade of Volterra, where the citizens assemble to watch the sunset, enjoy the view of the Colline Metallifere and escape from the cutting wind which torments them every day. What with the wind and the prison, this is the least gay of all the Tuscan towns.

CHAPTER 11

San Gimignano

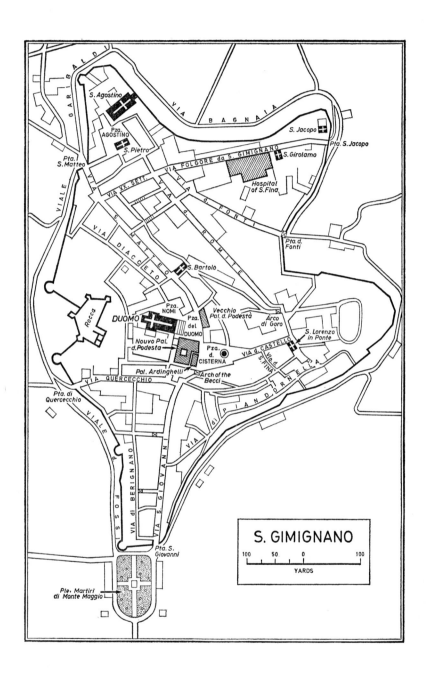

S. Agostino

Pza.
AGOSTINO

S. Pietro

Pta.
S. Matteo

VIALE

VIA XX. SETT

VIA DIACCETO

VIA GARIBALDI

VIA BAGNAIA

S. Jacopo

Pta. S. Jacopo

VIA FOLGORE da S. GIMIGNANO

S. Girolamo

Hospital
of S.Fina

Pta. d.
Fonti

VIA d. ROMITE

VIA d. FONTI

VIA S. MATTEO

S. Bartolo

Rocca

Pza.
NOMI

DUOMO

Pza.
del
DUOMO

Nouvo Pal.
d.Podesta

Pza.
d.
CISTERNA

Vecchio
Pal. d. Podesta

Arco
di Goro

S. Lorenzo
in Ponte

VIA d. CASTELLO

Pal. Ardinghelli

Arch of the
Becci

VIA QUERCECCHIO

Pta. di
Quercecchio

VIA di PIANDORNELLA

VIA d. S FINA

VIA di BERIGNANO

VIALE

FOSS

VIA S. GIOVANNI

Pta. S.
Giovanni

Ple. Martiri
di Monte Maggio

S. GIMIGNANO

100   50   0   100

YARDS

CHAPTER 11

San Gimignano

There is a town with the lovely name of Madrigal de las Altas Torres on the way to Salamanca. Similarly, S. Gimignano likes to call itself 'S. Gimignano alle Belle Torri,' for the little city is famous for its high medieval 'towers of nobility,' more of which survive there than in any other town in Italy. To-day there are fifteen left standing but according to tradition there were once seventy-two. S. Gimignano must have looked, in D. H. Lawrence's phrase, 'like an angry porcupine' or at the very least like Benozzo Gozzoli's St Sebastian in the Collegiata, who has no fewer than thirty-four arrows sticking out of his emaciated torso. These towers were built partly as keeps in the anarchic Middle Ages and partly as status symbols, with each noble trying to build a higher tower than his neighbour. In S. Gimignano the podestà built a tower in 1311 which was a hundred and seventy-eight feet high and he forbade anyone to build a higher one; so the arrogant Salvucci built twin towers side by side just to show what they could do if they wanted to.

The town freed itself from the rule of the Bishops of Volterra in the early twelfth century and became a free commune. But S. Gimignano, in the thirteenth century so prosperous that the Commune had to introduce sumptuary laws to restrain the extravagant luxury of the citizens, fell a prey to the internecine rivalries of its nobles, culminating in the fierce feud between the Guelph Ardinghelli and the Ghibelline Salvucci, which in 1352 induced the distracted citizens to 'give themselves in perpetuity' to the Florentine Republic, an offer which the cautious Florentines accepted only by one vote.

Climbing the hill and passing through the gates into S. Gimignano the traveller seems to have left the modern world behind him and to have entered a living and breathing thirteenth-century city. The **Via S. Giovanni,** paved with travertine and lined with thirteenth-century houses, leads under the Arch of the Becci into the **Piazza della Cisterna,** so called because of the thirteenth-century well in the centre of it. (Notice how in the course of eight centuries the soft ropes have cut channels inches deep in the hard stone.) The Piazza is paved with red tiles in a herring-bone pattern and surrounded by medieval palaces and towers. The tower at the south-west corner belonged to the Becci. On the west side is the Ardinghelli Palace, its towers pollarded almost to rooftop level when the family were driven into exile. On the south side of it is an excellent hotel and restaurant, La Cisterna, in what was once the Palazzo Mori-Checcucci.

Adjoining the Piazza della Cisterna is the Piazza del Duomo, the central square of the city. Immediately on the left is the Nuovo Palazzo del Podestà. On the right is the **Vecchio** Palazzo del Podestà, with a large loggia which in summer is used as an opera stage. In front are the twin towers of the Salvucci. Facing the Vecchio Palazzo, is a broad stairway leading up to the **Duomo** or Collegiata itself. A plain façade confronts one with two doors, a 'men's door' on the right and a 'women's door' on the left, and three circular windows above.

The Romanesque interior is almost entirely covered with frescoes by eminent Sienese and Florentine painters, but the light is not good and the best time to see them is the morning. On the entrance wall is a thirteenth-century Sienese fresco of St Nicholas of Bari giving the three golden balls as a dowry to the poor nobleman's daughters and so saving them from a life of ill-fame, and on the pillars by the door are a St Catherine attributed to Lippo Memmi, and SS. Jerome, Bernardino and

124

Frescoes at San Gimignano. *Above:* St Fina's funeral, with the towers of San Gimignano and Ghirlandaio's own portrait in the figure just behind the bishop. *Below:* St Augustine as a child, being handed over to the schoolmaster by his mother; on the right, the saint receives his first caning.

The towers of San Gimignano.

Antony Abbot by Benozzo Gozzoli. There are two very expressive wooden statues representing the Annunciation by Jacopo della Quercia. Between them is a St Sebastian by Benozzo Gozzoli dated 1465. Above are three frescoes of 1393 by Taddeo di Bartolo, showing the Last Judgment in the middle with Heaven and Hell on either side. The pillar beside the women's door is painted by Benozzo Gozzoli with the Assumption, St Augustine and St Bernard.

The left-hand wall of the nave is entirely covered with frescoed scenes from the Old Testament by Bartolo di Fredi of Siena, who concluded his work in 1356. The lunettes at the top tell the story of the Creation and the Eating of the Forbidden Fruit, continuing along the top row from left to right with the Expulsion, Cain and Abel, three panels of the story of Noah, two of Abraham and two of Joseph, which are continued in two panels at the left of the bottom row. Three scenes are then devoted to the story of Moses (notice particularly the Crossing of the Red Sea) and five to the misfortunes of Job. The saint dressed in nothing but a halo in the last scene under the organ is Job smitten by his devil-sent disease.

Some fifty years after Bartolo di Fredi had completed the left wall, Barna da Siena, a more considerable painter, was called in to decorate the right-hand wall. His work consists of twenty-two scenes from the Life of Christ. Chronologically, they start with the lunettes on the left, continue with the upper row, again starting from the left and continue with the lower row, this time reading from right to left. The series ends with a magnificent Crucifixion. Below are Roman horsemen and in the left-hand corner the Virgin swoons. Above, the figure of Christ stands out white and almost luminous against a black sky spangled with cherubim. The great Ghiberti was so impressed with this fresco that he called Barna 'most excellent among the other artists, most expert and most learned.' It was, alas, his last work for in 1410, according to Vasari, he fell from the scaffolding and died. The fresco was finished by his pupil, Giovanni d'Asciano. The master is buried in the Duomo which he adorned with these great Gothic paintings, always seeming on the verge of breaking through to the Renaissance.

At the end of the right-hand wall is the **Chapel of Santa Fina** (for which the sacristan sells tickets and turns on the light). S. Fina is S. Gimignano's own favourite saint. She was a child of ten who was stricken with a dire disease, which she interpreted as a punishment for her sin in accepting an apple from a little boy. She dedicated her sufferings to God and spent five years lying on her back on a hard oak table. The chapel was designed by Giuliano da Maiano and the altar, where the bones of the saint repose in a gilded box, is the work of his brother Benedetto. The enchanting frescoes are by Domenico Ghirlandaio and were painted in 1475. On the right wall St Gregory appears to the saint to announce that she would die on the day on which the Church celebrated his birthday. It shows a pleasant Renaissance interior with roses peeping through the window and two holy women in white wimples, only slightly surprised by the apparition of the saint. On the left wall is S. Fina's funeral, solemnised by the Bishop and attended by the clergy and the notables of the town. The towers of the city appear through the windows, framing the composition on either side. The painter has painted his own portrait in the figure behind the Bishop and beside him that of his brother-in-law and pupil, the Sangimignanese painter, Sebastiano Mainardi.

The ciborium on the high altar between two angels is the work of Benedetto da Maiano, as is the sculptured canopy in the Chapel of St Geminianus on the left. Beneath it is a reliquary containing the finger of St Geminianus, a holy Bishop of Modena, which according to the legend was stolen at his funeral by a Tuscan boy for the sake of the beautiful ring upon it and brought here to the city which made him its patron and took his name. The choir stalls are attributed to Antonio da Colle. In the loggia of the Baptistery just off the left aisle is a delightful Annunciation by Domenico Ghirlandaio. The font was made by Girolamo di Cecchino the Sienese in 1378.

Outside the Baptistery is the rather derelict-looking Piazza

126

Pecori, called after the local historian, once Provost of S. Gimignano, who wrote the *Storia della Terra di S. Gimignano*. It is surrounded by medieval houses, the finest of which is the Provost's Palace. On the other flank of the Duomo is the Piazza dell' Erbe or market square and at the upper end of it is the Rocca, the castle built in 1353 by the Florentines after the submission of the city. Cosimo de' Medici dismantled it in 1555 after the fall of Siena, when it was no longer needed. To-day it consists only of ivy-clad ruins, but the last surviving turret still affords a fine prospect of the town. The guardian lives in the house on the left.

The Palazzo Comunale in the Piazza del Duomo was begun in 1270 by Arnolfo di Cambio. The tower, the Torre del Podestà or Torre Grossa, was completed in 1311 and straightway became the yardstick for height which no private towers were allowed to exceed. The courtyard has on its right a large recess called the Loggia del Giudice, where justice was formerly administered. Three frescoes all remind the judge of the need for impartiality in his task. Taddeo di Bartolo's Holy Child, for example, holds a scroll on which is inscribed '*Diligite justitiam, qui judicatis terram*,' while Sodoma's fresco shows St Ivo, the patron saint of lawyers, dispensing justice. A travertine staircase leads out of the courtyard to the upper stories which house the Museum.

On the first floor is Dante's Hall, where on 8th May, 1300, the poet, at the head of an embassy from Florence, addressed the podestà and council and urged them to join the Tuscan League. The representatives of the guilds sat on the benches to the left, the Guelph leaders on the right, and the members of the town council at the far end. The great fresco of the *Maestà* or Majesty, as a Madonna with Saints and Angels was called at that time, is by Lippo Memmi. The Madonna sits on a golden throne surrounded by twenty-eight saints and angels. The kneeling figure is Mino dei Tolomei, the podestà responsible for the fresco. It is dated 1317; so Dante never saw it. Lippo Memmi was the pupil of Simone Martini, who had painted the great *Maestà* in the Palazzo Pubblico at Siena two years before, and Tolomei commissioned the work from him because he wanted to have something like the Sienese *Maestà* in S. Gimignano. It can at least bear comparison with Simone's masterpiece. It has two angels at the lower left and right, added later by Benozzo Gozzoli.

Through the door on the right of the *Maestà* is a small room lined with majolica jars from the Hospital of Santa Fina. They are of great interest to the student of ceramics, for they date from the fourteenth to the seventeenth century. Notice too the bust of Guido Marabottini, the first administrator of the hospital, by a follower of Donatello. The little room next to it with beautifully carved and inlaid seats was used for private sessions.

At the top of a short flight of stairs is the podestà's chapel, which contains six pictures, three by Pier Francesco Fiorentino, one by Mainardi and two of the School of Benozzo Gozzoli. A flight of stairs on the right leads up to the tower, from which there is a very fine view over the gentle Tuscan countryside as far as the main chain of the Apennines. On the second floor proper is the main picture gallery on the left and on the right the podestà's bedroom, decorated with erotic but unfortunately almost vanished frescoes.

By the entrance door of the Pinacoteca is a painted crucifixion of 1260, surrounded with scenes from the Passion, by Coppo di Marcovaldo, a Florentine prisoner who was captured at the Battle of Monteaperti and soon released on account of his artistic abilities. We know little more of him except that Cimabue was a close student of his work and was greatly influenced by it. The main gallery contains a number of first-class paintings, notably two *tondi* by Filippino Lippi showing the Annunciation and commissioned by the Municipality in 1483; Benozzo Gozzoli's two Madonnas with Saints, both signed and dated 1466. It is very interesting to compare them with Pinturicchio's great Madonna in Glory with SS. Gregory and Benedict, which hangs close by. Both the Florentine and the Umbrian share a pagan enthusiasm for the gay colours and the physical beauty of the earth and its inhabitants, not least their clothes and their horses, as also a conscientious skill in drawing. Sebastiano Mainardi and his pupil, Vincenzo Tamagni, who was later to collaborate with Raphael in the Loggie of the Vatican, represent the native painters of San Gimignano.

The second room, on the right, contains an interesting tabernacle door with scenes from the Life and Miracles of S. Fina by Lorenzo Gerini the Florentine. In the next room is a Madonna and Child attributed to Guido da Siena, which probably dates from 1259; a fragment of a fresco by Bartolo di Fredi; and two Taddeo di Bartolos.

The main street of S. Gimignano, the Via S. Matteo, runs due north from the square, through a double line of medieval palaces and churches, to the Porta S. Matteo. Just before reaching it, turn right to the Piazza S. Agostino. The single-aisled Gothic church of **S. Agostino** was completed about 1320. Immediately to the left on entering is the Altar of St Vincent with an attractive Madonna and Saints of 1494 by Francesco Fiorentino, with a tiny donor like a black mouse kneeling in the middle of them all. The fresco above is by Tamagni. The Chapel of S. Bartolo beyond it has a beautiful marble altar which took Benedetto da Maiano two years to make. S. Bartolo was a Sangimignanese saint who devoted his life to the lepers in the leprosarium at Cellole, about three miles out of the town, and died of their disease. The first of the three scenes from his life carved in bas-relief under the sarcophagus depicts the saint's great toe falling off. The others show his death and the casting out of a demon. Mainardi's frescoes on the left wall represent St Nicholas of Bari, St Lucia and St Geminianus, holding the town in his arms.

The right-hand aisle contains a *Pietà* by Bartolo di Fredi, a St Nicholas of Tolentino by Tamagni and a Mystic Marriage of St Catherine attributed to Salimbeni. On the High Altar is the Coronation of the Virgin, perhaps the masterpiece of Piero Pollaiuolo, completed in 1483. It is notable both for the lovely composition and the realistic portraiture of the characters. On the right as you face the altar is the Chapel of the Nativity with

Bartolo di Fredi's frescoes of the Life of the Virgin on the left-hand wall and Tamagni's altarscreen representing her Birth.

The choir is covered with frescoes which are probably the most important work of Benozzo Gozzoli, next to the famous chapel in the Riccardi Palace in Florence. They took him three years to paint and were completed in 1465. The seventeen scenes of the Life of St Augustine start chronologically in the bottom left-hand corner and then continue in the upper rows, also running from left to right. The first scene, it will be observed, is a double one. On the left a chubby little Augustine is handed over to the schoolmaster in Tagaste by his mother, St Monica, and on the right he receives his first caning. These frescoes were commissioned by Fra Domenico Strambi, a native of the town who was professor of philosophy at the Sorbonne and whose sepulchre is just on the left below Mainardi's fresco of St Geminianus blessing three illustrious citizens. Farther on, the altar of the Madonna of Favours bears a fresco of 1330 by Lippo Memmi showing the Virgin enthroned nursing the Child and St Michael killing the Dragon. It has been inexpertly restored in the past and little is left of the original. Beyond the pulpit of 1524 is a St Sebastian painted by Benozzo Gozzoli in 1464 to commemorate the end of a pestilence. The saint is shown interceding with God to bring the plague to an end and at his feet are the people of S. Gimignano. The Altar of the Cross has frescoes by Tamagni.

To visit the little church of **S. Pietro** in the Piazza S. Agostino, ask one of the Augustinians to walk across the brick-paved square with you and open it, for it is kept locked. It contains frescoes by Barna da Siena, assisted by Giovanni d'Asciano, of the Annunciation, the Temptation of St Antony, the Madonna Enthroned between Two Saints and an Adoration of the Magi. Proceeding down the Via Folgore da San Gimignano (he was a thirteenth-century poet praised by Dante) one arrives at one of the oldest hospitals in Italy, the **Hospital of Santa Fina,** built in 1253 with the offerings that the people laid at the feet of S. Fina when her body was exposed in the Duomo.

On the ceiling of the vestibule is a tempera painting attributed to Mainardi and on either side are busts of S. Fina and St Gregory by Pietro Torrigiani, famous as the man who broke the nose of Michelangelo. On the walls are saints by Mainardi.

Beside a small meadow at the end of the Via Folgore is little Romanesque **S. Jacopo,** an old Templar church probably dating in its present form from the thirteenth century. It contains interesting frescoes by an unknown Sienese artist. Below it, outside the Porta delle Fonti, are thirteenth-century arcaded fountains, formerly used for washing the wool which was the source of S. Gimignano's wealth in the Middle Ages. (Her wool merchants had their agents all over Italy, France and the Levant. It was this wealth which created the fine buildings which we now see and it was her subsequent poverty from the fifteenth century onwards which preserved them by preventing her from demolishing them and putting up new ones.) **S. Lorenzo in Ponte,** built in 1240, is frescoed by Cenno di Francesco Cenni, the painter of S. Francesco in Volterra. At No. 2 in the Vicolo di S. Fina, off the Via del Castello, is the house of the little saint and the cellar where she lay five years motionless on the oak table which may still be seen in the Chapel of the Hospital of S. Fina. She died on 12th March, 1253, and it is said that at her death violas suddenly bloomed between the grey travertine stones of the towers and that the miracle is repeated every year on the anniversary, no matter how hard the winter has been.

CHAPTER 12
Siena

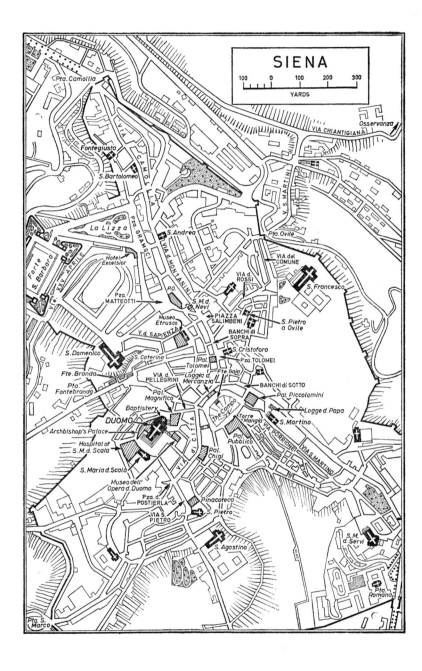

SIENA

100 0 100 200 300

YARDS

Pta. Camollia

Osservanza

VIA CHIANTIGIANA

Fontegiusta

S. Bartolomeo

VIA CAMOLLIA

VIA S. MARTINI

La Lizza

Pza. GRAMSCI

VIA d. MONTANINI

S. Andrea

Pta. Ovile

VIA del COMUNE

Hotel Excelsior

Forte S. Barbara

VIA XXV APRILE

VIA d. ROSSI

S. Francesco

Pza. MATTEOTTI

P.O.

S.M.d. Nevi

PIAZZA SALIMBENI

S. Pietro a Ovile

Museo Etrusco

V. d. SAPIENZA

BANCHI di SOPRA

S. Domenico

S. Caterina

S. Cristoforo

Pza. TOLOMEI

Fte. Branda

Pal. Tolomei

Fte Gaia

Pta. Fontebranda

VIA d. PELLEGRINI

Loggia d. Mercanzia

BANCHI di SOTTO

Pal. Magnifico

Pal. Piccolomini

Baptistery

The Campo

Logge d. Papa

DUOMO

Torre Mangia

S. Martino

Archbishop's Palace

VIA di CITTA

Pal. Pubblico

VIA PORRIONE

VIA S. MARTINO

Hospital of S.M.d. Scala

Pal. Chigi

S. Maria d. Scala

Museo dell' Opera d. Duomo

Pza. d. POSTIERLA

Pinacoteca

S. Pietro

S.M. d. Servi

VIA S. PIETRO

S. Agostino

Pta. Romana

Pta. S. Marco

CHAPTER 12

Siena

Although it is smaller than such modern industrial growths as Leghorn and Prato, Siena is beyond dispute the second city of Tuscany, whether from the historical or the artistic point of view. For several centuries she was the bitterest and most powerful rival of Florence in commerce and in war. She lacked, however, Florence's natural advantages, which were proximity to a navigable river, access to an important port and the command of several Apennine passes. Siena has no river and is cut off from the Tyrrhenian by mountains. A thousand feet above the sea, she crowns a steep three-pronged ridge among the low rolling hills which form the plateau of southern Tuscany. Since the buildings nearly all stand on the high ground, this ridge gives her a strange sprawling shape like a mutilated starfish or an inverted Y.

While other styles, Romanesque, Renaissance and Baroque, and other materials such as the light grey stone known as travertine, are also used, one's abiding memory of Siena is of a red-brick Gothic city (although it is arguable whether the term 'Gothic' can properly be applied to the Italian ogival style). She has sprouted some new suburbs where the ridges run out beyond the walls, but the central part of the city has changed very little since the Middle Ages. The old houses and palaces still line the narrow, winding streets of this city which has never been divided into rich and poor quarters. The palace of the nobleman and the little shop of the artisan have always existed cheek by jowl.

According to a legend such as cities seek to account for their origins with (like London with King Lud), Siena took her name from her founder, Senius, the son of Remus, who fled here with his brother Ascius from the persecution of their uncle Romulus. For this reason she shares her emblem with Rome, a she-wolf suckling Romulus and Remus; similarly, her colours are said to be black and white because Ascius rode a black horse and Senius a white one. The only thing certain among all these fairy tales is that there was first a small Etruscan settlement here and later on a Roman colony.

In the Early Middle Ages Siena was ruled first by an Imperial Count and then by her own bishops, who were direct tenants *in capite* of the emperor, and to whom the lawless barons of the *contado* outside owed fealty in their turn. The *milites* or knights upon whom the bishops had to rely for their authority in turn asserted their power, drove out the Bishop and substituted their own government by lay consuls. Being at the same time a direct fief of the Empire and the agelong enemy of the Guelphs who ruled Florence, Siena naturally took the Ghibelline side when the conflict between the Empire and the Papacy broke out. Her great merchant bankers (mainly composed of the defeated nobles of the *contado*, whom she compelled to live within her walls instead of levying tolls upon her commerce) had ramifications all over Europe and the Levant. These brought them into direct rivalry with the merchants of Florence. The enmity between the two cities was at bottom commercial rather than political.

In 1236 the bourgeoisie inserted themselves into the government of the patricians and formed the Council of the Twenty-Four, half nobles and half commoners. (All the governments of the Commune of Siena were composed of multiples of three, to allow equal representation of the three self-governing *Terzi* into which the city was divided—those of the Città, of Camollia

136

and of S. Martino, one for each of the three ridges she was built on.) A series of wars with Florence ensued, crowned in 1260 by the great victory at Monteaperti of the Sienese under Provenzano Salvani when, it is said, ten thousand Florentines were killed and fifteen thousand captured.

The political situation, however, changed rapidly and disastrously with the death of King Manfred of Sicily and the execution of his son Conradin by Charles of Anjou. In 1269 the Sienese were defeated at Colle Val d' Elsa, where Provenzano was killed. The Ghibelline cause in Siena was finished and a Guelph administration was installed. The all-party governments of the Thirty-Six, and then of the Fifteen, were succeeded by that of the *Nove*, all of them merchants, which ruled Siena until 1355 and gave it nearly seventy years of the good government celebrated by Ambrogio Lorenzetti on the walls of the Palazzo Pubblico.

This was the great period of Sienese art. In painting, Guido da Siena and his followers ensured the triumph of the Byzantine style over the earlier Romanesque in the mid-thirteenth century. Nevertheless, the real founder of the Sienese School was the great Duccio di Buoninsegna, who lived from 1260 to 1319 and was therefore a contemporary of Giotto in Florence. He breathed a new life into the Byzantine forms of which he was such a master. His greatest follower, Simone Martini, carried the naturalistic process yet farther, as did the brothers Lorenzetti, powerfully influenced by Giotto, whose work they had seen at Assisi. They were never heard of after 1348 when the Black Death came to Siena and is believed to have killed four-fifths of the population. Most of the great Gothic churches, palaces and city gates were built during this period. After the disaster of the Black Death the Nine were overthrown and there followed a confused century of rule by most of the other multiples of three, in which the artisans predominated.

'The city is all divided into factions and is governed more crazily than any town in Italy,' wrote the French historian, Philippe de Commines. In the midst of all the misgovernment

137

the great mystics who always seem to make Siena in some ways more like an Umbrian than a Tuscan city, St Catherine in the fourteenth century and St Bernardino in the fifteenth, preached peace and reformation.

Jacopo della Quercia, the sculptor, added lustre to the name of his native city. In painting, the Gothic tradition was carried on down to the end of the fifteenth century by artists such as Barna, who has left no works in Siena, Bartolo di Fredi and Taddeo di Bartolo, who inherited it from Simone Martini, Lippo Memmi and, more particularly perhaps, from the Lorenzetti. In the Quattrocento the most eminent names are those of Sassetta in the first half of the century, Vecchietta and Sano di Pietro, both of whom derived much from him, Domenico Bartolo, the Florentine-influenced Matteo di Giovanni and his follower, the delightful Neroccio di Bartolomeo Landi. That long underrated painter Antonio Bazzi, commonly called Sodoma, adorned the last half-century of the Republic. Sodoma, who was born a Piedmontese from Vercelli, brought the Lombard style of Leonardo da Vinci down to his adopted city and, for better or worse, diverted Sienese art into the main stream of Italian painting, from which it had so long been separated. His pupil, Domenico Beccafumi, is more properly to be classed among the Mannerists of the Florentine School.

In 1479 the party of the Nine or *Noveschi* returned to power. They were expelled, came back again and set up a government of ten Priori. Out of all the confusion Pandolfo Petrucci emerged as dictator. His sons were expelled after his death in 1512. After the usual period of anarchy, the mortal disease of the Sienese, the Spaniards installed a garrison in the city in 1531. In 1552 the Sienese rose and expelled them after three days of street fighting. The armies of Spain and Florence under the Marchese di Marignano moved to besiege the exhausted city and, after all the unclean animals and even the grass had been eaten and the 'useless mouths' had been expelled from the city to perish outside the walls, she was forced to surrender in April 1555. The ancient republic was then absorbed into the dominions of Cosimo de' Medici.

The river which Siena so sadly lacked was to some extent substituted by the medieval Via Francigena, the great highway which led from the Po Valley down to Rome and which ran through the centre of Siena. Indeed, it continued to do so until a few short years ago, when by-pass roads were constructed outside the walls. It enters the city from Florence by the Porta Camollia and runs due south as the Via Camollia, the Via Montanini and the Banchi di Sopra. Over the Camollia Gate is inscribed the Latin welcome: '*Cor magis tibi Sena pandit*,' which may be translated as 'Siena opens her heart to you wider (than this gate).'

Just off the Via Camollia, in the Via Fontegiusta, is the Renaissance church of **Fontegiusta.** (The *custode* lives in the little courtyard on the right.) The stained glass on the entrance wall is fifteenth-century work by Guidoccio Cozzarelli and the tabernacle on the marble high altar is the work of Lorenzo Marrina. The third altar on the right bears an Annunciation by Bernardino Fungai. The Assumption on the high altar is by Girolamo di Benvenuto, while the fresco of the Sybil announcing to Augustus the Birth of the Redeemer is the work of Baldassare Peruzzi, who lived at 176 Via Camollia just opposite the old Templar church of S. Pietro alla Magione. S. Bartolomeo in the Via Camollia contains a Madonna and Child by Vecchietta. Farther down, in the Via Montanini, S. Andrea has another Madonna by Vecchietta, and there is a beautiful *Maestà* by Matteo di Giovanni in the little Oratory of S. Maria delle Nevi on the right just before you come to the Piazza Salimbeni.

On the west side of the Via Montanini is a large open space, the **Piazza Gramsci,** from which there is a good view of the Cathedral roof and its lovely cupola. Beyond the Piazza is the Lizza, the local park of Siena, and at the side of it is the great Medicean fortress of Santa Barbara, built to cow the Sienese. From its ramparts you may see the towering bulk of Monte

Amiata, and the pointed hill of tower-crowned Radicofani where the bandit Ghino di Pacco seized the Abbot of Cluny. They are the twin sentinels which guard the southern borders of the Sienese. If you follow a signpost marked '*Enoteca*' to the left as you go in, you will find yourself in a series of cool rooms culminating in a bar, where you can—if you are staying in Siena long enough and your liver lasts out—sample all the wines of Italy. It is in fact the permanent wine exhibition of the Peninsula. An *enoteca* is a collection of wines (from the Greek οἰνοτεκον), just as a *pinacoteca* is a collection of pictures and a *biblioteca* of books. In the Viale 25 Aprile on the east side of the fortress a market is held every Wednesday morning, which brings the farmers flocking into town to buy clothes, shoes and household goods.

At the angle where the Lizza joins the Piazza Gramsci is the Hotel Excelsior which, being easy to find and with plenty of parking space, is to be recommended to the visitor of a day or two. Alternatively, there is the Continental in the Banchi di Sopra, easier to get at from south than from the north on account of a one-way street. For a longer stay there are the Park Hotel, a converted villa with a beautiful garden outside the Porta Camollia just off the road to Florence, and the Scacciapensieri a mile or two outside the Porta Ovile near the Convent of the Osservanza. The Pensione Ravizza in the Piano dei Mantellini out towards the Porta S. Marco is a converted palazzo with a garden and a view and is very well spoken of by those who have stayed there.

The best restaurant in town is reputed to be da Guido, to which a sign points from the Banchi di Sopra, just opposite the fashionable tea-toom, bar and cakeshop of Nannini. The Piazza del Campo is lined with restaurants such as the Mangia, the Campo, the Speranza and Zi' Rosa, where you may, if so disposed, raise your eyes from your plate to lift them up to the Palazzo Pubblico.

Beyond the Piazza Gramsci is the Piazza Matteotti, where the post office is. (There are some remarkable frescoes on the ceiling dating from the end of the nineteenth century, with allegorical figures holding wind-up telephones, express trains and other symbols of communication.) From the Piazza a street runs right-handed down to the great brick church of **S. Domenico** on the western edge of the city. It was built by the Dominicans in the thirteenth century. In about 1300 the southern end of the church was enlarged and the transept was built over the old church of S. Gregorio, which then became the crypt of S. Domenico. It is generally known as the Lower Church but there is almost nothing of interest in it. The entrance is from the Upper Church near the sacristy door beneath the large Nativity by Francesco di Giorgio Martini. (The *Pietà* in the lunette is by Matteo di Giovanni.) As befits a friars' preaching church, the rectangular whitewashed nave is very bare, with a high beamed roof, almost like a Dutch church. This was the parish church of St Catherine of Siena, who was born and lived in the Fontebranda valley just below. The Benincasas, St Catherine's family, are all buried in the Lower Church, which is also known as the Church of the Dead.

On the right as one enters the main church is the Cappella delle Volte, which derives its name from the vaulting of the ceiling. It was here that the saint entered her order of the Mantellate in 1368. At the far end of the chapel is a striking picture of her by her disciple Andrea Vanni, which may very well be a portrait from life. The rebuilt brick pillar between the two arches is said to be on the site of the one at which she used to linger in prayer and it is represented, richly decorated, in the Cappella di S. Caterina on the right wall of the nave. St Catherine's body is in S. Maria Sopra Minerva in Rome, but a Gothic reliquary in this chapel displays her mummified head, which derives a peculiar—and if one may say so without irreverence—rodent-like effect from its two white front teeth protruding from the drawn brown skin. The chapel is frescoed by Sodoma, and the St Catherine Swooning at the Pillar on the left of Giovanni di Stefano's tabernacle, is generally held to be one of his finest paintings. Its emotional feeling and its plastic quality certainly carry it far above the generality of the painter's works. On the other side of the altar is St Catherine in Ecstasy, and on the left wall the saint intercedes for the soul of an executed man called Tuldol—both by Sodoma. The fresco on the right wall of the saint curing a woman possessed of a devil was painted by Francesco Vanni in 1593.

The Cappella dei Tedeschi in the right transept is covered with memorial tablets of German students and others who died in Siena in the sixteenth and seventeenth centuries. The high altar and the two angel-candelabra are the work of Benedetto da Maiano. Behind, a window affords a lovely view of the Cathedral. The second chapel on the left of the high altar contains an attractive St Barbara enthroned between St Catherine of Alexandria and St Mary Magdalene, with an Epiphany in the lunette, by Matteo di Giovanni. Opposite is a Madonna, with a *Pietà* above it by Benvenuto di Giovanni. The damaged fresco half-way down the left wall of the nave is attributed to Pietro Lorenzetti.

From the square outside S. Domenico there is an exciting view of the Cathedral across the deep gully which runs down from the Fonte Branda, a spring which is first mentioned in the eleventh century. In 1246 the fountain was reconstructed in its present battlemented form like a sunken fort with three large Sienese arches. To the right of it is the narrow Vicolo del Tiratoio and at No. 15 on the right is the **Sanctuary of St Catherine,** into which the house of Benincasa the dyer was turned in 1464, three years after her canonisation by the Sienese Pope Pius II. Little attempt has been made to preserve a medieval house and there is not very much to see except for earnest devotees of the great saint who in 1939 was proclaimed Patroness of Italy. The whole house has been turned into a maze of chapels, oratories and loggias and except for an altarpiece by Fungai in the Upper Oratory, which was once the kitchen, the pictures are all very mediocre. The Chapel of St Catherine in Fontebranda, once her father's shop, is now the Chapel of the Contrada of the Oca or Goose. The wooden statue of the saint on the altar may be from the hand of Neroccio. Her cell, also on the ground floor, contains such personal relics as the stone which served her for a pillow, her night-lantern and a fragment of the walking stick with which she went to Avignon to persuade the Pope to return to Rome. Adjoining the sacristy of the Lower Oratory is the Museum of the Contrada of the Oca, which will interest above all the fans of the Palio.[1]

At no. 3 Via della Sapienza, which leads up from S. Domenico to the Banchi di Sopra, is **the Etruscan Museum,**[2] containing remains from all over Tuscany. Its main interest will be for the specialist. Next door to it is the very ancient church of S. Pellegrino alla Sapienza, rebuilt in the eighteenth century. From this point the Costa dell' Incrociata leads into the Piazza Salimbeni, at the far end of which is the handsome Gothic Palace of the Salimbeni, faced with pale grey travertine. (The Salimbeni were one of the great patrician families of Siena and long kept the town in a turmoil by their feud with the Tolomei.) The Palazzo Salimbeni is now the headquarters of the Monte dei Paschi di Siena, founded in 1624 and one of the oldest banks in Italy. It owes its curious name to the fact that its credit was based upon the revenues of the flocks (*paschi* or *pascoli*) of the Maremma.

A little farther down the Banchi di Sopra on the left a medieval arch leads into the Via dei Rossi, down a short street on the right of which is the church of **S. Pietro a Ovile.** It has on the right wall an early copy of Simone Martini's famous Annunciation in the Uffizi at Florence, possibly the work of Domenico di Bartolo, and a very good Madonna of the school of the Lorenzetti. The painted crucifix on the altar on the left is the work of Giovanni di Paolo.

At the end of the Via dei Rossi an archway on the right leads into a great square in front of the Gothic church of **S. Francesco.** Plain, bare and built throughout of red brick, it recalls S. Domenico on the other side of the city. (Both of them, to be candid, would be denounced as eyesores if they were modern factories instead of being medieval churches.) The scions of

[1]See page 146. [2]Closed on Tuesdays

143

both the Tolomei and the Salimbeni lie here side by side in death, including some of the eighteen Tolomei who were invited to a reconciliation banquet by the Salimbeni at a place still called Malamerenda or 'the wicked dinner' and then treacherously murdered. The church prides itself in particular on its Lorenzettis. In the chapel on the left of the high altar is Pietro Lorenzetti's great fresco of the Crucifixion, with its strong echoes of Giotto. On the right wall of the third chapel on the left of the altar is his brother Ambrogio's fresco of St Louis of Anjou at the feet of Pope Benedict VIII and opposite it the same artist's Martyrdom of the Franciscans at Ceuta.

If we continue straight on from the Via dei Rossi down the steep and ancient Via del Comune we come to the double Gothic Porta Ovile. Outside it on the right is the Fonte Ovile, one of the old fountains of Siena. Ahead the Via Chiantigiana runs up into the vine-clad Chianti hills from which comes some of the best-known Italian wine, and on a hilltop about a mile away rises the **Monastery of the Osservanza.** It was founded by St Bernardino and is the headquarters of the Observant sect of the Franciscans, who observe literally St Francis's rule of poverty in distinction to the Conventuals. St Bernardino was their Vicar-General. The Osservanza was destroyed by bombing in 1944 and rebuilt in 1949. It can be reached by a footpath to the left just after the level-crossing or by a motor road which branches left about a mile beyond it and is signposted 'Camping.' It contains a number of good della Robbias, notably Andrea's altarpiece of the Coronation of the Virgin. There are also a terra-cotta *Pietà* by Giovanni di Paolo and a Madonna and Saints by the 'Maestro dell' Osservanza,' who was long identified with Sano di Pietro.

Returning to the Banchi di Sopra, we come to the Piazza Tolomei with the travertine Gothic palace of the Tolomei, the oldest domestic building in Siena, on the right. On the left is the church of S. Cristoforo, where the municipal council used to meet before the Palazzo Pubblico was built and where it gave its proud defiance to the Florentine envoys on the eve of

Monteaperti. In the right transept is a very attractive painting of St George and the Dragon by Sano di Pietro.

Beyond Nannini's is the Croce del Travaglio, the traffic centre of the city, where the three arms of the Y all meet. From this point the Banchi di Sotto runs leftwards through the S. Martino quarter out to the Porta Romana and Rome, while the Via di Città runs straight on towards the Porta S. Marco and the Maremma. On the left is the Gothic and Renaissance loggia called the Loggia della Mercanzia, where the old commercial court used to be held. Beside it several arched-over alleys run steeply down to the great bowl of a Piazza called the Campo.

The Campo is the historic centre of the city and for many centuries was the scene of all its most dramatic events, comic and tragic, grave and gay—popular tumults, faction fights, Jew-burnings, horse races, solemn prayers for victory over the accursed Florentines, the triumphal procession of Duccio's *Maestà*, the eloquent sermons of St Bernardino and the dragging of the proud standard of the Lily at the tail of a donkey after Monteaperti. To-day it is the place where the people stroll in the cool of the evening and sit outside the numerous cafés which fringe it. The Campo is an enormous semicircle with the great Palazzo Pubblico forming the straight side or diameter and a road running all round it. The inner part, which is paved with red brick in a herring-bone pattern, slopes downwards to a central point just in front of the middle of the façade of the Palazzo Pubblico. It is shaped like a sea-shell and the resemblance is heightened by the fact that it is divided into nine parts in honour of the Nine by stone strips which radiate out from the centre of the diameter side like the ridges of a cockleshell. Equally, it may be likened to a delicate rose-pink fan with nine sticks of bone holding it open on the ground.

In the centre of the upper part of the Campo is the Fonte Gaia, which was called the Gay Fountain because of the public rejoicings which accompanied its completion in 1419. It used to be decorated with beautiful reliefs by Jacopo della Quercia which, being carved in soft stone, were suffering so badly from the weather that in 1868 they were replaced by copies. Among the earliest Renaissance sculptures in Siena, the originals are now to be seen in the loggia on the second floor of the Palazzo Pubblico. All round the Campo are high Gothic palaces and houses. The finest is the thirteenth-century Palazzo Sansedoni with its curving pink brick façade, its three-lobed windows and a tower which, before it was lopped off, once rivalled the Mangia opposite.

While most of the excitements of the Campo are things of the past and neither revolutions break out there nor are peace pacts made, it is still the scene of the famous Palio, a manifestation peculiar to Siena in which she can boast one of the oldest, and beyond question one of the most spectacular, festivals in Italy. The Palio is a horse-race which is run round the Piazza twice a year, on 2nd July in honour of the miraculous Madonna of Provenzano, and on 16th August in honour of Our Lady of the Assumption, the patroness and sovereign of the city. (In 1945, after years of deprivation, they held two extra ones to celebrate VE Day and VJ Day respectively.)

The dim origins of the Palio date back to the Middle Ages when the Campo was the scene of a number of more or less lethal contests played with quarterstaves, stones and other weapons, bullfights, buffalo races and so on. Of all these sports the horse race alone has survived. The Palio as it is to-day was actually instituted in July 1659, but a horse race in honour of the Assumption is first mentioned as far back as 1147.

Siena is divided into districts called *contrade*. These compete against each other in the race for the Palio. They are now reduced to seventeen, but formerly there were fifty-nine, each representing a parish. They are called after animals such as the Panther, emblems of war such as the Tower, or natural features such as the Forest. They are believed to have grown out of the various military companies or trainbands of the city which became obsolete after the loss of Sienese freedom. Their object was and is to arrange entertainments and celebrations and to keep the ancient traditions alive. They therefore represent a

146

living survival of the free spirit of the republic. They each have their own colours, their costumes, their chapels, their museum-cum-social-centres, their leaders or *Priori*, their chaplains or *correttori* and their *comparse*, the teams of young men, dressed in Renaissance costume, who play their parts in the Palio procession and on other occasions. When I talk of Renaissance costume, I mean furs and silks and velvets, real steel armour renewed every generation, and not the cheap finery we associate with English 'pageants.' All the year round boys and youths in back streets are to be seen practising the play with the flags or *sbandierata*, which is a prominent feature of the Palio. The *contrade* are the centres of fierce local patriotism and enthusiasm runs high as Palio time draws near and the streets are gay with the flags of the rivals. They have their own traditional alliances, enmities and border disputes like miniature republics within the city.

A few days before the race the Campo becomes transformed into the semblance of a racecourse. Wooden stands are put up all round it. Hangings appear from every window. Barricades bar off the course itself, which is the broad peripheral road running round the *nicchia* or shell in the middle. The track itself is covered with a layer of yellow earth for the animals to race upon. Each *contrada* appoints a captain, a sort of war-leader for the period of the Palio. He may do secret deals with the other captains to win or throw the race but it is so dangerous and dicey a course that the result remains anybody's bet, whatever may have been arranged or whatever money may have passed.

The horses are drawn by lot and distributed to the ten *contrade* which are running that year. There is not room for seventeen horses all at once, so that seven have to stand down. Their turn will come to race the following year together with three others chosen by lot. The jockeys are professionals; many of them, like the horses, come from the Maremma.

Three days before the great race the six trials or *prove* start. They are preliminary races designed to familiarise the horses and their jockeys with the course. (Seats for them can be had for a hundred lire or two as against several thousand for the

Palio itself.) On the great day each horse, with its jockey, is led into the church of the *contrada* and solemnly blessed by the priest. (If the horse treats the holy place with something less than respect, it is held to be a good omen.) By about four in the afternoon the Campo is filling up with spectators—citizens, peasants and tourists. The 'shell' in the centre, which constitutes free standing room, is filled with a solid mass of people, presenting a target which the pigeons, displaced for the afternoon, cannot possibly miss, and the stands are also jampacked when at five o'clock a gun goes off and the cavalcade begins with a ride past, first at a trot and then at a canter of mounted *carabinieri* in full dress, all with red and blue plumes in their Napoleonic hats.

Next there follows the slow procession of the *contrade* which lasts a good hour and a half. The hundreds of participants are all richly dressed in fifteenth-century style, and the splendid pageantry is probably without a rival in Europe. Heading the procession are six mace-bearers and behind them rides the standard-bearer of the Commune with a groom in attendance. He is followed by a band of thirty drummers and other musicians playing the March of the Palio; thirty-six standard-bearers with the flags of the old Sienese cities and castles; representatives of the guilds and corporations with more flags; the Captain of the People accompanied by centurions, all mounted on richly caparisoned horses.

After all these preliminaries follow the *comparse* or teams of the different *contrade*, each headed by a drummer and two flag-bearers or *alfieri*. Then the captain in armour with helmet and drawn sword marches escorted by two attendants. He is followed by a page bearing the standard of the *contrada*, likewise with two attendants. The rear is brought up by the jockey, helmeted and costumed, riding upon a parade horse called a *soprallasso*, and followed by the *barbero*, the actual horse which is to race, led by a groom. The ten *contrade* which are in the contest come first, followed by the seven which are not and who march without the horses. Then come halberdiers in chain-mail and leather jerkins,

148

Horizontal white and green 'tiger-stripes' cover the nave of the Duomo in Siena. Another unique feature of the Cathedral is its multi-coloured marble floor, composed of graffiti and designed by some of the leading artists in Siena. 56 pictures cover the floor.

Donatello's 'Banquet of Herod', showing the head of John the
Baptist being brought to Herod on a plate: one of the gilded bronze
bas-reliefs surrounding the basin of the 15th century octagonal
marble font in middle of the Baptistery, originally designed by
Jacopo della Quercia in 1417–30.

who escort a triumphal chariot drawn by four great milk-white oxen. Sitting in it are pages and trumpeters and four magistrates of the town, the *Provveditori di Biccherna*. Above it floats the Palio itself, the great silken banner with the painting of the Madonna which is the prize to be competed for and which has given its name to the race.

The procession takes over an hour and a half to pass any given point on account of the frequent halts made to enable the Pinturicchio-clad *alfieri* to show their skill at the *sbandierata*. This dipping, waving and throwing of multicoloured flags is intended as a salute and is performed three times by each *comparsa* at definite points along the route in honour of the Archbishop, of the prefect and of the people of Siena. The legerdemain and agility displayed by the flag-wavers are fascinating to watch. The flags, which must be kept always in motion and never allowed for a moment to hang loose or to touch the ground, are thrown about, caught behind the back, crossed between the thighs, under the legs and behind the neck, tossed from one *alfiere* to the other and hurled high in the air and caught again in the left hand before they touch the ground. This last gesture is the *alzata* or 'hoisting,' which forms the finale to each *sbandierata*.

Then, when the procession is finished, the jockeys ride out from the Cortile del Podestà in the Palazzo Pubblico and each is handed the *nerbo* or bull-whip with which he is allowed to belabour not only his own horse but the others as well and hit his rival jockeys over the head. No holds are barred and I have heard it described as 'the dirtiest race in the world.' It is also one of the most dangerous, for the jockeys ride bareback, without saddle or stirrups. When they have coaxed their excited horses into position in front of the starting rope, the *mossiere* or starter lets it fall and they race at top speed for three breakneck rounds of the Campo. Those who want to see broken necks in the literal sense should take their seats at the very dangerous *curva di S. Martino*, whose sides are cushioned with mattresses. It is a right-angled corner with a steep descent on the other side, and

149

it is rare that the Palio finishes without one or more riderless horses racing like mustangs alongside the others, their long manes and tails flowing in the slipstream.

Amid delirious excitement, with the shouting and the cheering interspersed at one place with embraces and at another with fisticuffs, the crowds pour on to the course. If he is lucky the winning jockey is carried off in triumph by his supporters, but his dangers are not over, for sometimes the object of the crowd seems to be to lynch either him or one or two of his rivals, and the riders are swiftly surrounded by strong squads of police, who hustle them out of harm's way. The Palio itself is carried in triumph by the winning *contradaioli* to the baroque church of S. Maria di Provenzano in July or to the Cathedral in August, where a *Te Deum* is sung in thanksgiving for the triumph. Then the banner goes to swell the trophies in the museum[1] of the winning *contrada*. Later on, a banquet is held in the main street of the *contrada* to celebrate the victory, at which the horse is, rightly enough, the guest of honour with its own table and its own menu of carrots and sugar.

Dominating the Campo is the beautiful **Palazzo Pubblico** or Town Hall. With its slightly curved façade and the tall tower at the corner, it is a masterpiece of Gothic architecture, the upper stories made of rose-red brick and the ground floor of grey travertine. It was built between 1288 and 1309. The large circle with the kris-like rays and the letters Y.H.S. in the centre is the monogram of Christ designed by St Bernardino as part of his campaign to reclaim Italy for God and it stands for '*Jesus Hominum Salvator*,' Jesus, the Saviour of Men. When an unfortunate man who made dice, cards and gaming boards complained that his ban on such 'vanities' had ruined him and left him and his family to starve, the saint gave him the very profitable commission to manufacture these tablets, which may still be seen on many houses in Siena and one of which he always held in front of him when preaching.

[1]The easiest of access is the museum of the Goose, which is in the Sanctuary of St. Catherine, as is the chapel.

The original building was three stories high but in the six-teenth century a fourth was built over the central part. The openings in the ground floor are in the form of the double arches known as 'Sienese arches,' while the two upper stories have Gothic windows with three openings. The black and white shield in the spandrels above them is the Balzana, the ancient coat of arms of the city. The building at the left corner of the façade is the Cappella di Piazza, in front of which St Bernardino used to preach, with the men and women divided by a canvas barrier, and which was built as a thanksgiving for the departure of the Black Death. (It is difficult to resist the reflection that there would have been more reason for gratitude if the plague had never come at all, although in that case no tangible monument to its absence would have been erected.)

The most striking feature of the Palazzo, if not indeed of all Siena, is the high **tower** which rises close to the Cappella and is called the Mangia after its first bell-ringer, a spendthrift who was nicknamed Mangiaguadagni or 'Eat up one's earnings.' Built between 1338 and 1348, it is 334 feet high but so slender that it looks even higher. The entrance to it is in the adjacent Cortile del Podestà at the side of the Cappella di Piazza. The chamber which holds the great bell called Sunto (because it was christened S. Maria Assunta) and the machicolated traver-tine platform beneath it unfold like a white flower at the top of the long stem of red brick.

The entrance to the interior is near the right-hand end of the Palazzo. You take your ticket for '*Il Museo*' at the little window just on the left as you go in. The ground floor rooms, with frescoes by Sano di Pietro (a magnificent Coronation of the Virgin which many experts believe to be his finest work), Vecchietta and Sodoma, are used as offices and can only be visited by special permission. The rooms we have come to see are on the first floor.

The first hall is called the Sala del Mappamondo after a Mappa Mundi by Ambrogio Lorenzetti, which was formerly on the wall here. On the two end walls are very beautiful frescoes by Simone Martini. At the far end of the room is the great *Maestà* which established his fame. It is signed and dated 1315, when the painter was in his early thirties. It has fallen a victim to the damp on the walls but after several restorations it still stands out as a masterpiece. Beneath a canopy silhouetted against a blue background like an evening sky, the Madonna, holding the Child in the act of benediction, sits upon a Gothic throne. Below, two angels offer her flowers. On either side are the four patron saints of Siena, Ansanus, Crescentius, Victor and Savinus, and other saints to the number of thirty-two. It is interesting to compare this *Maestà* with that of Duccio di Buoninsegna in the Museo dell' Opera del Duomo and to notice how the still half-Byzantine forms of the master are attaining to something like naturalism in the hands of the pupil.

Facing the *Maestà* on the opposite wall is Simone Martini's magnificent fresco of 1328 showing the Sienese captain Guidoriccio (or Guido Riccio) da Fogliano riding to the siege of Montemassi. With forts and encampments on either side, the centre of the picture is occupied by the figure of the soldier riding across the hard grey earth with a commander's baton in his hand. The background is almost monochrome and serves to show up to best effect the brilliant colours of the central figure, whose costume and whose horse-trappings are of a vivid orange with black lozenges, like some bright poisonous snake. Below Guidoriccio is the well-known Byzantine Madonna by Guido da Siena. It is perhaps the most important surviving work of the predecessors of Duccio. It is signed and dated 1221— rather improbably since that happened to be the year of the painter's birth. Modern scholars assign it to the second half of the century. The St Ansanus and the St Victor on either side are the work of Sodoma.

The long wall facing the windows is covered by monochrome frescoes, on the right the di Andrea brothers' Battle of Poggio Imperiale against the Florentines and on the left Lippo Vanni's Defeat of the Breton Free Company at Sinalunga. The two Sienese *beati* on the pillars at the far end belong to the school of Riccio; the St Catherine is by Vecchietta, the St Bernardino by Sano di Pietro, and the Blessed Bernardo Tolomei by Sodoma.

Beyond this wall is the chapel decorated, as is the ante-chapel, with frescoes by Taddeo di Bartolo. The scenes all round are taken from the Life of the Virgin. The upper ones are in bad condition and difficult to see. All round the chapel are exquisite wooden choir-stalls, inlaid with twenty-two scenes depicting the Articles of the Creed, which occupied Domenico di Niccolò from 1415 until 1428 and earned him the name of Domenico dei Cori. The Holy Family with St Leonard over the altar is by Sodoma and dates from 1536.

The door beneath the Guidoriccio in the Sala del Mappa-mondo leads into the Sala della Pace, in which Ambrogio Lorenzetti has painted the greatest cycle of profane frescoes which had come down to us from the Middle Ages. It is also known as the Sala dei Nove, because it was the seat of government of the Nine, to whom the artist dedicated these frescoes. They were painted between 1337 and 1339.

The wall on the right shows Good Government, symbolised by an old king dressed in the black and white of Siena and surrounded on either side by symbolic figures of the Virtues. The figure in white lolling ungracefully on the divan at the far left is Peace, after whom the room is named. Over the King's head hover Faith, Hope and Charity, and at his feet the great she-wolf of Siena nuzzles two naked cherubs. Below, the Sienese soldiers lead captives in chains. Beyond Peace sits Justice, draw-ing inspiration from Wisdom above her. Ribbons running down from her scales are gathered by Concord, who passes them on to the twenty-four Counsellors of Siena. The legend below them points out rather sententiously that 'to govern well the King never turns his eyes away from the faces of the Virtues seated round him. Therefore his subjects willingly give him taxes, dues and lands without war.'

The entrance wall shows the Effects of Good Government, both in the town and in the countryside. Medieval Siena is shown with her squares and her streets full of trade and chaffering; girls dance to the sound of tambourines; merchants sit at their counters counting their gold in peace. Outside the walls the peasants work unmolested, ploughing and harvesting and bringing their produce into the city to sell. Others are shown hunting and fishing.

Opposite is a badly damaged fresco depicting Bad Government and its results. Bad Government, a diabolical, horned, black figure is surrounded by all the Vices, Tyranny, Cruelty, Fraud and so forth, while Justice is bound and trampled underfoot. On the left, even more damaged, are the Effects of Bad Government—desolation, murders and robberies. While the symbolism is taken from scholastic philosophy, these frescoes, together with some small pictures in the Pinacoteca, make it clear that Ambrogio Lorenzetti was the first of the great landscape painters, even if his figure painting cannot bear comparison with that of his brother Pietro.

In the next room, the Sala dei Pilastri, notice a small Neroccio di Bartolomeo Landi immediately on the left of the door, which shows St Bernardino preaching in the Campo of Siena and casting out a devil. Among the medieval boxes in the cases in the middle of the room is the great treasure-chest of Siena, *la cofana della Biccherna*. In the glass case opposite the door is the gold rosebush presented to the city by Pius II. (He was indeed *pius* in the full Latin sense of the word towards the city in whose territory he had been born, towards his actual birthplace and towards his family.) Another case shows the bell from S. Cristoforo which was rung to announce the victory of Monteaperti.

Now we go back to the Sala del Mappamondo and through the door on the left of the entrance hall to the frescoed Sala dei Cardinali, which contains a Madonna and Child disputed by the scholars between Guidoccio Cozzarelli and Matteo di Giovanni. Rossellino's fine marble portal on the left leads to the Sala del Concistoro, the Consistory, with frescoes in the vault by Beccafumi showing scenes from classical history. The Judgment of Solomon over the door is by Luca Giordano and on the left wall are three large Gobelin tapestries from designs by Charles Le Brun.

The other door out of the Sala dei Cardinali leads into the Sala di Balia and is completely frescoed with scenes by Spinello Aretino of the life of Pope Alexander III who reigned from 1159 to 1181 and was born a Bandinelli from Siena. The town of Alexandria which he is shown as founding on the far half of the right-hand wall is, of course, the Alessandria in Piedmont and has nothing to do with its Egyptian namesake. Below it the prostrate figure at the feet of the Pope is the emperor making his submission. The large naval battle on the entrance wall shows the defeat of Barbarossa by the Venetians off Punta Salvore in Istria.

Across the small hall beyond the far door is the Sala Monumentale frescoed with scenes from the life and particularly the battles of King Victor Emmanuel II, whom even his own painters have not been able to portray as anything but a comical figure, like a dwarf by Velazquez. One of his little uniforms is shown in a wall cabinet. From the hall a staircase leads up to the open Loggia, with the remains of Jacopo della Quercia's sculptures from the Fonte Gaia. The fresco of the Madonna and Child is by Ambrogio Lorenzetti. Four stories below (for the Palazzo is built upon a steep slope) is the market-place and beyond, across the Val Montone, is a view past the high brick campanile of S. Maria dei Servi out to the open country.

To get to **S. Maria dei Servi** (and it has some of the best paintings in Siena) turn right on coming out of the Palazzo and then right again along the Via Porrione. Soon we come to the large Renaissance loggia called the Logge del Papa, which was built in 1462 to a design of Antonio Federighi on the orders of Pope Pius II and dedicated to his Piccolomini relations. The church of S. Martino next door was built in 1537 but Fontana's baroque façade was only added in 1613. On the second and third altars of the right wall are altarpieces by Guido Reni and Guercino, much darkened by time. The polychrome wooden

155

statue of the Madonna is dubiously attributed to Jacopo della Quercia.

Follow the Via Porrione almost as far as the Porta Romana to the thirteenth-century church of S. Maria dei Servi. A many-windowed Romanesque campanile, with *monofore* increasing to *quadrifore*, rises behind the unfinished façade. The transepts and the apse are Gothic but the Renaissance aisles were probably designed by Baldassare Peruzzi, who returned to his native Siena after working with Raphael in Rome. Over the second altar on the right is the *Madonna del Bordone*, a large Madonna and Child by the Florentine Coppo di Marcovaldo, whose crucifix we saw at S. Gimignano. Signed and dated 1261, it constituted the ransom which he paid for his freedom after being made prisoner at Monteaperti. On the third altar is the Birth of the Virgin by Rutilio Manetti, a Sienese follower of Caravaggio, and on the fifth a spirited Massacre of the Innocents by Matteo di Giovanni, an artist who rather specialised in this macabre subject. The Madonna and Child in the lunette above ranks among his finest works. The Adoration of the Shepherds on the right wall is by Taddeo di Bartolo.

Beneath the altar of the right transept lies the more than usually gruesome mummified body of the Blessed Francesco Patrizi, his hand stretched out as though he were alive. The Madonna and Child over the sacristy door is the work of Duccio's nephew, Segna di Buonaventura, and the fresco of the Massacre of the Innocents (two in one church!) in the adjacent chapel is by Pietro Lorenzetti. It is badly faded but still gripping, as the distraught mothers are held back by the soldiers and Herod watches in lonely state from his balcony. The Madonna on the altar is by Lippo Memmi.

The Coronation of the Virgin over the high altar was painted by Bernardino Fungai in 1500. The second chapel on the left contains more frescoes by Pietro Lorenzetti, which well display his power of depicting character and emotion, as in, for example, the fascinated horror with which Herod regards the head of the Baptist on the right-hand wall. Facing it on the left is the same

156

Madonna and Child by Duccio, Museo dell'Opera del Duomo, Siena.

Detail from the Canonization of St Catherine, in the Piccolomini
Library of the Duomo, Siena.

painter's Death of St John the Evangelist, also somewhat damaged. Over the altar in the left transept is Giovanni di Paolo's *Madonna della Misericordia* of 1436. It is not one of his happiest works.

We now return by way of the Via S. Martino and the Via Porrione to the Loggia della Mercanzia in the Via di Città. Just past the Logge del Papa in the Banchi di Sotto is Bernardo Rossellino's Renaissance **Palazzo Piccolomini** on the left, now the seat of the State Archives, with sixty thousand parchments dating from 736 onwards, some of great historic and personal interest, arranged in three rooms. Along the walls are the *Tavolette di Biccherna*, the wooden covers of the account books ot the Biccherna or Exchequer, many of them painted by the most eminent painters of the day, including the Lorenzetti.

Turn left at the Loggia della Mercanzia. The Via dei Pellegrini on the right off the Via di Città leads to a small triangular piazza. On the left is the Palazzo del Magnifico, the Palace of the dictator Pandolfo Petrucci, while the far side is occupied by the façade of the Cathedral **Baptistery,** or S. Giovanni as it is often called, for it is practically a church on its own. This baptistery was built on to the end of the Cathedral, where the ground dips sharply down to the Valle Piatta, and the chancel was then constructed above it. Internally, therefore, it occupies the position of a crypt and externally it forms the lower part of the apsidal front. The façade was built in the fourteenth century in the purest Gothic style, with three great portals, a gable over the central one, and buttresses dividing them. The material used is white marble, picked out here and there with red or flamingo-pink.

The interior is attributed to Camaino di Crescentino and his son Tino di Camaino. The ceiling carries a number of frescoes by Vecchietta of apostles, prophets and sibyls, while the Articles of the Creed in the other vaults are the work of his pupils. The Life of Jesus in the apse is by Michele di Matteo of Bologna and pupils of Vechietta. The lunette on the left depicting the

Miracles of St Anthony is attributed to Benvenuto di Giovanni. The most conspicuous feature of the Baptistery is the great octagonal marble font in the middle. Jacopo della Quercia is believed to have been responsible both for the original over-all design and for the handsome marble ciborium which rises in the middle.

The Baptistery is very dark, but there is a man with a portable lamp who will light up the beautiful bas-reliefs of gilded bronze round the basin of the font. In the first one is Zacharias being expelled from the Temple, by Jacopo della Quercia; in the second, the Birth of John the Baptist, by Turino di Sano; in the third the Baptist preaching, by the same artist; in the fourth, Ghiberti's Baptism of Christ; in the fifth, his Arrest of the Baptist; and in the sixth Donatello's Banquet of Herod. Three of the four bronze angels on the ciborium are also by Donatello and the fourth is by Giovanni di Turino.

On the left of the Baptistery a tall flight of stairs, and on the right a sloping street, the Via dei Fusari, lead up to the Piazza del Duomo itself, which occupies one of the highest points of the city. **The Cathedral,** which was probably begun about 1150 and took more than a century and a half to build, spans the transition from Romanesque to Gothic, but the two styles are blended harmoniously together. The great façade is the most highly ornate part of an otherwise rather austere Romanesque cathedral, the plainness of the flanks relieved only by horizontal Pisan-style stripes of white marble and of the very dark green known as *verdescuro di Prato.*

These tiger-stripes cover the whole of the nave and of the high campanile, whose six stories of windows increase from one to six lights (*esafore*) as they rise to the summit. One of the most beautiful features of the Cathedral is the cupola, which rests on delicate superimposed arcades supported by slender columns. It is difficult to find a place to see it at close quarters, although, as I have said, there are good distant views from S. Domenico and from the Piazza Gramsci.

The lower part of the façade, dedicated to the Old Testament, is basically Romanesque with Gothic influences and the upper part, dedicated to the New Testament, is Gothic. Striped white, green and red, both carry a wealth of statues, bas-reliefs, mosaics, gables and finials. Giovanni Pisano was responsible for the lower portion, although it was only completed in 1333, some twenty years after his death. The bas-relief over the round main door is believed to be by Tino di Camaino and represents the story of Joachim and Anna. The lateral pillars and many of the statues were the work of Giovanni Pisano and his pupils. Many of the statues have been removed to the Museo dell' Opera del Duomo across the piazza to protect them from the weather and have been replaced by copies. Original are the prophets on the lower part of the left-hand pillar, and David and Solomon on the sides of the central arch. The bronze door in the middle by Enrico Manfrini dates from 1958 and represents God and Man glorifying the Virgin. It was the gift of the Monte dei Paschi. On the sides are prophets and women of the Old Testament. Below are scenes from the life of the Virgin and above are saints and popes. The large bas-reliefs in the centre panels represent the Assumption and the Coronation of the Virgin.

The upper part of the façade above the cornice was not added until after the New Cathedral had been half built and then abandoned. Its most prominent feature consists of three gables, of which the central one is the highest. It rises above a great rose window. This upper part is richly and completely Gothic with no Romanesque features like the lower. The mosaics in the gables were made in Venice in the nineteenth century. On the right is the Nativity; in the middle the Coronation of the Virgin; on the left the Presentation of the Virgin. The façade is not a completely happy creation on account of the basic disharmony between the upper and the lower parts, above and below the cornice, built as they were at long intervals and not altogether married up.

The building adjoining the Cathedral on the north is the Archbishop's Palace, and opposite the façade is the **Hospital of S. Maria della Scala,** one of the oldest in Italy even if one rejects the legend of its foundation in 832 and assigns it, as most scholars do, to the end of the thirteenth century. Every day between half past twelve and half past one it is open to visitors, who may walk straight through to the ward in front, the Pellegrinaggio or Pilgrims' Hall, now occupied by the sick. The walls are appropriately covered with a series of frescoes illustrating the nursing of the sick and the care of the poor and of orphans. The contemporary types and costumes are of particular interest. Most of them were executed by Domenico di Bartolo between 1440 and 1443. Others are by lesser known painters. It was here that St Catherine and St Bernardino used to come to nurse the plague-stricken.

Next door to the Hospital is the fifteenth-century church of **S. Maria della Scala,** also called the Annunziata after a wooden statue by a follower of Tino di Camaino. The Risen Christ in bronze on the altar is the work of Vecchietta, and the choir-gallery on the right has been ascribed to Baldassare Peruzzi. A door on the left leads to the underground Oratory of St Catherine, with the cell where she used to rest after a long day tending the sick in the hospital next door. The terra-cotta portrait of the sleeping saint is by Vecchietta; the triptych of the Madonna Enthroned with the Baptist and St Andrew in the sacristy by Taddeo di Bartolo.

S. Maria della Scala derives its name from the flight of steps leading up to the Cathedral façade just in front of it, and it is now time for us to mount them and go in by the right-hand of the three doors, the one which is usually open. Before doing so notice the graffiti let into the pavement representing the Robing of the Ecclesiastical hierarchy. They are reproductions of the originals now in the Museo dell' Opera del Duomo.

One's first impression as one steps out of the sunlight into the high, rather dark interior, Romanesque in form but more Gothic in spirit than most of the original buildings of the city, is of the striking effect of the black and white horizontally striped marble which covers practically the whole of its surface up to the blue vaulting, spangled with gold stars. All round the cornice at the top of the columns are fanciful terra-cotta busts of the first hundred and seventy-one Popes from St Peter to Lucius III, who succeeded to his chair in 1181. It is interesting to learn from Augustus Hare that the bust of the mythical Englishwoman, Pope Joan, who is said to have succeeded Leo IV as Pope John VIII in 855, was only expunged of its label 'Johannes VIII, Femina de Anglia' in 1600; the guide will still show you the head which is supposed to have been hers.

The unique feature of the Cathedral is its floor, which is entirely composed of graffiti, designed by some of the leading artists of Siena and inlaid with many-coloured marbles. There are fifty-six different pictures and they cover the whole floor of the great Cathedral like a carpet. The sibyls and so forth near the entrance door are visible at all times but most of the more elaborate and valuable scenes under the cupola are covered for protection with a wooden flooring which is supposed to be removed on the Eve of the Assumption on 15th August until 15th September (but was not during the two successive Assumptions on which I have hopefully visited the Cathedral). Usually, however, the three scenes in the left transept are corded off and left uncovered. They are Benvenuto di Giovanni's Deposition of Ahab, Matteo di Giovanni's Massacre of the Innocents and Antonio Federighi's Battle of Bethany. Beccafumi was the most prolific of the designers and was responsible for thirty-five of the scenes. Pinturicchio, Neroccio, Domenico di Bartolo and Domenico dei Cori were among the other contributors to this great gallery of stone pictures.

The rose-window on the entrance wall represents the Last Supper and was executed in 1549 to the designs of Perin del Vaga, the assistant of Raphael, by Pastoriono dei Pastorini, the greatest of the Sienese glassworkers. The Pope depicted in the act of benediction at the right-hand end of the façade wall is Camillo Borghese of Siena, who took the title of Paul V and who completed St Peter's at Rome. The Pope in the left-hand corner is Marcellus II, a Cervini of Montepulciano.

The fourth altar in the left aisle is the great Piccolomini Altar designed and constructed by Andrea Bregno the Lombard in 1481. It is thought that Michelangelo carved the four statues of SS. Peter, Paul, Gregory and Pius in the niches, while the Madonna in the niche above is believed to be an early work by Jacopo della Quercia. The marble-framed panel of the Nursing Madonna is generally credited to Paolo di Giovanni Fei and dates back to the end of the fourteenth century.

We have now reached a corner of the Duomo practically dedicated to the alliterative names of the two Pius Piccolomini and of Pinturicchio, for just beyond the Piccolomini Altar is the entrance to the **Piccolomini Library,** which Pinturicchio decorated and above which is his enormous fresco of the Coronation of Pius III. The two beautiful marble arches of the entrance were carved by Marrina in 1497. In the altar under the arch on the right is a bas-relief of St John the Divine in his old age by Vecchietta. Through the arch on the left one enters the library. (The ticket will admit one also to the Cappella di S. Giovanni in the transept nearby.)

Cardinal Francesco Piccolomini, afterwards Pope Pius III, built the library in 1495 to house the books and honour the memory of his uncle Pius II. Well lit and airy, it contains in cases round the walls a collection of missals and antiphonaries with magnificent illuminations by such artists as Liberale da Verona and Girolamo da Cremona, which alone are reason enough to visit the library. The ceiling is painted with mythological and allegorical subjects and grotesques by Pinturicchio's pupils, while the walls are entirely covered with the Master's delightful scenes from the life of the humanist and diplomat, Æneas Sylvius Piccolomini, later to be Pope Pius II, still perfectly preserved and as brilliant as the day they were painted. If they cannot boast of any great inventive or dramatic power, they are at least wonderfully gay and decorative.

The first scene, on the right by the window, shows the young Æneas Sylvius setting out from Talamone in the train of Cardinal Capranica, behind whom he rides, for the Council of Basle. In 2, as the figure on the right with the three plumes in his hat, he heads an embassy from the Council to King James of Scotland to try and persuade him to invade England. In 3 he is crowned poet laureate by the Emperor Frederick III. In 4 he is received by Pope Eugenius IV as Ambassador from the Emperor, and in the background is ordained priest by the Pope at the age of forty-two. In 5, by now Bishop of Siena, he introduces the Emperor Frederick to Princess Eleonora of Portugal, whose betrothal he had arranged. The column with the two coats of arms stands to this day outside the Porta Camollia, which is shown in the left background, with Siena Cathedral on the right. In 6 he receives the cardinal's hat from Pope Calixtus III. In 7, elected to succeed Calixtus after a stormy conclave in 1458, he has the ceremonial tuft of cotton burnt in front of him in St John Lateran. In 8, already bent and ill, he urges the princes assembled at Mantua to undertake a crusade to recover Constantinople from the infidel. (The Turks shown in several of these later scenes are intended to symbolise his zeal for the crusade.) In 9 he canonises St Catherine of Siena, shown lying at his feet. The two figures on the left at the bottom of the lower scene are the young Raphael and Pinturicchio himself, wearing a red hat. The white-robed Dominican on the extreme right is said to be Fra Angelico. In 10, the dying Pope sees the Venetian galleys sail into the harbour of Ancona, just too late, for the troops assembled there for the Crusade have already dispersed. The figure in the orange robe is the Doge of Venice, and the bearded man in the green hat is the Greek Despot of the Morea. Disappointed and sad-dened at the failure of his plans, the Pope retired to the church of S. Ciriaco, which is shown in the background, and shortly afterwards died.

The circular **Chapel of St John the Baptist** in the left transept just round the corner is Renaissance work by Giovanni di Stefano. The arm of the Baptist, presented to Pius II by the Despot of the Morea, Thomas Palaeologus, is treasured here. (There are other arms at Dubrovnik and in the Chapel Royal at Madrid, while yet a fourth arm, it is recorded, was thrust into the mouth of a great dragon at Antioch.) The octagonal font (for this is a supernumerary baptistery) is ascribed to Antonio Federighi. The bronze statue of the Baptist in the central niche was made by Donatello in 1457. The St Catherine of Alexandria in the niche on the right is by Neroccio and the St Ansanus on the left by Giovanni di Stefano. Both date from 1487. The panels on the eight walls were painted by Pinturicchio at the beginning of the sixteenth century but only five of the frescoes are as he created them. The genuine Pinturicchios are, lower left, Alberto Aringhieri, Rector of the Works of the Cathedral, as a youthful Knight of Malta; the Birth of St John the Baptist; and on the right Alberto Aringhieri as an old man. On the upper left is St John in the Desert and on the upper right St John preaching. The other panels have been remade by Rustici and Maccari.

The statues of the two Popes in this transept represent the two Piccolomini, Pius II on the right and Pius III on the left. The wooden crucifix is fourteenth-century work and therefore cannot have been carried, as tradition would have it, on the war chariot or *carroccio* of the Republic at Monteaperti.

In the **Chapel of St Ansanus** behind the pulpit is the Gothic tomb of the distinguished jurist, Cardinal Riccardo Petroni, by Camaino and his son Tino. It dates from 1314, the year in which Giovanni Pisano is believed to have died. Four caryatids support the sarcophagus, which is adorned with reliefs of the Incredulity of St Thomas, the Risen Christ and the Appearance to St Mary Magdalene. Above is the recumbent effigy of the Cardinal himself and above that again are three gables with statues of St Peter, the Madonna and Child and St Paul. Beneath the wooden cover on the floor in front of it a bronze slab covers the tomb of Bishop Pecci and was executed by Donatello in 1426. (The sacristan will show it you.)

The white marble **pulpit** is the work of Nicola Pisano, assisted by his pupils, chief among whom were his son Giovanni and Arnolfo di Cambio of Colle Val d'Elsa, who built the Palazzo Vecchio, in Florence. It may be regarded as transitional

164

One of the Frescoes by Sodoma (1477–1549) covering all four walls of the Cloister of the Abbey of Monte Oliveto Maggiore, on the life of St Benedict of Norcia, founder of the Benedictine Order. The wicked priest Florentius attempts to poison the souls of Benedict's monks by introducing naked women into the monastery. When the abbot saw the fresco he ordered it to be destroyed, so Sodoma agreed to clothe the women.

Capital with the story of Daniel, in the Abbey of Sant 'Antimo.

in style between Nicola's own Romanesque pulpit in the Baptistery at Pisa and Giovanni's later Gothic pulpit in the Cathedral there. It was begun in 1265, only half a dozen years after the pulpit in the Pisan Baptistery. It would seem as though Nicola was already feeling the Gothicising influence of the younger generation, or else that he left a great deal of the work to Giovanni and Arnolfo. Octagonal in shape, the pulpit rests upon eight columns. There is a central column supported by figures who represent the seven liberal arts.[1] On the architrave of the exterior columns are represented the Sibyls. The panels, reading from left to right from the top of the stairs, represent the Visitation and the Nativity; the Adoration of the Magi; the Presentation in the Temple and the Flight into Egypt; the Massacre of the Innocents; the Crucifixion; the Salvation of the Elect on Judgment Day; and the Casting of the Wicked into Hell.

The door to the **sacristy** is on the left behind the pulpit but special permission must be obtained to visit its treasures, such as a bust of Alexander VII by Melchiore Caffà, the pupil of Bernini, and three panels by Sano di Pietro, including one of St Bernardino preaching in the Campo and another of him in the Piazza S. Francesco. Both are of considerable historical and topographical interest. Giovanni di Turino has a holy water stoup of marble, gilded bronze and coloured enamels.

Notice the iron plate in front of the high altar at the top of the three steps up to the chancel. If you lift it up you will find yourself looking perpendicularly down into the Baptistery far below. The windows of the apse, representing the Death, Assumption and Coronation of the Virgin, are believed to be the oldest pieces of stained glass in Italy. They are the work of Dona and Giunta di Paolo from designs specially made by Duccio, whose mighty *Maestà*, now in the Museo dell' Opera del Duomo, stood on the high altar until 1506. The present **high altar** is a handsome and elaborate construction designed by Baldassare Peruzzi, and is surmounted by a great bronze tabernacle by

[1]See page 75.

Vecchietta, formerly in S. Maria della Scala. The upper two angels bearing candelabra are by Giovanni di Stefano and the lower pair by Francesco di Giorgio Martini. On the right of the altar is a lectern of 1558, and behind are carved and inlaid choir stalls. The intarsia was the work of Fra Giovanni da Verona and comes from the Olivetan monastery of Monteoliveto Minore outside the Porta Tufi, where Bernardo Tolomei, the founder of the Order, died. The two handsome orchestra-lofts on either side are sixteenth-century work. The picture of the Assumption in the apse was painted by Bernardo Cesi in 1594, and the two Old Testament scenes on either side by Ventura Salimbeni in 1608.

The central cupola is supported by six columns. The two immensely long poles attached to the pair nearest the nave are, according to tradition, the flagpoles borne on the *carroccio* at the Battle of Monteaperti. The gilded statues at the top of the columns represent the saints of Siena, Catherine, Bernardino, Ansanus, Victor, Crescentius and Savinus, and date from 1481.

The circular **baroque chapel** in the right transept which corresponds to St John's Chapel in the left transept dates from 1661. It was built by Alexander VII, who was the Sienese-born Fabio Chigi. The altar and the statues of the Madonna and St Jerome just inside the door are from the hand of Gian Lorenzo Bernini, greatest of all the baroque sculptors. The chapel is also called the Chapel of the Madonna del Voto from a thirteenth-century painted panel which is attributed to Guido da Siena but which is kept covered. The two statues of Popes represent the two Sienese pontiffs, Alexander III and Alexander VII, and balance the two Piccolomini Popes in the opposite transept.

Near the Chigi Chapel, in the right aisle, is the door which leads to the bell tower, from the top of which there is a magnificent view over southern Tuscany. (The staircase only goes up to the third floor and the remaining three must be climbed by ladder.) The tomb of Bishop Tommaso Piccolomini over the door is the work of Neroccio Landi, sculptor as well as painter. Next door to it is the Porta Chigi which leads out into the Piazza, facing the New Cathedral. It has a modern bronze door, the work of Vico Consorti, which was presented in 1946 by Count Guido Chigi as a thank-offering to the Virgin, the Sovereign and Protectress of Siena, for saving her city from destruction during the War. The bas-relief above it represents Our Lady of Pardon and belongs to the school of Donatello.

This great Cathedral, which was created when the power and the wealth of the Republic were at their zenith, failed to content the ambitious Sienese and it was not even finished before they began to build a still larger one, of which the original was to have been only the transept. Its white and black marble columns and its pointed Gothic windows stand like a great skeleton on the south side of the Cathedral. The building had already reached the level of the clerestory when it was discontinued after 1348. There seem to have been two reasons for this. Firstly, the Black Death had crippled the resources of the city; and secondly the experts came to the conclusion that the columns as built were too light for the weight they would have to bear.

The dangerous portions were pulled down and the spaces between the columns filled with the red brickwork which we see to-day. The unfinished nave became a piazza (now, like all the others except only the Campo, a car park) and was later dedicated to the greatest of Sienese sculptors, Jacopo della Quercia. On the wall is a plaque composed by the critic Adolfo Venturi, which runs as follows: 'This square flourishes in the name of Jacopo della Quercia who by breathing life into stones near here for the Fonte Gaia threw the bridge of glory between Giovanni Pisano and Michelangelo.' At the far end of the Piazza Jacopo della Quercia rises the immensely high façade which the Sienese call *Il Facciatone* and which cuts into the blue Tuscan sky almost as deeply and as sharply as the campanile itself. From the foot of it there is the best near view of the lovely cupola of the Cathedral.

Between the arches of the left nave is the **Museo dell' Opera del Duomo** or Museo dell' Opera Metropolitana, which contains such works of art belonging to the Cathedral as are not

167

displayed there. The ground floor contains mainly weatherworn sculptures by Giovanni Pisano and his pupils which once adorned the façade of the Duomo. There are also a few classical sculptures such as a Roman copy of Praxiteles' Three Graces, which formerly stood, rather incongruously, in the Piccolomini Library in the Cathedral. The iron screen which divides the room dates from the fifteenth century and comes from the Hospital of S. Maria della Scala.

The first floor is occupied by the administration and on the second floor is the great glory of the Museum, and indeed of the whole School of Siena, the Duccio Room. Air-conditioned and without windows, it is draped with dark green curtains and each picture has its own individual lighting. At the far end is the great wooden panel, or panels, of the *Maestà*. When, after three years' work it was completed in June 1311 in the painter's studio by the Stalloreggi Gate,[1] it was carried to the Cathedral amid the wild rejoicing of all the citizens and escorted by the Nine, the magistrates and the clergy. (The story told by Vasari of the Rucellai Madonna in S. Maria Novella in Florence seems to have been based on this.) They mounted the painting on the high altar of the Cathedral, rather ungratefully replacing the Madonna of the Large Eyes which, so their fathers devoutly believed, had given them the victory at Monteaperti.

The panels were originally painted on both sides, but in 1795 the Madonna and Saints on the obverse were separated from the numerous small scenes from the Passion which formed the reverse and also from the predella and other smaller paintings on the front. The majority of these scenes are in this room, five are in the National Gallery in London, four are in the National Gallery in Washington and one is in the Frick Collection in New York, while six of them seem to be lost altogether.

The great Madonna herself with the Child in her arms fills the entire end wall of the room. She sits, surrounded by angels and saints, on a Romanesque throne, on the base of which is the Latin inscription: 'Holy, Mother of God, be thou the cause

[1]Now 89 Via Stalloreggi.

of peace to Siena, and be thou life to Duccio because he hath painted thee thus.' On either side kneel the four patron saints of Siena. At the top are panels of those ten Apostles who are not already depicted among the saints in the main picture.

On the right-hand wall hang several Madonnas by Duccio and his pupils. Opposite the *Maestà* are the scenes from the Passion which formerly formed the back of the altarpiece and on the left wall hang the scenes from the lives of Christ and the Virgin which were formerly at the top and the bottom of the anterior face. All these scenes are well worth studying in detail. Notice in particular the great Crucifixion which formed the centrepiece of the reverse side. The most beautiful panel, I think, is that of the Three Maries at the Tomb. They stand in anguish on the left of the picture, robed in red, purple and green respectively, while an angel in white points to the empty tomb. 'They have taken away my Lord and I know not where they have laid him.'

On the third floor is a roomful of pictures memorable chiefly for some attractive works by Matteo di Giovanni. In the centre are cases of illuminated missals and choir-books. The next room is devoted mainly to rich ecclesiastical vestments and altar-cloths. At the end is a window affording one of the finest views in Siena, and down a short flight of stairs just below a door leads by way of two spiral staircases up to the Facciatone, with an even wider panorama. Both these rooms afford good close-ups of the upper parts of the New Cathedral, and here and there in the Museum itself one comes unexpectedly upon a bit of the original structure itself, glittering white marble with black stripes and Gothic decorations.

The top story contains another small gallery of pictures including a Sano di Pietro Madonna and four panels by Ambrogio Lorenzetti depicting SS. Catherine of Alexandria, Benedict, Francis and Mary Magdalene. There is a delightful little Giovanni di Paolo showing St Francis appearing at the Council of Arles. The most notable object is the Large-Eyed Madonna, *la Madonna degli occhi grossi*, as the Sienese call the

Madonna delle Grazie. It is painted on wood in very slight relief and shows the Madonna full face holding up the Child in front of her. It dates from the first half of the thirteenth century and is Romanesque in style. The eyes are only large because they are wide open and thus contrast with the almond eyes of the Byzantine School which was soon to succeed the Romanesque. It is of great human and historic interest, since it used to stand on the high altar of the Cathedral and was the actual Madonna in front of which the Sienese prayed on the eve of Monteaperti when they proclaimed Our Lady the Sovereign of Siena. Later it lost its place to Duccio's *Maestà* and was relegated to the Chapel of the Madonna del Voto.

The street beneath the Facciatone leads into the Via di Città. Just down on the left may be seen the handsome grey travertine front of the **Palazzo Chigi** (or **Saracini**), as it curves in to match the curve of the street. In 1930 the owner, Count Guido Chigi, turned it into a musical academy, and a school for young musicians is held there every summer. The Palazzo Chigi contains the finest private collection of pictures in Siena. If the rooms are not being used for other purposes, as they generally are in the summer, and if you can find the porter and get him to show you over the palace, you will find the only Botticelli in Siena, a Madonna with Two Saints. There are three Sassettas, an Epiphany and two Madonnas, and other works by Neroccio di Bartolomeo, Sano di Pietro, Matteo di Giovanni and Vecchietta.

Farther up the hill, the Via di Città peters out as though it were a stream rising in the Piazza di Postierla. From here the Via S. Pietro to the left leads to the Picture Gallery or **Pinacoteca** in the Palazzo Buonsignori, one of the last of the red brick Gothic palaces to be built in Siena, just before you come to the church of S. Pietro. When you visit the gallery, remember to begin at the top and work downwards to the bottom like a Stilton cheese. The primitives, which are also much the best pictures, are arranged on the second floor because it has the most light to see them by. The first floor is rather dark and the morning is the best time to visit the gallery.

On the way up to the second floor, however, pause on the first not only to rest your legs but to go into the little room of new acquisitions and loans not included in the catalogue. It is up four or five steps on the right of the landing and then to the right again. On the left-hand wall, and that perhaps only temporarily, hangs the gallery's solitary example of one of Siena's greatest masters. Simone Martini is completely unrepresented in the Pinacoteca except by this very lovely but badly damaged Madonna, which is on loan from the parish church of Lucignano d' Arbia. By the time this book is published Simone's Madonna may have been returned to Lucignano, and other loans or new acquisitions may hang on the walls of this little room. But it is a covert worth drawing on the way upstairs. Besides the Simone, they have recently had a Pollaiuolo and a Signorelli on loan in this room.

If I seem to devote little space to this collection, the only one in the world where the great School of Siena can be properly studied, it is for the sole reason that it is so well labelled that a detailed commentary is almost superfluous, although I recommend buying, if only as a souvenir, the profusely illustrated pocket guide by Dr. Enzo Carli, the director. It is enough to say that the gallery is arranged as far as possible chronologically, so that the first two rooms on the second floor are devoted to Guido da Siena and his Byzantine followers. (Look at the curious flower-like trees, like giant dandelions, in the Raising of Lazarus. No. 8.) The next two rooms contain some outstandingly beautiful Madonnas by Duccio and his followers. My favourite is the somewhat damaged Madonna dei Francescani, with the three tiny friars crouched like rabbits on the floor. It is an iconographical rarity in that the Virgin inclines her head towards her right shoulder, contrary to the tradition by which she bends towards her left.

The sixth room is devoted to the Lorenzetti brothers, who are well represented here. While I incline, on the whole, to prefer Pietro for his power of conveying emotion and his superior portraiture, it is certain that the two small landscapes by

171

Ambrogio (No's. 70 and 71) are among the most breathtakingly beautiful things in the gallery. Probably intended to adorn some chest or *cassone*, they were painted a couple of centuries and more before it occurred to anybody else to depict a landscape for its own sake. One represents a castle with a little black nut-shell of a boat floating on wonderful blue-green water, and the other a little walled and towered city by the seashore. Both have been said to represent the Sienese harbour of Talamone in the Maremma, but nobody will ever know for certain whether either of them do.

There are several hundred Sienese pictures in the Pinacoteca and one finds oneself feeling sometimes how much more effective most of them must have looked in their own churches instead of crowded side by side on the walls of a gallery. The counter-argument, of course, is that it would require immense labour to go round visiting them in their native habitats, whereas here they can be compared with one another and studied at leisure. Even while one applauds the desire of the authorities to assemble the most complete collection of Sienese paintings possible, one finds oneself rather guiltily feeling that three rooms full of that rather pedestrian painter, Sano di Pietro, are as good as a feast. There is such a thing as æsthetic indigestion.

That excellent painter Taddeo di Bartolo spans the transition from the Trecento to the Quattrocento.[1] The glories of Sienese painting, Duccio, Simone Martini, the Lorenzettis and Lippo Memmi were dead. All the same, a number of good, even if not great, painters, flourished in the fifteenth century. Sassetta in the first half of the century is probably the finest of them, but he is not represented here at his best. (Perhaps one can judge his quality as well in the National Gallery in London.) But look at his spirited No. 166, showing St Antony being beaten by devils. Paolo di Giovanni Fei has a wonderful fourteenth-century domestic scene in the Nativity of the Virgin, the major work of the

[1] In Italian the fourteenth century is the Trecento—the thirteen hundreds—or the *Secolo 14*; and the fifteenth century likewise is the Quattrocento or the *Secolo 15*.

Above: Arezzo's fan-shaped Piazza Grande, with (from left to right) the church of Pieve di S. Maria, the 18th century Tribunal, and the Palazzo della Fraternita dei Laici. *Below:* The Church of S. Maria della Grazie just outside Arezzo.

The Romanesque Church of the Pieve di S. Maria, begun in the
12th century and completed in the 14th. Below are five blind arches,
above three loggias of gradually diminishing size, with no two
columns alike. Towering above is the 'belfry of a hundred holes'.

curious and talented painter who taught his art to Sassetta. It dates from the last decade or two of the fourteenth century. Bartolo di Fredi has some powerful paintings with lovely decorative horses.

Giovanni di Paolo contributes a very original and striking painting of Christ and a Flight into Egypt where instead of the usual gold background the mountainsides are gilded by the setting sun. This piece comes very near to being a landscape painting. Matteo di Giovanni, that delightful artist of the later Quattrocento, has a number of lovely fair-haired Madonnas with sloe Byzantine eyes, pointed Florentine faces and long thin Sienese hands. Neroccio di Bartolomeo Landi was in some ways the most fascinating painter of the later Quattrocento and was one of the last representatives of the fey, mystical tradition of the Sienese School. It is hardly credible that No. 281, his long-necked, black-hooded, highly stylised Madonna with the dimly portrayed saints in the background should be almost contemporary with the works of Botticelli. It was painted about 1475 but it is still in the direct and close tradition of Simone Martini. So far apart were the two Schools of Siena and Florence even as late as this.

On the first floor are some good Sodomas and Beccafumis. Sodoma's Christ at the Column, a fragment from a larger work, is acknowledged to be one of his finest works, surpassing even the St Catherine in S. Domenico. It is equally remarkable for its emotional and for its formal and plastic qualities. Of the non-Sienese Pinturicchio is represented by a charming *tondo* of the Holy Family with the Infant St John, probably a late work. The portrait of Queen Elizabeth of England may or may not be the work of Federigo Zuccari, who worked at her court. There is a highly controversial Dürer, Portrait of an Old Man, signed and dated, for the authenticity of which Dr. Carli goes out of his way to vouch. Amateur art critics, however, have scrawled angry 'No's' all over its label and substituted such names as Lucas van Leyden and Marinus van Romerswael.

On leaving the Pinacoteca turn left along the Via S. Pietro

and go through an archway, the so-called Porta dell' Arco, which once marked the limit of the town in this direction. The church on the other side of a dusty square is **S. Agostino,** and the convent buildings beside it are now a school, the Convitto Tolomei. The entrance is through the door on the left in the porch. The church dates from the thirteenth century but the interior was entirely rebuilt by Vanvitelli in 1755. Over the second altar on the right is a very typical Crucifixion by Perugino with an attractive landscape in the background.

Just beyond it is the entrance to the Piccolomini Chapel, a miniature picture gallery in itself. Over the altar is a finely coloured and beautifully preserved Adoration of the Magi by Sodoma. It is one of his best altarpieces. On the wall to the right hangs a gruesome Massacre of the Innocents by Matteo di Giovanni, who is believed by some to have painted his own portrait in the figure beneath the outstretched arm of the diabolically scowling Herod. Notice the impish glee of the two elder children as they watch the slaughter from the balcony behind. ('But, Mummy, you promised I could see the pig being killed.') Facing it on the left-hand wall is a very untypical triptych by Simone Martini. In the centre is the figure of the Blessed Agostino Novello, whose ashes rest beneath the high altar of the church. He is receiving inspiration from an angel whispering in his ear. On either side are representations of four of his miracles. On the far wall, opposite the altar, is a recently discovered fresco of the Madonna Enthroned among Saints by Ambrogio Lorenzetti. Damaged though it is, some of the colours are wonderfully preserved. The wooden Madonna beneath it dates from the fifteenth century, but its authorship is disputed.

CHAPTER 13

The Southern Sienese

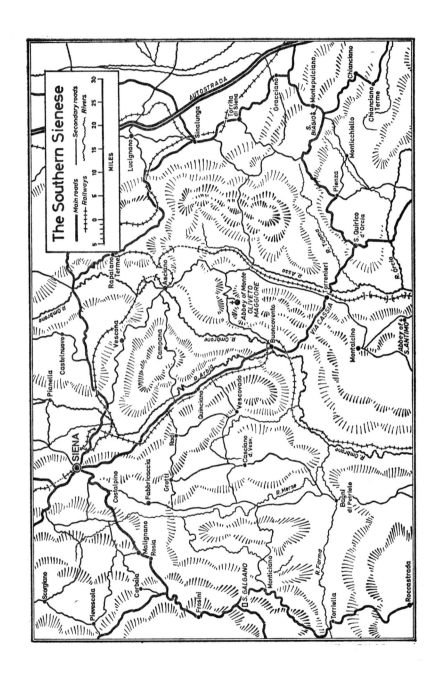

The Southern Sienese

Main roads
Secondary roads
Railways
Rivers

MILES
0 5 10 15 20 25 30

AUTOSTRADA

Lucignano
Sinalunga
Torrita di Siena
Gracciano
S. BIAGIO
Montepulciano
Chianciano
Chianciano Terme
Monticchiello
Pienza
S. Quirico d'Orcia

Rapolano Terme
Asciano
Abbey of Monte OLIVETO MAGGIORE
Buonconvento
VIA CASSIA
R. Tuoma
R. ASSO
R. Orcia
Abbey of S. ANTIMO
Montalcino

R. Ombrone
Vescona
Campana
R. Ombrone
R. Arbia
Quinciano
Vescovado

Castelnuovo
Pianella
SIENA
Costalpino
Fabbricaccia
Grotti
Rosi
Cascicano d. Vesv.
R. Merse
R. Ombrone

Scorgiano
Plevescola
Cerbaia
Malignano
Rosia
S. GALGANO
Monticiano
Frosini
Bagni di Petriolo
R. Farma
Torniella
Roccastrada

CHAPTER 13

The Southern Sienese

In 1313 a Sienese nobleman called Bernardo Tolomei forsook the world and with it his lectureship at the university, gave away nearly all his possessions and with two companions, Ambrogio Piccolomini and Patrizio Patrizi, went out to a small property which he had retained for himself in the *crete*, the eroded clay hills to the south-east of Siena. The district was then known as 'the desert of Accona,' although any Arab would laugh at such a description of these cornfields and woodlands. If they are a desert, it is only by comparison with the rich lands which stretch from Siena up to Florence and Arezzo and which are one of the loveliest regions in Europe. The Chianti country itself is limestone but the remainder of the triangle consists mostly of gently rolling tufa hills, with occasional outcrops of travertine rock. It is rich in vineyards, cornfields, olive groves and fruit farms, mostly owned and run on a sharecropping basis (*mezzadria*), in which 53 per cent goes to the peasant and 47 per cent to the landlord, who has to keep the farms in good repair. Everywhere there are little woods of ilex and umbrella pine, and unexpected avenues of cypresses lining the horizon or leading up to a farm. Many of the hill-tops are crowned with a manor house or a monastery, or else by a clump of pines, ilex or cypresses. Dragging the ploughs and pulling the lumbering wagons along the roads are the great white Tuscan oxen, or more often cows, for horses and mules are rare in Tuscany. The peasants drive and guide them more by shouts than anything else, for man and beast have perfected a simple common language. It is very hard to make oneself believe that this fantastically beautiful landscape existed before the early Italian artists came to paint it. But so it is. Art has copied nature this time and not nature art.

Anyhow, it was in this delectable desert that Bernardo founded the Abbey of **Monte Oliveto Maggiore** and the Olivetan Congregation within the Benedictine Order. The best way to get to it is by driving from Buonconvento on the Via Cassia through hilly country, broken up by ravines and precipices where the earth has been washed away to reveal the bluish clay, until the great red-brick monastery appears on a spur ahead to the right. It is reached by way of a battlemented gatehouse like a fort with a many-coloured Madonna of della Robbia, Crowned between Two Angels over the portal and (mercifully, for it can be a thirsty walk back from the abbey in the sun) a little restaurant-bar on the left.

A steep and stony road runs down between the cypresses to the abbey itself, and to the left of it a brick-paved footpath. The great fishpond between them dates from 1533. The entrance to the abbey is just beyond the church, and leads into the great cloister, which is frescoed on all four sides with scenes from the life of St Benedict of Norcia, the founder of the Order, by Luca Signorelli and Sodoma. The story closely follows the account of St Gregory. Chronologically the series begins at the south-east angle (which is the second corner on the left) with the scene of Benedict leaving his home to enter the schools of Rome. The third scene, showing one of the saint's early prentice miracles, is interesting because the jaunty, swarthy gallant in the foreground is a self-portrait of Sodoma, a lover of gaiety and of jests who earned himself the nickname of Il Mattaccio, the Crazy Fellow. At his feet are some of the many pets which he brought with him to assuage the boredom of his long stay in the monastery, two tame badgers and a raven which he had taught to talk. 'The dwelling of this man appeared like Noah's Ark itself,' wrote Vasari, who furthermore described Sodoma as a 'gay and licentious man' and his life as 'eccentric and beastly.' He painted twenty-six frescoes here in all, completing the work of his predecessor, Luca Signorelli, who had tired of the task after only eight and gone away to paint his masterpiece at Orvieto.

There is no need to detail the scenes one by one, for each has its subject clearly inscribed beneath it. Norcia is the town in the background of the first scene, Rome of the second and Subiaco of the fourth. Some of these background landscapes are the most fascinating parts of the pictures and many of Sodoma's might almost be taken for Chinese work—especially the one with the willow-pattern bridge and two funny little boats rocking on the river. Particularly frustrating for two painters who took such delight in bright colours must have been the necessity for filling up their foregrounds with massive groups of monks in dead-white habits. They made the best of their opportunities in such scenes as the twelfth, with its crowd of armed men and horsemen and the monuments of Rome in the background.

In the end corner of the south wall is the scene of how the wicked but resourceful priest Florentius, foiled in an attempt to poison Benedict in the previous scene, tries instead to poison the souls of his monks by introducing a number of naked women into the monastery. From characteristic diablerie Sodoma would not let anyone see the scene until it was completed. The abbot, as he very well knew he would, ordered the fresco to be destroyed, but eventually a compromise was arrived at when Sodoma agreed to put some clothes on the women—a striptease in reverse. John Addington Symonds, who praises the 'delicacy and naiveté, almost like a second Luini, but with more of humour and sensuousness' of these frescoes, singles out for special mention this one which 'carries the melody of fluent lines and the seduction of fair girlish faces into a region of pure poetry.'

The next fresco round the corner is by Sodoma and after that follows a series of eight by Luca Signorelli, which he began in 1497. Notice particularly the sadly discoloured twenty-fifth scene, where a pair of monks break bounds and dine in the house of two lady friends, only to be rebuked by St Benedict in the top right-hand corner. The twenty-seventh scene, St Benedict unmasking the deception of Totila, King of the Goths, offers Signorelli the same chance of painting bright colours that the reception of Maurus and Placidus gave Sodoma.

The frescoes on the north side are all by Sodoma. At the end of them a passage leads through into the church, a baroque building dating in its present form from 1772. Its best feature is the magnificent intarsia choir-stalls inlaid with street scenes, birds and miscellaneous objects in *trompe l'œil* cupboards by Fra Giovanni da Verona, who made the choir-stalls in Siena Cathedral. The Nativity of the Virgin behind the high altar is by Giacomo Ligozzi, also a Veronese. The Chapel of the Sacrament, off the left transept, has a punning modern altar which plays on the name of the abbey. Below is the Mount of Olives in silver, with olive-wood tree trunks and branches on either side, and above is an olive-wood tabernacle flanked by olive-wood candlesticks.

The famous library of the abbey is up a staircase leading off the middle cloister, which in turn is reached by a door in the south side of the great cloister near the fresco of the bad women. You cannot miss the stairs, for everything beyond them is firmly marked '*Clausura*,' which means the private part of the monastery; here no women are admitted. The library contains a large number of books dating from the earliest days of printing, and in glass cases in the middle are illuminated choir books of the fourteenth and fifteenth centuries. At the top of the stairs at the end of the room is the old pharmacy of the abbey, with a collection of seventeenth century majolica jars.

The refectory is seventeenth-century, with frescoes, and in the Chapter Room there is a fine Madonna of the Sienese school of the fourteenth century.

A number of small chapels and grottoes are scattered through the wooded grounds, and in a building behind the apse of the church is the praiseworthy Institute of Book Pathology, where the monks restore old bindings, parchments, maps and early

The discovery and identification of the true Cross, one of the frescoes at the Church of San Francesco at Arezzo, by Piero della Francesca. The Empress Helena, mother of Constantine, locates three crosses hidden by the Jews in Jerusalem – one of them the cross on which Christ was crucified. In the background, beyond the sloping mountains, is the 15th century town of Arezzo, surrounded by walls and towers.

The hill town of Poppi, in the upper region of the Arno valley, known as the Casentino. Crowning the summit of the hill is the castle of the Counts Guidi – a square fort with its tower jutting up from it. It now houses the communal offices and a library rich in manuscripts.

books. One need not, I think, be an anti-clerical to wish that all monks could be so usefully employed.

There are two roads out of Monte Oliveto. One leads to Buonconvento and the other to Asciano, where Domenico di Bartolo was born. Both are small towns which, as so often in Tuscany, boast not only good pictures in their churches but also their own little picture gallery. It is breathtaking to think of the wealth of art which the Senese, the *contado* of Siena, must have contained, when one reflects upon the hundreds of works which have been drained off to the Pinacoteca in Siena and other collections, and the number which are still left in these little towns.

S. Francesco in Asciano (to get in apply to the *Parroco* or parish priest next door to the Collegiata) is frescoed by Giovanni da Asciano, the pupil of Barna da Siena, while the twelfth-century Collegiata contains a Madonna by Pacchia on the right wall and a *Pietà* of the School of Sodoma on the left. On the left of the handsome Romanesque church is the Museum of Sacred Art, a former oratory, which one can have opened for one by ringing the bell marked '*Parroco*' at the house next door. There is a box in the gallery for voluntary contributions, so that there is no need to offer him anything '*per i poveri*.'

On the right of the entrance is a polyptych of the Madonna and Saints with a predella of the life of St Catherine of Alexandria, an early work by Matteo di Giovanni, and next to it an attractive Assumption by the same artist. The pride of the gallery is a St Michael and the Dragon by Ambrogio Lorenzetti, which comes from the Abbey of Rofeno. Notice the dramatic force of the composition and the seven snake-heads of the dragon, like those of Naga, the seven-headed cobra of Eastern mythology. Giovanni di Paolo contributes an Assumption; and the Maestro dell' Osservanza a Nativity of the Virgin, once believed to be by Sassetta, with a domestic scene well worth close examination as a picture of a late medieval house. At the end of the corridor is a Madonna, believed to be a very early Barna. In the second room are a Madonna with Saints attributed to Taddeo di Bartolo and on the side walls detached frescoes by Giovanni da Asciano.

Buonconvento, which in coaching days was the first (and by all accounts wretchedly uncomfortable) staging post out of Siena on the road to Rome, is a small walled town, where the Emperor, Henry VII of Luxembourg, Dante Alighieri's 'Lamb of God,' died in 1313 and with him the last hope of the vanquished Ghibellines. Over the high altar of the *pieve* or parish church of SS. Peter and Paul is a Madonna by Matteo di Giovanni; on the right wall of the chancel is a Madonna with Saints by Sano di Pietro and on the left another by Pacchiarotti.

Close by is a small Pinacoteca, which contains a polyptych of the Madonna by Sano di Pietro; a Madonna and Child by Segna di Bonaventura; and an Annunciation by Girolamo di Benvenuto, together with works of lesser importance and some examples of the goldsmith's art. The wooden statue of a Pope probably represents Paul V.

Continuing eight miles down the Via Cassia towards Rome and turning off at Torrenieri, we come to the fairy-like hill-top city whose towers we saw on the skyline as we drove down the road or from the window of our railway carriage. This eyrie was the last relic of the Sienese Republic when in 1555, after the fall of the city, nearly seven hundred Sienese families, exhausted though they were of everything except courage after a siege lasting over a year, migrated on foot hither to **Montalcino.** There the black-and-white standard of the republic, which is still to be seen in the Rocca, flew for another four years until the French garrison under Blaise de Montluc retired in 1559 in accordance with the harsh terms of the Treaty of Cateau Cambrésis and Montalcino was forced to submit to Florence.

The centre of the little city is the Piazza del Popolo with a handsome Renaissance loggia and beside it the curious Palazzo Comunale, very narrow, with the high brick-topped tower which one sees from so far away. Nearby is a good inn, the Albergo del Giglio. Behind it is the Piazza Garibaldi, with the fourteenth-century church of S. Egidio. Beyond and above, on the top of the hill, stands the great Rocca. It was the last of all the Sienese castles, and to it the jutting spur with the Medici arms was added by Cosimo de' Medici—the last humiliation to the vanquished republic.

In front of the Palazzo Pieri-Neri at 31 Via Ricasoli, which runs from the entrance to the Rocca, is the Episcopal Seminary with a Museum of Sacred Art. Among its contents, besides works by followers of Simone Martini and Ambrogio Lorenzetti, are an Assumption by Girolamo di Benvenuto, a Madonna by Bartolo di Fredi and a silken standard representing the Crucifixion by Sodoma. There are also a number of wood carvings. The great Romanesque church of S. Agostino next door contains fourteenth-century frescoes by unknown artists.

From the Piazza del Popolo a signpost points to the Civic Museum, which is in the broad tree-shaded Piazza Cavour. If it is shut, you ring the bell for the custodian. It contains a small but good picture gallery (although for myself I would be somewhat wary of some of the attributions). Bartolo di Fredi is represented by a Deposition and by a Coronation of the Virgin, Sano di Pietro by a Madonna and Child and Luca di Tommè by another Madonna. There are two della Robbia altar fronts, some interesting majolica vessels of the thirteenth century and two bibles, one of which also dates from the thirteenth century. The guardian of the Civic Museum will show you the little Archæological Museum two doors away, which contains some broken Etruscan pottery and some interesting frescoes. At the side of the Museo Civico is a little belvedere with a view over the dappled uplands as far as Siena and beyond. It needs little imagination to think the thoughts of those diehard Sienese patriots, as they sat there of an evening more than four centuries ago and gazed at the beloved city lost to them for ever.

Some six miles from Montalcino, along the road which turns off near the Rocca outside the walls, is the **Abbey of S. Antimo,** one of the oldest and loveliest Romanesque churches in Tuscany. Legend attributes its foundation to Charlemagne, but the present building was begun in 1118. The church is usually open in the summer but in the winter the guardian has to be routed out from the village above on the hill, Castelnuovo dell' Abate. His name and address are stuck up on the church door, but ask anyone in the village for *il guardiano dell' Abbazia.*

The church is built partly of travertine and partly of alabaster, of which there are quarries just on the other side of Castelnuovo. There is a satisfying semi-circular apse and a carved south door. On the walls of the campanile are curious sculptures of the Madonna and Child and of an Assyrian-looking winged bull with a woman's head. The lovely interior is a simple basilica with two side-aisles separated by columns, some of alabaster and some of travertine. Do not miss the carved capital of Daniel in the lions' den on the second column on the right. A Romanesque crucifix hangs on the left of the main door and there is a Romanesque Madonna of painted wood over the high altar. In the apse are some much repainted frescoes by Spinello Aretino and in the sacristy on the right monochrome frescoes of the fifteenth century. The crypt contains a *Pietà* attributed to Sodoma. The farm buildings on the right incorporate remains of the original Benedictine monastery.

The other great abbey of Southern Tuscany is **S. Galgano,** a vast red-brick, ruinous Gothic church just off the road to the Maremma. After Fossanova and Casamari in the mountains behind the Pontine marshes, it is probably the most important Cistercian abbey in Italy. In the thirteenth century the abbey possessed all the land round about, having ousted the local Benedictine abbeys, and rich properties farther afield. In the fourteenth century it was twice sacked by the White Company of the English *condottiere,* Sir John Hawkwood, and soon after it decayed and fell into ruin. When the monastic orders were suppressed the monks, who had supplied arbitrators, judges, doctors and architects to Siena, Volterra and the rest of Southern Tuscany, were dispersed; the church was disaffected and in 1816 the monastery became a farm and the materials diverted to its construction.

The great church was begun in 1224 on the model of the Cistercian houses in Burgundy. (It is one of the few ogival buildings in Tuscany to which the term 'Gothic' can be applied without reserve.) The steeple and the roof have long fallen in and the wide three-naved interior stands naked to the weather, a rather pathetic relic reared up high over this empty countryside. On the right of the church are the refectory, the chapter house and what is left of the cloister. They are now turned into farm buildings.

The road between the thermal spa of Chianciano Terme and the little town of S. Quirico d'Orcia[1] on the Via Cassia leads through two small architectural gems some eight miles from each other. They are the fifteenth-century city of Pienza and the largely sixteenth-century city of Montepulciano, both the creations of Florentine architects. **Pienza** was known as Corsignano when Æneas Sylvius Piccolomini was born there, the son of the lord of the village. When he was raised to the Papacy as Pius II in 1458, he remembered his birthplace, renamed it Pienza in honour of himself and commissioned the Florentine architect Bernardo Cambarelli, called Rossellino, a disciple of Leon Battista Alberti, to rebuild the village in the contemporary style.

Popes can pay for fast construction and between 1459 and 1462 a group of handsome Early Renaissance buildings sprang up round the Piazza Pio II, which is in its own way one of the finest 'period pieces' in Italy. One entire side of the square is occupied by the Cathedral. On the right is the great Palazzo Piccolomini, with a handsome arcaded courtyard, loggia and hanging garden. The state rooms on the first floor may be visited daily between 10 a.m. and 12.30, and between 3 p.m. and 6 p.m. They contain a number of portraits and collections of weapons and majolica. The building was probably modelled on Alberti's great Rucellai Palace in Florence (but not so closely as to prevent Rossellino in his æsthetic excitement from forgetting the kitchens, which had to be added later). In front of the Papal

[1] S. Quirico was that same Judas the Jew who was tortured by St Helena to make him reveal the secret of the True Cross, was converted and became Bishop of Jerusalem.

Palace is a very beautiful stone well-head, also designed by Rossellino. Opposite the Cathedral is the Palazzo Comunale and the Palazzo Ammannati. (Cardinal Ammannati of Pavia was one of those whom the Pope invited to come and build here.) On the fourth side of the Piazza are the Bishop's palace and the Museum.

The Cathedral, unfortunately, was built upon the brow of a steep clay slope, and the apse has chronically shown signs of wishing to slide down it into the Val d'Orcia. The high interior, with its three naves in the style of the *Hallenkirchen* which Pius had admired in Germany, is of a striking beauty and there are still one or two very attractive monuments left, notably the travertine altar on the right by Rossellino, which used to contain relics of St Andrew, the patron saint of Pienza. (In the nineteenth century the body of the saint was exchanged by the men of Patras with the Tsar of Russia in return for a new water supply.) There are Madonnas with Saints by Sano di Pietro, Giovanni di Paolo (with a fine *Pietà* in the lunette) and a lovely Assumption, in which Vecchietta has shown that he can rise to the level of a great painter. Particularly delightful is the angelic choir at the feet of the Virgin, who bear her to heaven on a white cloud. The saints on either side are SS. Catherine, Lucy, Calixtus and Pius I.

The Diocesan Museum of Sacred Art is just beside the Cathedral. It was formerly the house of the canons. The first room on the right on the second floor contains the principal treasure of Pienza. It is the great cope of Pius II, one of the most exquisite and best preserved of all medieval embroideries. It is agreed by all authorities to be *opus anglicanum*, English work of the first half of the fourteenth century. It somehow found its way to Greece and in 1462 was presented to the Pope by Thomas Palaeologus, the last Despot of the Morea. In 1963 it occupied the central place of honour in the exhibition of English medieval embroideries in the Victoria and Albert Museum. *Opus anglicanum* was England's most famous artistic production of the Middle Ages and was so widely sought after on the Continent that it far exeeded in the number of pieces all the other kinds of embroidery in the great Vatican inventory of 1295.

The Pienza cope consists of three concentric semicircles. The inner one shows five scenes from the life of the Virgin. Mark the grace of the Madonna in the Coronation scene in the centre, the lovely draperies and the angels with censers hovering overhead. The central ring of scenes consists of nine scenes, also from the life of the Virgin, with the ancestors of Christ in the spandrels. The outermost zone of all consists of six scenes from the life of St Margaret of Antioch on the left and seven scenes from the life of St Catherine of Alexandria on the right. In the spandrels are the twelve apostles. The backgrounds are of gold thread, worked with heraldic beasts, fleur-de-lys, scrolls and so forth.

The other rooms contain some Flemish tapestries of the fifteenth and sixteenth centuries and, among the pictures are a Madonna della Misericordia by Bartolo di Fredi and a Madonna with Saints by Vecchietta, with a most attractive Annunciation in the lunette. There are choir books, illuminated by Sano di Pietro (one initial contains a miniature, if not a caricature, of Pius II) and other painters, and some manuscripts and incunabula.

The Bishop's Palace next door was once the palace of Cardinal Rodrigo Borgia, the father of Lucrezia and Cesare, who later became Pope Alexander VI. He was one of the cardinals whom Pius had invited to follow him to Pienza, where he must have been abysmally bored. The Palazzo Comunale on the other side of the road was restored in 1900.

Some three miles from Pienza is the **Castello of Monticchiello,** which is notable not only for its striking position on a rocky hill but for a Madonna and Child by Pietro Lorenzetti in the church of SS. Leonardo and Cristoforo. Montepulciano can be easily reached from Pienza by way of Monticchiello, although it is not on the main road.

Montepulciano crowns the top of a long, narrow, steep-sided hill and was long a Sienese stronghold, albeit the inhabitants

187

generally favoured Florence. The town has long been celebrated for its magnificent red wine, and the Tuscan poets sing of '*Montepulciano dove il vino e Re!*' (Lunch at the Albergo Marzocco, highly praised by J. A. Symonds a century ago, just inside the gates on the left and sample the *vino nobile*, as it is called.) Montepulciano's most famous son was the poet Angelo Poliziano, known in English as Politian, the friend of Lorenzo the Magnificent, who took his name from his native city.

Before climbing the hill follow the signpost to S. Biagio at the foot of it. At the end of an avenue of magnificent cypresses which frame it, pale golden against the blue sky, is the lovely Renaissance church of S. Biagio or Blaise. It is the work of Antonio Sangallo the Elder, who was sent by the Florentines to fortify the city, and was begun in 1518. It is entirely built of white travertine, which has acquired a golden patina with the passage of time. It is in the form of a Greek cross with a semi-circular apse. It was to have had two campanili but only one has been completed. The loggiaed building to the east of the church was designed by Sangallo as the canonry. The guardian of the small museum which it contains holds the keys to unlock S. Biagio, but the interior is not very impressive. 'The Madonna of S. Bagio, in whose honour this shrine is erected is reported to have brought a whole herd of cattle to their knees by the attractive manner in which she winked her eyes,' says Augustus Hare, nevertheless.

The city wriggles along its hill-top like a caterpillar on a twig and is traversed by one main alimentary canal, so to speak, which starts as the Via Roma and runs straight ahead from the main gate, goes by various names and is lined by a number of Renaissance palaces and churches mostly built by Florentine architects of the early sixteenth century. It is thus sixty or seventy years later than Pienza. The Palazzo Avignonesi at 37 Via Roma is by Vignola, who also built the Palazzo Tarugi opposite at No. 32. The elder Sangallo built the Palazzo Cocconi at No. 28 and Michelozzo the handsome church of S. Agostino, which contains a S. Bernardino by Giovanni di Paolo and a Madonna

188

The great 'Resurrection' fresco at Sansepolcro, by Piero della Francesca, who was born in Sansepolcro.

The church of S. Maria al Calcinaio, Francesco di Giorgio's elegant
Renaissance church, just outside Cortona.

of the Girdle by Baroccio. The street reaches the far end of the town, where S. Maria dei Servi has an elegant baroque interior by Father Andrea Pozzo, and then doubles back on itself to the Piazza Grande, the main square of the town.

The Cathedral on the right has never had its façade completed and presents a rather bleak exterior. Inside is a fine airy Renaissance interior containing no fewer than seven dismembered fragments of Michelozzo's tomb of Bartolomeo Aragazzi, the secretary to Pope Martin V. (Two others are in the Victoria and Albert Museum.) Over the high altar is Taddeo di Bartolo's great triptych of the Assumption, painted in 1403. Steps at the back of the altar allow one to examine this magnificent work at close quarters. As well as the central theme of the Assumption, it contains an Annunciation and a Coronation of the Virgin, a number of scenes from the Passion and the Old Testament, and figures of the saints and the doctors of the Church. Taddeo di Bartolo was always at his best on an intimate scale, and the small scenes of the predella are worth studying in detail. The statues of Faith and of Science on either side of the altar are by Michelozzo.

On the left as one comes out of the Cathedral is the Palazzo Comunale, built at the end of the fourteenth century. Steep and narrow stairs lead up to the roof and the tower with a view over Tuscany and Umbria which stretches on a clear day from Siena to Assisi. The other two sides of the square are occupied by sixteenth century Renaissance palaces. Opposite the Palazzo Comunale is Sangallo's Palazzo Contucci and opposite the Duomo is the same architect's Palazzo Tarugi. A curious feature of the latter is the little window over the front door, which is designed to enable the people inside to inspect their callers before letting them in. On one side is a very handsome well-head of 1520, bearing lions and griffins and the arms of the Medici. It is almost certainly by Sangallo.

From here the Via Ricci leads down to the red-brick Palazzo Neri Orselli Bombagli, which houses the Museo Civico. On the first floor are two altarpieces by Andrea della Robbia; one is

189

dedicated to God the Father and the other to the Madonna. In the large room adjoining and the one which lies above it are a St Francis by Margaritone d'Arezzo, two or three portraits by Bronzino, a couple more by Sustermans and a Holy Family with St John by Sodoma. Perhaps the best picture in this rather mediocre collection is a Nativity by Girolamo di Benvenuto. The interest of Montepulciano consists less in its individual treasures than in the dignified Renaissance palaces and churches crowning the steep hill nearly two thousand feet high, where the people of Chiusi are said to have sought refuge during the barbarian invasions and 'where wine is king.'

CHAPTER 14

Arezzo

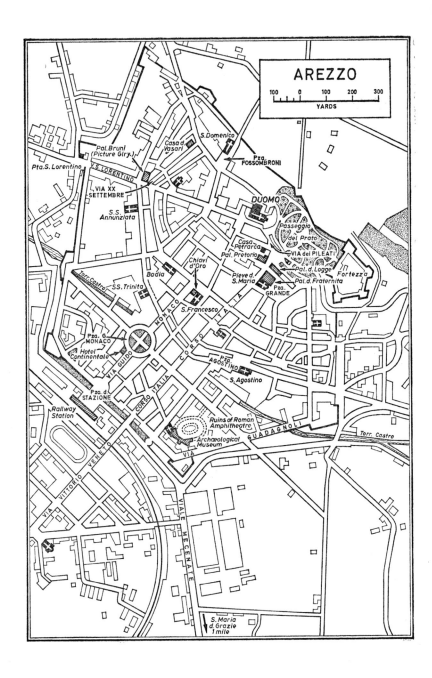

AREZZO

100   0   100   200   300
YARDS

S. Domenico

Casa d.
Vasari

Pal. Bruni
(Picture Glry.)

Pta. S. Lorentino

Pza.
FOSSOMBRONI

V. S. LORENTINO

VIA XX
SETTEMBRE

S. S.
Annunziata

DUOMO

Passeggio
del Prato

Casa
Petrarca

Pal. Pretorio

VIA del PILEATI

Chiavi
d'Oro

Pal. d. Logge

Badia

Pieve d.
S. Maria

Pal. d. Fraternita

Fortezza

Torr. Castro

S. S. Trinita

Pza.
GRANDE

S. Francesco

MONACO

Pza. G.
MONACO

Hotel
Continentale

VIA GUIDO

CORSO

Pza.
AGOSTINO

S. Agostino

Pza. d.
STAZIONE

CORSO ITALIA

Railway
Station

Ruins of Roman
Amphitheatre

GUADAGNOLI

Torr. Castro

Archæological
Museum

VIA

VENETO

VIA VITTORIO

VIALE MECENATE

S. Maria
d. Grazie
1 mile

CHAPTER 14

Arezzo

The eastern part of Tuscany consists of four valleys with the provincial capital, the ancient city of Arezzo, crowning a small hill which rises out of a fertile plain near the point where three of them meet. Westward the Valdarno Superiore, which despite its name comprises the middle reaches of the Arno, runs down to Florence; to the north the upper valley of the same river, known as the Casentino, leads up to its source high on Monte Falterona; to the south the Val di Chiana forms a wide expanse of rich farmland stretching down to Umbria; eastwards, beyond one of the minor ranges of the Apennines, is the Alta Val Tiberina, where the stripling Tiber runs out of twin lakes on the slopes of Monte Fumaiolo just over the border of Romagna.

Arretium was one of the twelve lucumonies or kingdoms of the Etruscans and subsequently became an important Roman city. It was famous all over the early Empire for its 'coralline' ware—terra-cotta vases, bowls and goblets ornamented in relief with floral decorations, banquets, dances, sacrifices and mythological scenes. So called because they were the colour of dark coral, they were first made about a hundred years before Christ and went out about the middle of the first century AD. (Attractive modern copies are to be bought in some of the shops of Arezzo.) A comprehensive collection of them is to be seen in the Museo Mecenate.[1] This excellently arranged and labelled archæological museum has been installed in an old Olivetan

[1]Closed on Wednesdays.

C.G.T.   N   193

monastery built on the ruins of the Roman amphitheatre. The collection of Etruscan bronze statuettes is rated one of the finest in the world. The museum is called after the distinguished Aretine, Maecenas, friend of Augustus and protector of Virgil and Horace, whose name has passed into all languages as a synonym for a munificent patron of the arts. It lies at the foot of the hill in the flat modern part of the city, which contains, in front of the railway station, two bronze reproductions of the famous Chimera of Arezzo, which was unearthed here in 1553, was carried off by the Duke to Florence and is now to be seen in the Archæological Museum in that city. One of the most famous bronzes of ancient times, it is generally supposed to be Etruscan but some archæologists believe it to be Greek. The Chimera is represented as an angry lion. Well it may be angry, for its own tail in the form of a serpent is seizing in its jaws a goat's head which grows out of its spine.

Continuing between the two autophagous Chimeras up the Via Guido Monaco, we come to a broad piazza of the same name and on the left-hand corner is an excellent modern hotel, the Continentale. The other Category B hotel is the older Chiavi d'Oro (which, when I first stayed there long before the days of sanctions, was called the Inghilterra) farther up in the Piazza S. Francesco. It has no dining-room, but one can eat quite well in the Buca di San Francesco, just on the other side of the Basilica of S. Francesco next door. The monument in the square commemorates Count Vittorio Fossombroni, the engineer who drained the Val di Chiana and restored health and prosperity to this part of Tuscany.

The city of Arezzo takes great pride in the famous men to whom it has given birth. Since the modern traveller, however, can neither touch the shade of Maecenas for a few hundred pounds, ask Guido Monaco how on earth he came to invent musical notation, persuade Petrarch to recite his sonnets or Pietro Aretino his bawdy verse, nor even gossip with the garrulous ghost of Vasari, he comes here mainly to see one of the world's acknowledged masterpieces—Piero della Francesca's great frescoes in the church of **S. Francesco,** whose raw, unfinished façade faces on to the eponymous Piazza, next door to the Hotel of the Golden Keys.

The spacious nave, single in the usual style of the friars, is lavishly frescoed by artists such as Parri Aretino and his father Spinello, who painted the Annunciation at the end of the wall on the right and the Guasconi Chapel in the right-hand apse. Without any merits greater than a pleasing facility, they are representative of the short-lived Gothic school of Arezzo, which was a synthesis of those of Florence and Siena. The Aretine school was not of much significance in itself and was soon absorbed by that of Florence—unless, indeed, we are to include in it that lone wolf, Piero, who really belonged to no school at all. The son of a shoemaker, he was born in 1415 at Borgo San Sepolcro in what was then Papal territory, studied under Domenico Veneziano in Florence, worked in Rome and a number of cities in east-central Italy, died in 1492 and was buried on the very same day that Columbus discovered America.

Now a certain rich merchant of Arezzo called Baccio left instructions on his deathbed that the 'great chapel' or apse of S. Francesco should be decorated in his memory. The work was given to a mediocre late-Gothic Florentine artist called Bicci di Lorenzo. Having painted the frontal arch and the vaulting, he very considerately died and left the wall space free for Piero who, fresh from triumphs at the courts of Sigismondo Malatesta at Rimini and Federico Montefeltro at Urbino, was called in to finish the work. With one or two interruptions, it took him from 1452 until 1466. He painted two prophets, one on each side of the window, high up under the vaulting, and a typically architectural Annunciation at the bottom on the left. The remaining space was devoted to the long and intricate Story of the Holy Cross, as related by the medieval hagiographer, Jacopo da Voragine. Voragine's *Legenda Aurea* was a best-seller in the Middle Ages and was translated and published in English by Thomas Caxton, but since the legend is no longer familiar nowadays, it will be necessary to explain the frescoes in some detail if they are to mean anything much except a magnificent tapestry of weird hats and prancing horses, and a vision of rich, glowing colours which, when they were painted, earned the chancel the name of 'the enchanted garden.'

The lunette at the top of the right-hand wall shows the death of Adam, with Eve supporting his head. He tells his son Seth to go to the gates of Paradise to ask for the oil of mercy which had been promised him long ago. Instead the Angel gives him a twig from the Tree of Good and Evil, which Seth plants in his dead father's mouth. Many centuries pass and the Queen of Sheba, on her way to visit King Solomon, has to cross a bridge over the Pool of Siloam, which is built of the wood of the Tree from Eden. Struck by a sudden revelation, she recognises its destiny, falls on her knees and worships it in the left half of the scene below, which is among the finest of the whole cycle for drawing and colour. On the right, she is received by King Solomon who, foreseeing the ruin of his people, orders it to be buried. (Notice how often the same models reappear over and over again, as in the case of Sheba's and Helena's ladies-in-waiting. The figure in blue on Solomon's right is thought to be a self-portrait of the artist.) Centuries later the Jews, however, dig up the wood and from it fashion the Holy Cross upon which Christ was crucified.

The bottom row shows, by the window, a weirdly foreshortened angel appearing in a dream to the Emperor Constantine and telling him to put his faith in the Cross—'*In hoc signo vinces*'— as he illuminates the emperor's tent with an unearthly golden radiance. For chiaroscuro and composition this fresco is perhaps the masterpiece of the chapel. The damaged panel adjoining shows the Battle of the Milvian Bridge just outside Rome, where Constantine holds up a small golden cross and thereby puts to flight the forces of his rival, the Emperor Maxentius, whose horse is seen trying to scramble out of the Tiber—the little limpid Tiber of Piero's own San Sepolcro.

The panels on the left are not consecutive, and chronologically the middle two precede the lower one, which is presumably placed there to balance the battle scene opposite. The Jews had hidden the three crosses in Jerusalem, but the Empress Helena, the mother of Constantine, finds them by lowering a certain Judas, who knew their whereabouts but would not reveal it, into a well and keeping him there until he agrees to 'talk' and, as is shown in the highly geometrical fresco by the window in the middle row, is pulled up—partly by the hair. St Helena is now faced by another problem: which of the three crosses is the actual one on which Christ was crucified? This she solves, as is shown in the central panel, by holding the crosses over a newly dead corpse. Two of them have no effect but the third one restores it to life. The city in the left background represents fifteenth-century Arezzo, while the street scene on the right is taken from Borgo San Sepolcro.

Helen took a part of the True Cross to Rome and left a part in Jerusalem, but in the seventh century Chosroes, King of Persia, captured Jerusalem and carried off the Cross to Persia, where he made it into a throne and had himself worshipped as a god. The Greek Emperor Heraclius thereupon raised an army, invaded Persia and, as we see in the bottom panel, overthrew Chosroes, who is shown on his knees on the right calmly waiting to be beheaded. The lunette at the top shows the emperor barefoot, returning the Cross to Jerusalem. In the words of James Elroy Flecker,

> *A thousand swinging steeples shall begin as they began*
> *When Heraclius rode home from the wrack of Ispahan,*

but the walls of Jerusalem closed in the victor's face, so the legend goes, and only parted to receive him when he came humbly on foot and divested of his imperial pomp.

The Legend of the Cross did indeed provide Piero with a subject spanning the millennia and perfectly suited to his gifts. Vivid colour and unerring composition, satisfying mass and spacing, a number of exotic figures whose costumes owe something to the fifteenth century and much to the artist's vivid imagination—all these explain why Arezzo has become one of the focal points for art-lovers visiting Tuscany and why Piero, whose frescoes in Rome and Ferrara have all perished, holds the exalted position which he does in the world of art.

A block away from S. Francesco runs the Corso Italia, the principal street of the town and dominating it is the very remarkable Romanesque church of the **S. Maria della Pieve** just at the foot of the hill which leads up to the Cathedral. Its tall campanile, once much higher, is perforated with scores of *bifore*, which have earned it the name of the 'belfry of a hundred holes' and make it look like a giant dovecote, or perhaps one should say an eaglecote. Below are five blind arches at the bottom and then above them three loggias gradually diminishing in size. No two of the columns are alike and the one in the centre of the top row is the effigy of a saint or a caryatid. The church was begun at the beginning of the eleventh century and not finished until 1330. The six large granite columns of the portico are Roman. Round the intrados of the central door are carved the figures of the months. The handsome interior is adorned only by the rich decoration of the capitals and a number of loggias and blind arches. The chancel is raised high above the nave and on the altar is a great polyptych by Pietro Lorenzetti showing a Madonna and Child with Saints, with the Annunciation and the Assumption above. It is signed and dated 1320.

The apse of the Pieve is in the Lombardic style of the Duomo of Pisa, semicircular with blind arches below and two loggias above. It opens on to the beautiful fan-shaped **Piazza Grande**. Next to the apse is the eighteenth-century Tribunal and the Palazzo della Fraternità dei Laici, a Florentine building which, added to over several centuries, happily combines the Gothic and Renaissance styles—but then the Renaissance architect was Bernardo Rossellino, who also carved the beautiful Madonna della Misericordia in the lunette. Beside it at the top of the slope is Vasari's Palazzo delle Logge and from this point the Piazza sweeps down to an arc of medieval houses and open shops, with contemporary towers and balconies.

Every year on the first Sunday in September the Giostra del

Saracino, the Joust of the Saracen, takes place in the Piazza. It is a revival of an old medieval game called the Quintana or Quintain, which afforded useful military training in the days when firearms had not been invented and knights could afford to be bold. For the joust the houses of the Piazza are beflagged— green and white on the north side, yellow and red on the east, green and red on the south and blue and yellow on the west, for the square is the traditional centre of the city where the four wards composing it all meet. Each owns a side, and the stands erected all round are decorated with the shield of their quarter. At the highest corner of the square, next to Vasari's Loggia, stands a wooden automaton in the form of a tall Saracen king. On his left arm hangs a shield divided into squares which are numbered one to five; his outstretched right arm holds a triple thong and at the end of it hang three leather globes the size of cricket balls. Beside him stand two live 'Saracens,' whose duty is to untwist the cat-of-three-tails after use.

The four wards compete against each other and from early morning the streets are filled with processions of foot soldiers in medieval costume, each representing one of the four quarters. Knights on caparisoned horses in the colours of their ward are led along by grooms. Beautiful medieval ladies ride in the procession, their make-up by Elizabeth Arden and their costumes out of the Duc de Berry's *Book of Hours*. In the afternoon everyone assembles in the Piazza Grande. After parades by the costumed captains, standard-bearers, drummers, trumpeters and soldiers of the wards, eight knights, two for each ward, charge at full gallop up a gravelled runway which has been laid diagonally across the Piazza and lunge with their lances at the shield of the blackamoor. Each one tries to hit the square with the highest number. The Saracen rotates smartly on his axis when his shield is hit and if the knight is not very spry he is knocked off his horse by the cricket balls. Each knight is entitled to one charge but in the event of a tie the leaders ride it off. Feeling runs high and the joust occasionally culminates in a free fight between the different wards.

From the Pieve the **Via dei Pileati** runs up a steep hill to the castle and the Cathedral past the fourteenth-century Palazzo Pretorio, whose façade is encrusted all over as though by molluscs with the shields and the coats of arms of the Florentine governors. Just beyond it is the house where Petrarch is said to have been born. Rebuilt in the sixteenth century and restored again after the War, it is now the seat of the Accademia Petrarca di Lettere, Arti e Scienze. At the top of the ridge are the dismantled Medicean fortress and a park with a good view from the ramparts over the plain to the mass of the Pratomagno and the Apennines to the north. There the Aretine housewives sit gossiping beside their perambulators, while the children run races round the great white monument to Petrarch in the centre.

At the side of the Passeggio del Prato, as it is called, is the **Duomo,** a fine piece of Italian Gothic built between the thirteenth and the sixteenth centuries, with a façade which was only added in the twentieth. It contains some of the best stained glass work in Italy, a country admittedly poor in that art. All the windows of the right aisle are the work of Guillaume de Marcillat who, having been involved in a homicide case in his native France, settled and worked in Arezzo in the sixteenth century. His great innovation was to treat a window as a narrative picture and no longer as pure decoration. If his pictures are not very striking in themselves, they can certainly become so when painted on glass with the Italian sun streaming through them. In addition to the glass of the Duomo, Marcillat was responsible for the windows in SS. Annunziata and the great rose window in S. Francesco showing St Francis before the Pope. He also painted the first three vaults in the nave of the Cathedral.

For the elaborate high altar sculptors were brought from Siena. At the back of the panelled reredos is the great Ark of S. Donato, which contains the relics of the patron saint of Arezzo, martyred in the reign of Julian the Apostate. Agostino di Giovanni and Agnolo Ventura, who collaborated in the building of the Campanile at Siena, have decorated the front with bas-reliefs of the Virgin and two saints. There are a number of fourteenth-century reliefs at the back, of which the upper band by the same two artists depicts scenes from the life of S. Donato, and the lower, by Betto di Giovanni and Giovanni di Francesco, scenes from the life of Christ and the Virgin. The stained-glass window of the Assumption behind was made by Ascanio Pasquini in 1953.

On the left side of the chancel is a fresco by Piero della Francesca of St Mary Magdalene, in which we see the same massive, pouting, sulky model who did duty for the Virgin in the Annunciation in S. Francesco. Beside it is the great tomb of Bishop Guido Tarlati, said to have been designed by Giotto, with sixteen sculptured scenes from his life. They mostly show battles and the storming of castles—for Arezzo was ruled in the Middle Ages by a series of warlike Count-Bishops, whose hands were apter to handle the mace than the crozier. As direct vassals of the Empire like the Patriarchs of Aquileia, they had the right to say mass with a helmet and a sword lying on the altar. Guido Tarlati succeeded to the bishopric in 1312, not long after the disastrous defeat by the Guelphs at Campaldino, in which Bishop Guglielmo Ubertini and many of the Aretine nobles were slain and Dante fought for the Florentines. The great chapel of Our Lady of Comfort, just off the left aisle, is almost a separate church. It is noteworthy for several excellent works by Andrea della Robbia, notably the Assumption, the Madonna Adoring the Child and a polychrome Crucifixion with SS. Francis and Donato. The late seventeenth-century monument just outside the grille is that of the Aretine scientist and poet, Francesco Redi, who wrote a dithyramb poem in praise of wine entitled 'Bacchus in Tuscany.' (The verdict of this expert was, in Leigh Hunt's translation,

Give ear and give faith to the edict divine:
Montepulciano's the king of all wine.)

Not far from the Cathedral is the quiet, shady Piazza Fossombroni and at the end of it stands the Romanesque church of S. Domenico, founded by the Tarlatis in 1275. It was designed, if Vasari is to be believed, by Nicola Pisano and is adorned with a number of frescoes by Spinello and Parri and their followers. Spinello himself painted the frescoes on the left of the entrance wall, and Parri those on the right. The dramatic thirteenth-century wooden Crucifixion over the high altar is attributed to Cimabue.

In the **Via XX Settembre** is Vasari's house, which he bought and frescoed himself. More of Vasari's work is to be found in the church of the Badia in the Piazza Principe Amedeo, whose interior he transformed. He designed the high altar of marble, wood and travertine as a tomb for himself and his family, with whose portraits he adorned some of the panels. He painted the Assumption on the right wall of the choir, while the crucifix nearby is the work of the Sienese Segna di Bonaventura.

The fifteenth-century **Palazzo Bruni** in the Via S. Lorentino now houses the Medieval Museum and the Picture Gallery.[1] In the great courtyard and the adjoining rooms on the ground floor is a well arranged collection of medieval sculpture. The picture gallery is in the *piano nobile* up the baroque staircase. The first room contains, in addition to an interesting Madonna of the school of Guido da Siena, the famous portrait of St Francis by the thirteenth-century master, Margaritone d'Arezzo, showing the saint's face framed in an oval hood and his hand held up in benediction. The picture is believed to have been painted about forty years after his death. Notice too Niccolò Gerini's *Pietà* with the symbols of the Passion. The second room contains a very delightful lunette of the *Pietà* by Spinello Aretino dated 1395 and an attractive and very Byzantine angel by Guariento of Padua. The third room is devoted to Spinello and his son Parri. Look in particular at the latter's very elegant Angel Musicians and his *Madonna della Misericordia* with the predella intact.

Pass through the so-called sacristy to the Early Renaissance rooms. Look at Rossellino's terra-cotta maquette for a *Madonna*

[1]Closed on Mondays.

della Misericordia and the two St Rochs by Bartolomeo della Gatta, a talented fifteenth-century Florentine who made his home in Arezzo. One of them contains a good view of Arezzo in the background. (One wonders how many cities of the period were so often painted as Arezzo. One calls to mind also the Piero background to the Invention of the True Cross here in S. Francesco and Giotto's fresco of St Francis driving out the devils from Arezzo in the Upper Church of Assisi.) There is a tondo of the Adoration by Luca Signorelli and two Madonnas by the same artist. Such was the admiration of the Aretines for Signorelli that when he painted a Madonna for the Guild of S. Girolamo the members bore it on their shoulders in triumph all the way from Cortona to Arezzo 'as was no more than his due, for he had always lived more like a lord and an honoured gentleman than a painter,'[1] writes his kinsman Vasari, in whose father's house, when little Giorgio was eight years old, 'that good old man' had stayed in Arezzo. Do not miss the head of St Benedict by the sixteenth-century Aretine master, Domenico Pecori. There follows a room containing a very rich collection of majolica from all over Italy and even from Spain.

The second floor is devoted to the sixteenth-century painters, and notably the indefatigable Vasari. Worthy of notice are his John the Baptist near the door of the first room and his St Roch on the right of the door into the second room. At the end of the second floor are a number of small rooms devoted to the mannerists, the baroque painters and nineteenth-century masters down to Fattori and the *macchiaioli*. Pietro Benvenuti has a striking portrait of the great engineer, Count Fossombroni, who might almost have been the twin brother of the Duke of Wellington.

Just outside the town, about twenty minutes' walk down the Via Mecenate, is the exquisite little church of **S. Maria delle Grazie.** The story goes that there was a spring there called the Fons Tecta which in ancient times had been sacred to Apollo

[1]Vasari spoke in very similar terms of Ambrogio Lorenzetti, whose ways 'were in all respects worthy of praise, and rather those of a gentleman and a philosopher than a craftsman.'

and where ever since then pagan rites had been carried on. Mothers used to dip their ailing children in the spring to make them strong and healthy. One day the formidable St Bernardino came to preach in Arezzo and heard of these infamies. He had the fountain destroyed and the grove cut down, and he built an oratory on the site. At the end of the century Benedetto da Maiano added the enchanting loggia in front with its eleven graceful arches. The high altar inside is the only known work in marble by Andrea della Robbia; the fresco in the centre of it is the work of Parri di Spinello and represents the Madonna to whom the church is dedicated. Fortunately the saint's activities had no effect upon the infant mortality rate of the city, for it is on record that the healings continued under the new dispensation.

CHAPTER 15

The Casentino

The Casentino

Main roads — Secondary roads ———— Railways ++++++ Rivers ⌇⌇⌇

MILES
5 0 5 10 15 20 25 30

M. Lóggio
M. d. Frati
M. d. Zucca
Conv. di M. Casale
Sansepolcro
S. Giustino
Pistrino
Selci
Citerna
Pieve S. Stefano
R. Tiber
R. Tiber
M. Penna
Chiusi di Verna
Caprese Michelángio
LA VERNA
M. il Castello
CASENTINO
Chitignano
Anghiari
Misciano
Tartigliano
Biforco
Bádia Pratáglia
Camáldoli
Rássina
Sùbbiano
Chiavéretto
Capolona
Borgo a G.
Quarata
R. Arno
EREMO di CAMÁLDOLI
Moggiona
Líerna
Sóci
Bíbbiena
Talla
Indicatore
Prátovécchia
Póppi
Castel Focognano
Castiglión Fib.
Stia
R. Arno
Castel S. Niccolò
Borgo alla Collina
Raggiolo
PRATOMAGNO
S. Giustino
Ponticino
Céthca
Montemignáio
Loro Ciuffenna
Terranuova-Bracciolini
Varco
Reggello
Castelfranco di Sopra
AUTOSTRADA
Levane
Montevarchi
Pélago
Tósi
VALLOMBROSA Saltino
Léccio
Reggello
Figline Vald.
Giovanni Vald.
R. Arno
Carìglia-Monastero
Rufina
S. Elléro
R. Arno
Pontassieve

CHAPTER 15

The Casentino

The Casentino, as we have seen, is the uppermost stretch of the Arno Valley and it deserves a chapter to itself on account of the religious associations which have made it a popular place of pilgrimage. It is enclosed on the north and east by the Apennines and cut off on the west from Central Tuscany and the Valdarno by the mountain massif of the Pratomagno, round the foot of which the Arno curves in a great loop. The Casentino is shut in by high mountains which in places leave barely room for the river, the road and the railway to run side by side. They are covered with thick forests of fir, beech and chestnut and are the haunts of wood-cutters and swine-herds, for the Casentino produces timber for all Tuscany and is famous for the ham and the salami of the pigs which feed upon the beechmast. High up among the forests are the shrines of La Verna and Camaldoli, for these green fastnesses, far from the chronic commotion in the valleys below, have always attracted those who seek for a spiritual retreat. Camaldoli, Vallombrosa and La Verna have filled their needs.

The Casentino broadens out into a rich agricultural plain near **Bibbiena,** where there is a triptych by Bicci di Lorenzo in the church of SS. Ipolito e Donato and where I once stayed in the Albergo Bei Amorosi, the Inn of the Beautiful Lovers. Cardinal Dovizi, better known as Cardinal Bibbiena, the famous secretary of Leo X, was born in this town and took his name from it. A few miles up the valley is **Poppi,** which presents a striking appearance from a short distance away, for the summit of the little hill rising out of the plain is crowned by the perfectly preserved castle of the Conti Guidi, which was built for them by Arnolfo di Cambio. A square, battlemented fort with a square tower jutting up from it, it now houses the communal offices and a library rich in manuscripts and incunabula. In the Middle Ages the Counts Guidi, who ruled the Casentino, together with large tracts of country near Pistoia, were one of the greatest of the feudal houses whom the Tuscan cities had to overcome in their struggle to free their trade. The only families to be mentioned in the same breath with them were the Malaspina far away in the Lurigiana and the Aldobrandeschi in their impregnable strongholds on Monte Amiata.

From Bibbiena a road runs up to **La Verna,** perched on a height visible for many miles around and just below the ridge of the Apennines. La Verna, or Alvernia, is the most sacred place in Tuscany, for it was there that St Francis of Assisi received the Stigmata, the five wounds which made him in the words of a mannered Victorian poet 'co-transforate with Christ.' In 1213 St Francis was at Montefeltro in Romagna, where he met a certain Count Orlando of Chiusi in the Casentino who, being told that he was in need of a solitary place for prayer and meditation, offered him a mountain which he owned called La Verna, 'which is very solitary and wild and only too well suited for anyone who wants to make penance in a place removed from men or who desires a solitary life. If you like it I will willingly give it to you and your companions for the salvation of my soul.' So the first Franciscans went up to the mountain, escorted by fifty armed men to keep away wild beasts, scaled a sheer cliff, the *crudo sasso* or 'raw rock' of which Dante speaks, and built themselves cells on the summit.

Foot-travellers can still enter by a path up the face of the cliff—by the front door, so to speak—from the hamlet of La Beccia below, but an asphalt road spirals up behind the hill, so that motorists can save themselves the climb. Just outside the monastery is a refectory where simple meals can be obtained. There is also a guest-house or *foresteria*, where male pilgrims can book accommodation in advance. Females have to stay with the sisters in the convent below in La Beccia.

The first primitive chapel in La Verna was S. Mari degli Angeli, which Count Orlando built for St Francis in 1216. The oldest part of the existing *Chiesina*, as it is usually called, is the altar and choir, the rest having been added later to meet the needs of the growing congregation. The good count's bones rest under the pavement. Over the altar is an Assumption by Andrea della Robbia, while his son Giovanni was responsible for the Deposition and the Nativity, also in this chapel.

The only artistic attraction of La Verna is the collection of della Robbias, the work of that gifted Florentine family who, with their workshop and their pupils, went on turning out hundreds of statues and reliefs in glazed terra-cotta for nearly a couple of centuries. Usually they consist of white figures on a blue ground but very often they are polychrome. The founder of the school, Luca della Robbia, was born in 1400 and his work was carried on by his nephew Andrea and afterwards by Andrea's five sons, of whom the best known are Giovanni and Girolamo.

We go now from the *Chiesina* across the little paved square known as the Quadrant to the Basilica, which was begun in 1348 by Count Tarlato di Pietramala. Of the fifteen della Robbias in La Verna, six are in this church, including the Annunciation, perhaps the greatest work of Andrea della Robbia, and his only less beautiful Nativity and Ascension. In the Chapel of the Relics are a piece of cloth stained with blood from the wound in St Francis's side, and drinking vessels and a table napkin used by the saint when he was the guest of Count Orlando.

Outside the basilica is the little Chapel of the *Pietà* with a polychrome della Robbia of the Deposition, whence an arch to the left leads to the covered and glassed-in Corridor of the Stigmata. Down it the friars pass twice a day, at two in the afternoon and at one in the morning, to pray in the Chapel of the Stigmata. Half-way down on the right is a dark, cold grotto known as St Francis's Bed, because he used to go there to pray and when he was tired lie down to sleep on the cold stone. Next we pass through the Chapel of the Cross to the Chapel of the Stigmata itself, which was built in 1263 to cover the holy place where St Francis traditionally received the Stigmata in his hands, his feet and his side. The actual rock on which the saint is said to have been standing is roped off in the middle of the floor. The end wall is covered by a lovely Crucifixion by Andrea della Robbia, expressly made to fit the space.

Two small oratories open off the Cappella della Croce and a steep stair leads down to the Precipice, the cleft where the Devil tried to throw St Francis over the cliff and the rock 'received the saint into itself, as if he had put his hands and face into liquid wax.' Next, off the Corridor of the Stigmata, is the First Cell of St Francis, which Count Orlando built for him when he first came to the mountain in 1214. Several paths lead up into the forest and to the peak which overhangs the monastery, whence, says Ariosto, 'one can descry both the Slav and the Tuscan seas.'

Also in a vast fir-forest close to the main ridge of the Apennines is neighbouring **Camaldoli,** the mother house of the Camaldolensians, a widely spread Order within the Benedictine Rule, founded in 1012 by St Romualdo, a rich Lombard nobleman of Ravenna, who was said in his lifetime to have founded a hundred monasteries and hermitages. He was given the site, nearly three thousand acres of forest, by a gentleman of Arezzo called Maldolus, from whom it took its name of Campus Maldoli. A road from Poppi leads up to the monastery and thence climbs to the yet more famous Hermitage or Eremo.[1] The monastery proper consists of two large buildings, in one of which the monks live, while the other is the guest-house which is used for meetings and conferences of priests and Catholic laymen. There are a couple of small hotels here and the place is popular with summer visitors from the plains. The baroque church is richly frescoed

[1]There was no saint called Elmo. Castel Sant' Elmo at Naples was called after the Sacro Eremo at Camaldoli; also presumably St Elmo's Fire.

by Vasari and Sante Pacini of Florence. Women are not allowed in the monastery proper.

A couple of miles higher up through the great fir woods is the famous hermitage. The baroque church with the twin towers on the right contains two attractive tabernacles by Gino da Settignano and a della Robbia Madonna and Saints. Guillaume de Marcillat, the glass-worker of Arezzo, is buried here in the Chapel of the Rosary. Beyond it—no women admitted—are the cells of the twenty white-robed hermits, consisting of five cottages in each of four parallel streets. Each *cella* has a portico with a wooden seat, a vestibule, a living-room with a bed in an alcove, a table, a cupboard and a fire-place, a study with a table and a book-shelf, an oratory with a small altar, a wood-store and a washroom. In front is a garden, where the hermit grows flowers and vegetables. The hermits are bound to silence except at certain times; they eat no meat; and they rise at half past one in the morning, file through the winter snow to the church for Matins and Lauds and at intervals all through the day they attend the other offices of the church.

Vallombrosa is yet a third place of religious significance in this region. High up in the woods on the western slope of the Pratomagno, it is technically just outside the Casentino but spiritually a part of it. It is best known to the English-speaking world on account of its literary associations with Milton, who wrote,

> *Thick as autumnal leaves that strew the brooks*
> *In Vallombrosa, where the Etrurian shades,*
> *High over arch'd, imbower.*

and Elizabeth Barrett Browning, who wrote of Milton that

> *He sang of Adam's paradise and smiled,*
> *   Remembering Vallombrosa. Therefore is*
> *The place divine to every English man and child,*
> *   And pilgrims leave their soul here in a kiss.*

Whether or no the last two lines be as literally true as they are literarily deplorable, Vallombrosa is a beautifully situated place, all the more so for being surrounded by great beechwoods, which are at their best in the young fresh green of spring and the golden glory of autumn. (The records in the archives show that the monks planted forty thousand beech trees in the three years between 1750 and 1753 alone.) Many Florentines come up here in the dog days. There is a hotel just opposite the monastery gates, open from June to September, and a number of others in the mountain resort of Saltino close by.

The story goes that in the early years of the eleventh century a young Florentine nobleman named Giovanni Gualberto, being sworn to avenge his brother's murder, came upon the killer unarmed in a narrow street near S. Miniato. The murderer fell on his knees and begged forgiveness, reminding him that the day was Good Friday, when Christ prayed for his enemies. The future saint forgave him and embraced him, took to the religious life and with some other monks came up to Vallombrosa and built cells and afterwards a wooden church. This was almost exactly at the same time as St Romuald was founding Camaldoli just across the Pratomagno. As at Camaldoli, the builder of the monastery founded an order operating within the Benedictine rule, and by the time S. Giovanni Gualberto died in 1073 at the age of eighty-eight the Vallombrosan Order, like the Camaldolensian, was spreading all over Italy. The Abbots of Vallombrosa enjoyed the rank of marquis, and the order was famous in particular for its miniaturists and illuminators.

Almost nothing is left of the original monastery and in their present form the seventeenth-century buildings contain little of interest even for connoisseurs of the baroque. Since the suppression of the monastery in 1866 only four monks are allowed to remain on to say the offices of the church. I felt little temptation to leave my soul here in a kiss, whatever that may mean, for there is a feeling of great sadness about Vallombrosa, despite the splendour of the autumn woods.

CHAPTER 16

The Border Towns

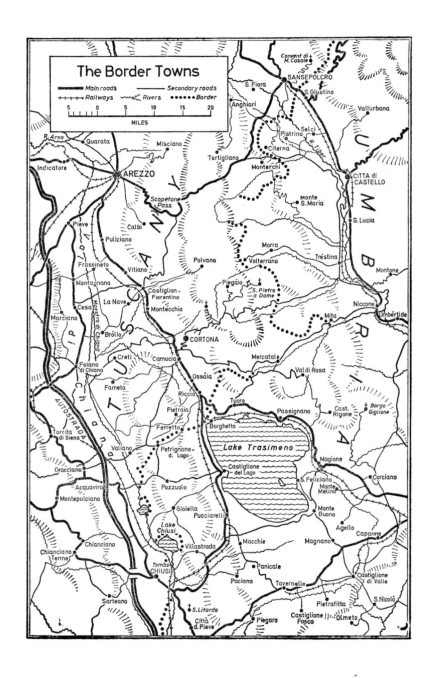

The Border Towns

In marked contrast with the Apennine bulwarks which divide her from Emilia on the north, Tuscany has no natural frontier with Umbria. The sister regions blend imperceptibly into each other in a land of low hills and broad valleys, and as a result there are a number of little historic cities which lie along the border. Chiusi, for example, is within a few hundred yards of Umbria, and Sansepolcro and Cortona are not much farther away. Their links are as much with Perugia as with Arezzo.

'Macaulay's schoolboy' knows that the Etruscan king

> Lars Porsena of Clusium
> By the Nine Gods he swore
> That the great house of Tarquin
> Should suffer wrong no more.

And indeed **Chiusi,** as Clusium is now called, is of interest solely on account of its Etruscan remains, for in the Middle Ages it was almost extinguished by the malarial exhalations from the swamps which the neighbouring Val di Chiana had become. Formerly one of the greatest of the Etruscan lucumonies, it is surrounded by a number of tombs which have already supplied specimens to half the museums of Europe and still left enough to stock an excellent little museum in the city itself. It is just at the side of the Cathedral (an ancient basilica with Roman columns but very much rebuilt), which has a big guarded car-park in the Piazza in front of it.

The Museum is smaller but more interesting than that of

Volterra for, whereas the Volterra finds all date from the very late period of Etruscan art, those of Chiusi trace its whole history from the beginnings. The Villanovian period from the ninth to the beginning of the seventh century BC, is represented by terracotta cinerary urns in the typical biconical form found in the old well-tombs. Of the seventh and sixth centuries are the *canopi*, which are cinerary jars with lids shaped like rude human heads, as well as two of the rare masks of pierced sheet-bronze supposed to represent the dead man. Of the same archaic period are the long-haired female divinities called *xoana*, the lions and the sphinxes which stood guard at the entrance to the cemeteries. In the sixth and fifth centuries the vases tend to take the form of rough busts with a serious attempt at portraiture. The final stage is marked by the incinerary urns and the sarcophagi with reclining figures of the deceased on the lids.

It is curious to note, especially in view of the Etruscan preoccupation with the disposal of the dead, that urns and sarcophagi are often found together in the same tomb, as in the Tomba della Pellegrina here in Chiusi, for the Etruscans practised cremation and inhumation side by side. (The older form, cremation, remained the standard form of body disposal in the inland cities, but inhumation became the common practice on the coast.) Some of these urns, with their stock mythological scenes, nearly all representing some form of violent death, have retained their original colours and are very attractive in a garish sort of way. Many of the recumbent forms on the lids reach a high standard of realism, for Etruscan art, whose fault was to be only too meekly imitative, was at its best in portraiture. A fine example is No. 361, a coloured figure of a woman with a pointed nose and red lips, whom one might have met at a cocktail party in Chianciano Terme the evening before.

Do not fail to look for a cippus (No. 2269) in the corridor near the entrance with a very lovely bas-relief of funeral scenes; and there are some interesting bronzes and glass-work and a golden tiara in the central halls. But, when all is said and done, the pride of the Museum is its vases. The most typical form of

216

Etruscan pottery, and one for the manufacture of which Clusium was the chief centre, was the black *bucchero* ware, which was apparently produced by mixing specially fine clay with powdered charcoal. (It derived its name from the black Peruvian pots which the Spaniards were sending to Europe and which they called *bucaros*.) The *bucchero* vases date from the early period of Etruscan art, the slim ones from the seventh century BC and the heavy ones from the sixth and fifth. The Museum has also several rare black *foculi*, trays with raised edges and various little pots on them which may have been meant to hold either toilet articles or food for the dead man to use in the underworld.

To visit the tombs which lie just outside the town, ask the guardian of the museum to lay on the *custode delle tombe*, who will show you round. (Tip him, of course.) The two or three most interesting are all close to each other, and a trip by car or taxi will take about an hour. You follow the Chianciano road and then turn right down the Via delle Tombe Etrusche. The late Tomba della Pellegrina, called after the farm it is on, is formed by a corridor with urns in niches at the sides, which leads to three cells containing sarcophagi. (Possibly the former belonged to children, poor relations or dependents while the latter belonged to the heads of the family.) A few yards farther on, under a tall cypress, is the early fifth-century Tomba della Scimmia, called the Monkey's Tomb from a tethered monkey depicted on the wall. It is the most interesting on account of the paintings which adorn the walls. They show the deceased, a lady sitting beneath a parasol, watching her own wake in the form of the funeral games given in her honour, with wrestling and horse-racing, fluteplayers and buffoons. The Tomba del Granduca, of about 200 BC, was found on the property of the Grand Duke at the beginning of the last century. The walls and vaulting of its single room are lined with blocks of travertine and no longer naked tufa like the earlier tombs. It contains the urns of the Pulfua Peris family. There are frescoes of athletes in the fifth-century Tomba della Colle, but that is on the other side of the city.

The **Val di Chiana,** the Clanis of the ancient writers, runs roughly from Lake Chiusi and Lake Trasimene to the Arno just below Arezzo. So sluggish was the Clanis that the Florentine engineers in later centuries had no difficulty in reversing its flow and making it run into the Arno instead of the Tiber. Little wonder that in the Dark Ages, when drainage was neglected in favour of pillage, it became a malarial swamp. Under the dynasty of Lorrains it was drained by that Count Fossombroni whom we have met at Arezzo. Now it is a rich and fertile plain, especially famous for its beef-cattle, which end up as *bistecca alla fiorentina.*

The chief town of the Val di Chiana is **Cortona,** a city so ancient that it has been called 'the grandmother of Rome,' for it was from Cortona that the 'heaven-born' Dardanus departed to found Troy, and from Troy that the pious Æneas came to Latium. Oblong in shape and surrounded by walls, some of them Etruscan, it lies upon the mountainside like a colossal counterpane spread out to dry upon a sloping roof. The modern city covers only the lower half of the *enceinte,* while the upper consists mostly of gardens and open spaces, with a thick wood of cypresses at the very top above S. Margherita.

A winding road leads up from the valley, where is Francesco di Giorgio's delightful Renaissance church of S. Maria al Calcinaio. We enter the city at the Piazza Garibaldi and on the right is the old church of S. Domenico. The fresco in the lunette over the main door is attributed to Fra Angelico, who lived for some time in the attached convent during a spell of exile from Florence. The Madonna and Child in the right-hand apse is a late work of Luca Signorelli. The great polyptych on the high altar by Lorenzo di Niccolò Gerini was presented by Cosimo de' Medici in 1438, and the Assumption near the left apse is considered the best work of his fellow Florentine, Bartolomeo della Gatta.

From the Piazza Garibaldi the Via Nazionale leads into the Piazza della Repubblica and the rather arbitrarily restored Palazzo Comunale, on the right of which a narrow street runs through to the Piazza Signorelli. In front rises the Palazzo Casali. (The Casali were lords of Cortona in the fourteenth century.) We go through into the courtyard and up the stairs on the right into the Museum of the Etruscan Academy,[1] evidently a body of catholic tastes, for its collections range from Egyptology to numismatics and from jewellery to illuminated missals. Its main attraction, as might be guessed, is its Etruscan section and in particular one of the most famous Etruscan bronzes in the world, a great lamp nearly two feet across which was discovered in a neighbouring field in 1840. It has sixteen burners and is curiously ornamented by a circle of eight ithyphallic satyrs alternating with eight sirens, and by waves with dolphins sporting in them. In the centre is a Gorgon's head.

There are also some good pictures including Madonnas by Pinturicchio and Antoniazzo Romano and, of all curious things to find here, a self-portrait by Zoffany. The most controversial object in the museum is a Greuze-like picture of the Muse Polyhymia painted on slate. It is a measure of the naturalism of ancient portraiture that the art experts cannot yet decide whether it is an ancient Greco-Roman painting or whether it is seventeenth century.

At the side of the Palazzo Casali a yellow sign points to the Duomo, which probably dates from the eleventh century but has been completely reconstructed in the Renaissance style by followers of Sangallo. Opposite it on the other side of the square is the Diocesan Museum in the former church of the Gesù— really two churches, a baptistery above and an oratory below. It contains a first-class collection of pictures such as one rarely finds in these country museums. We turn first into the baptistery on the right of the entrance. Over the marble font is one of the greatest pictures Fra Angelico ever painted, a very beautiful Annunciation. Notice the odd detail of the Expulsion from Eden in the top left-hand corner, the culmination of that primeval

---

[1]Being a private museum, it is usually closed in the winter, when few visitors come to this high, gaunt city, where the north wind cuts as sharply as at Volterra, but the travel bureau below can often rout out a *custode.*

sin to whose forgiveness the Annunciation was the prelude. The one ushers in, as the other ends, a theological era. In the predella are scenes from the life of Mary. On the right-hand wall is another Fra Angelico, a triptych of the Madonna and Child with Four Saints, and with scenes from the life of St Dominic in the predella. Both pictures come from the church of S. Domenico just by the city gate. On the same wall hang a crucifix on wood by Pietro Lorenzetti and a delightful triptych by Sassetta, somewhat damaged by damp. On the other two walls and in the larger room across the passage hang no fewer than nine paintings by, or at least attributed to, Luca Signorelli, who was Cortona's most famous son. My favourite is the Communion of the Apostles, but I confess that for me they only serve to show that a man may be supreme as a painter of frescoes and yet be unsatisfying on wood or canvas. Signorelli was a painter who needed space above all. In the second room also there are a Madonna of the school of Duccio and an admirable *Maestà* signed by Pietro Lorenzetti. G. M. Crespi's Ecstasy of St Margaret here is considered to be the masterpiece of this late Bolognese painter. The crucifix at the bottom of the stairs to the lower church is by Pietro Lorenzetti, and the oratory itself is frescoed with uninspiring designs by Vasari.

As you go out into the Piazza del Duomo once more, be sure to look at the lovely view over the hills, endless ranks of silver-grey olive-trees on the slopes to the north, and to the east the level green plain of the Chiana stretching away in the distance. Except for a slightly more extensive view (and air travel has made us more blasé about views than our grandfathers), there is little to be gained by toiling up the steep lanes to the top of the town. (The Medicean fortress at the apex is four hundred and fifty feet above the Piazza Garibaldi.) Except for the actual Gothic tomb of the saint inside it, the great church of S. Margherita dates only from 1856.

Thirteenth-century St Margaret of Cortona, unloved in childhood and very much in need of love, became enamoured of a handsome young gallant from Montepulciano and for nine years lived with him very happily without benefit of clergy. When his faithful hound led her one evening to his mangled corpse, Margaret repented of her sin, went to Cortona, where she became a Franciscan tertiary, and lived a life of extreme asceticism, hoping thus to atone for her lover's sin as well as her own. She ate only the refuse from other people's tables and busied herself in caring for the sick. It was not until 1728 that she was officially canonised by the Church, but the Cortonesi, who loved her, jumped the gun by four hundred years, dedicating a church to her in the fourteenth century.

Over the wooded Scopetone Pass a road leads from Arezzo to a twenty-five mile long strip of the Upper Tiber Valley which has long been attached to Tuscany, although physically it is a part of Umbria. In fact, it is just at the point where Tuscany, Umbria, Romagna and the Marches all meet. Its only town of any consequence is **Sansepolcro,** famous in art-history as the birth-place of Piero della Francesca and the home of his fresco of the Resurrection, beyond any doubt his noblest work. The town was originally called Borgo San Sepolcro on account of two pilgrims from Jerusalem who founded an oratory here to house some relics of the Holy Sepulchre, and now that it is plain Sansepolcro the inhabitants still call themselves Borghigiani. There is little of architectural interest in Sansepolcro and one goes there, unless one has business with the great Buitoni *pasta* concern upon which the little city largely lives, to see this one picture.

However one enters Sansepolcro, one soon finds oneself in the central square, which is called the Piazza Torre di Berta after a medieval tower blown up by a German mine in 1944. About a hundred yards on the right up the Via Matteotti is the Duomo, once the Camaldolese abbey to which the town belonged for two hundred years but now altered almost out of recognition. The Ascension on the altar to the left of the chancel is attributed to Perugino. A little farther up the street on the left, at the end of a row of fifteenth-century houses, is the former Municipio, which now houses the Picture Gallery. Facing us in the main hall

221

is the fresco of the Resurrection, which Aldous Huxley, no rash, mean or inexperienced judge, went so far as to call the greatest picture in the world.

Framed between bare, black trees against the background of a winter landscape at daybreak, Christ steps from the tomb holding the banner of the Cross and gazing out with the eyes of one who has been three days among the dead. At his feet slumber the four Roman soldiers on guard over the tomb. The second figure from the left may be a self-portrait of the painter. Try not to notice that the group has been 'fudged' and that the bearded guard with the round hat can obviously have no legs. Surrender yourself instead to the overpowering mystical force of the fresco.

There are three other Pieros in this and the following room, a polyptych of the *Madonna della Misericordia*, recently restored in Rome, with many saints and a predella showing five stories from the Passion; a figure of St Louis of Toulouse; and a fragment of a saint discovered in 1955 in the old church of S. Chiara. There are Two Saints by Luca Signorelli, and SS. Peter and Paul by Matteo di Giovanni. According to some scholars, Perugino's Assumption may have been painted from a design by Piero; others believe it to be a schoolpiece.

Like Siena and Arezzo, Sansepolcro has its own annual day of pageantry, when every year on the second Sunday in September a crossbow match is held against the men of Gubbio, who come over for the occasion. The bows, some of them ancient and some of modern construction, are so heavy that they have to be supported, and the *balestrieri* to sit, upon a kind of wooden bench. Unless one happens to be a fan of shooting with the crossbow or arbalest, the Palio dei Balestrieri is of interest mainly because the bowmen are all dressed in costumes of the period of Piero della Francesca, if not actually copied from his paintings, as a form of honour paid by his native city. Alas, he died blind and could not see his characters actually walking through the streets of his beloved Borgo.

There is a great Piero at Monterchi on the road back to Arezzo.

Do not go right up into the little walled town but go on till you see the walls of the cemetery on the left. Turn up a cypress-lined lane between tobacco-fields. The *custode* lives in the cottage just on the right of the little chapel and he will let you in to see the *Madonna del Parto*—Our Lady of the Childbirth. It shows the pregnant Virgin parting her blue robe with her fingers and holding her belly to feel the stirring of the unborn Messiah. She stands beneath a plum-coloured brocade canopy held up by two angels dressed in blue and plum respectively. For rich and sober colour and superb design it is a remarkably splendid fresco and one not to be missed. Monterchi lies only two miles off the Arezzo-Sansepolcro road.

Città di Castello, the first town in Umbria, might have been a great place of pilgrimage for art-lovers but it has frittered away its birthright for driblets of pottage. The youthful Raphael used to work there for Vitellozzo Vitelli, lord of the city. The great *Sposalizio* which he painted for the church of S. Francesco is now the pride of the Brera Gallery in Milan; the Coronation of St Nicholas of Tolentino and the Coronation of the Virgin were bought by the Popes and now adorn the walls of the Vatican; the Crucifixion in S. Domenico was sold to Lord Dudley in 1809 and is now in the National Gallery; the Adoration of the Magi hangs in Berlin. Augustus Hare mentions two Pieros, a Coronation of the Virgin in S. Cecilia and a Madonna and Child with Saints in the Municipio, but if they were ever in fact there they have vanished or at any rate been downgraded from their former attribution.

The Cathedral is not of much interest but if you can find someone to let you into the treasury, you will see a good silver altar frontal and a collection of early Christian communion vessels. The Picture Gallery is at the end of the Via Giovanni Muzi on the first floor of one of the Vitelli palaces. The first room is devoted to primitives and the second contains a St Sebastian by the ubiquitous Luca Signorelli. The third has Ghirlandaio and a standard painted by Raphael at the age of sixteen, showing the Creation of Eve on one side and the Trinity on the other. Half perished as it is, this is the only surviving relic of the young genius in the city where he painted so much. It must once have been very beautiful but there is little of it left to judge by. Apart from a good Head of Christ by Justus van Ghent, there is not much to see in the remaining rooms and any historic interest the pictures might have had is lost by the fact that they are all unlabelled.

Though it has some pleasant old streets and palaces, Città di Castello is not really worth making a special pilgrimage from Perugia or Arezzo to visit, but if you do so, I would suggest lunching at the Albergo Tiferno in the Piazza Raffaelle Sanzio just by S. Francesco. Tifernum was the ancient Latin name of the place and the inhabitants still call themselves Tifernati in the baffling way of Italian cities—like the Borghigiani of Sansepolcro.

Appendix

APPENDIX I

Gubbio

PUBLISHER'S NOTE : Mr. Lyall was also to have written on Umbria in this book, calling it *The Companion Guide to Tuscany and Umbria*. At the time of his death he was revising the manuscript of what he had written on Tuscany and had drafted the first Umbrian chapter—on the town of Gubbio. We include it here as the last piece of writing by this most modest, entertaining and likeable of men.

Gubbio is best known to the world at large on account of its Wolf. The *Fioretti di San Francesco* relate that St Francis was sojourning here when the town was terrorised by 'an exceeding great wolf, terrible and fierce, the which not only devoured animals but also men' and which lived just outside the Porta Victoria so that 'none durst go forth from that place.' The saint went out fearlessly, met Brother Wolf, made the sign of the cross over him and reproved him for his misdeeds. The great beast lay down, bowed his head and made other signs of penitence. St Francis proposed a treaty of peace by which the wolf would refrain from attacking the people of Gubbio and they in turn would feed him. The wolf gave him a paw in token of agreement and walked with him into the city 'in the fashion of a lamb.' There, in the presence of the astonished people of Gubbio, the wolf confirmed its agreement by once more laying its paw on the hand of the saint. The treaty was honourably kept on both sides. Unmolested and unmolesting, Brother Wolf walked freely in and out of the houses 'and never did any dog bark behind him,' while the citizens provided for his needs and were 'sorely grieved' when two years later he died of old age—or possibly (but this is not in the *Fioretti*) of overeating.

The importance of Iguvium as a centre of the ancient Umbrians is demonstrated by the discovery of the famous bronze tables known as the *Tabulæ Eugubinæ*, which were found under the Roman theatre in

227

1444, and its importance in Roman times is proved by the size of that same theatre, in which classical plays are still given to-day. (They were doing the *Amphitryon* of Plautus there the last time I was in Gubbio.) The city has through much of its history shared the fortunes of the Marches and for two or three centuries it belonged to the Montefeltro Dukes of Urbino and to their successors, the della Rovere, until the last of that dynasty bequeathed his duchy to the Church in 1624. Gubbio only became a part of Umbria in 1860.

The city is well worth the drive over the rough mountain road from Perugia, less on account of any individual works of art which it contains than because, more than almost any place of its size in Italy, it preserves the character of an unspoilt medieval city. As you breast the last hill on the road from Perugia, its noble rectangular palaces rise in tiers up the mountainside like an early cubist painting. Especially in the northern and eastern parts of the city there are entire streets of thirteenth- and fourteenth-century houses. Many of them still have the curious *porta del morto*, the dead man's door, a narrow door beside the broad main door, which is traditionally supposed to have been used only for bringing a coffin out of the house. Some prosaic scholars, however, say it was simply the entrance to the living quarters above the warehouse or workshop on the ground floor, used when the latter was evacuated or blocked up in time of trouble. But the legend is picturesque and one hopes it may be true. The town is built on the lower slopes of Monte Ingino and the upper part consists of two or three long parallel streets connected, as at Assisi, by steep ramps or staircases.

Gubbio was a minor centre of the arts. Like several other towns in this part of Italy—Deruta, Pesaro, Gualdo Tadino and Faenza, which has given its name to faience—it was long famous for its ceramic production. In the early sixteenth century a certain Maestro Giorgio Andreoli brought with him from his native Lombardy the secret of a ruby lustre which made the city famous. He was granted handsome privileges in return for setting up an industry here. The secret of the glaze has been long lost, but there is a good example in the Palazzo dei Consoli and there are several in the Victoria and Albert Museum and the Wallace Collection in London. Gubbio had its own school of painting founded in the thirteenth century by the half-mythical Oderisi whom Dante met in Purgatory. (The path of salvation is a narrow one indeed. Oderisi was sent to Purgatory for excess of zeal and pride in his chosen art of miniature-painting. Had he displayed too little zeal, he would doubtless have been sent down to the Inferno on a charge of sloth.) The Siena-influenced Guido Palmerucci was the principal painter of the fourteenth century, and Ottaviano Nelli of the fifteenth. The best of the Eugubine painters, he may be said to belong to the Gothic school of Gentile da Fabriano and like him derived much from the miniaturists.

Gubbio, with some six thousand people to-day, cannot fill its medieval walls. It is said that it once had thirty thousand inhabitants and it is known to have sent a thousand cavaliers to the First Crusade. Its form of government varied during the Communal period—now Consuls, now Priors. Most curious of all was an official called the Constable, who was a dictator elected every year for the twelve days of the Feast of St Ubaldo in May. In 1384 the city solved its internal problems by surrendering itself into the power of Count Antonio da Montefeltro and thenceforward shared the fortunes of Urbino.

In the level plain at the bottom of the hill is a large open space called the Piazza dei Quaranta Martiri, who were not the Forty Martyrs of Sivas commemorated in the Albanian port of Santi Quaranta, but forty hostages shot by the Germans no longer ago than June 1944 as a reprisal for partisan activities in the neighbourhood. From here there is a good view up the hill to the great square Palace of the Consuls and the Pretorio. Above, at the rim of the city, are the Ducal Palace and the Cathedral, and behind them rise the steep slopes of Monte Ingino, studded with slender cypresses.

At one side of the Piazza is the great thirteenth-century Gothic church of S. Francesco, the work of Fra Bevignate, the architect who designed the Great Fountain at Perugia. Unlike most Franciscan churches it has three aisles, and the apse at the end of the left one contains frescoes of the life of the Virgin by Ottaviano Nelli, which were only discovered in 1942. Fourteenth- and fifteenth-century frescoes by unknown artists decorate the other walls. On the other side of the Piazza is a long covered portico or colonnade dating from the fourteenth century and called the Weavers' Gallery, because it was used by the members of the Weavers' Guild to spread out their wares.

From here we go north across the brook through an old medieval quarter, past the beautifully preserved Palazzo Bargello of 1300, until we come to the very typical Via dei Consoli with its double line of medieval houses and its pottery shops (for the art has recently been revived in Gubbio—without, it would seem, producing a Maestro Giorgio). It takes its name from the Palace of the Consuls on the right. This imposing Romanesque building rises three hundred feet from the level of the Via Baldassini at its foot, on the west side. In front of it is the large open Piazza della Signoria with a balustrade overlooking the city and opposite is the Palazzo Pretorio, which now contains the communal offices and archives. The architect, Gattapone of Gubbio, designed the two palaces and the square as an architectural whole and he has very well succeeded in his aim. The height of the Consuls' Palace is emphasised by its straight, unbroken wall spaces, set off by a loggia at the top story, crowned by machicolations and battlements and a slender belfry.

Entering by a beautiful fan-shaped flight of steps from the Piazza, we find ourselves in an enormous hall designed for public assemblies and covering almost the entire extent of the building. Called the Salone dell' Arengo ('Harangue,' not 'Herring'), it contains among other things some restored frescoes by Guido Palmerucci, the pupil of Oderisi and master of Martino Nelli, the father of Ottaviano. In the small museum just off it are the much studied and discussed Eugubine Tables. These are seven leaves or sheets of bronze, some of which are inscribed in Latin characters and others in Etruscan, but all of them in the Umbrian tongue. They date from about 200 B.C. and appear to be the rules of a body of priests called the Attidian Brethren. Had they only been written in Etruscan instead of in Umbrian, scholars might very possibly have deciphered that language by now. In the Sala del Consiglio on the top floor is a collection of pictures mainly by Eugubine masters. Oderisi has left no known works behind him, but Palmerucci, with a lovely tondo of the Madonna and Child, the Nelli, the Nucci and their followers are all well represented here. You can step out on to the loggia and enjoy a good view over the medieval roofs of the city.

From the Via XX Settembre, which the Via dei Consoli has by now become, the Via Ducale leads steeply up to the Cathedral and the Ducal Palace. The Duomo dates from the thirteenth century and has an impressive Gothic interior. It contains little of interest apart from some sixteenth-century paintings by the two Nucci of Gubbio, Timoteo Viti of Urbino, the first master of Raphael, and two pupils of Perugino, Sinibaldo Ibi and Eusebio di S. Giorgio.

Opposite it is the entrance to the Palazzo Ducale, a delightful little palace in the style, on an infinitely smaller scale, of the Ducal Palace at Urbino. It was built about 1470 by Duke Federico Montefeltro and it is thought that it may have been actually designed by Luciano Laurana, the Dalmatian architect of the Urbino palace. Other authorities attribute it to Francesco di Giorgio Martini of Siena. Allowed to fall into ruin in the last century but now well restored, it is built round a delightful arcaded Renaissance courtyard, in which the elegant colonnade is of white stone and the pavement of red brick. Above, up the staircase on the right, are a series of well proportioned rooms with carved doors, chimney-pieces and ceilings in the manner of Urbino, with the monograms of the Dukes Federico and Guidobaldo and the badge with the oak leaves of the della Rovere. The travelling coach of the Dukes is preserved here.

It was in this little palace that Battista Sforza, the wife of Federico, died soon after giving birth to a son. The story goes that she offered her life if God would give her an heir after she had produced eight daughters. Federico, riding night and day, just arrived in time to see her fulfil her part of the bargain. Their likenesses, she pale and distinguished-looking with fair hair drawn tightly back and he with his round red hat and his sword-slashed nose, are familiar to us from the Piero della Francesca portraits in the Uffizi. There are probably no Renaissance princes we feel we know so well as these Montefeltro Dukes and their Duchesses. The cultivated court of his son Guidobaldo at Urbino, where they sat discussing such subjects as philosophy, Platonic love, the classics and the character of the gentleman until dawn broke in the sky, has been perfectly described by Baldassare Castiglione in his book *The Courtier*. Federico, made a Knight of the Garter in 1474 by Edward IV of England, was one of the greatest *condottiere* generals in Italy, but in spite of that he, like his son Guidobaldo, contrived to be a humane and enlightened ruler of his little state, the Renaissance despot at his best. When he was away campaigning, Battista held the reins of government in her capable hands. Gubbio chose wisely when she threw in her lot with Urbino rather than with Perugia.

We go down again to the Via Savelli della Porta, the parallel street below the Via XX Settembre and turn lefthanded towards the Porta Romana. The little sixteenth-century church of S. Francesco della Pace on the left is said to mark the spot where Brother Wolf used to sleep after he was tamed by St Francis. On the right is the church of S. Maria Nuova, which may be the work of Gattapone and which contains the acknowledged masterpiece of the Eugubine school, Ottaviano Nelli's tempera painting of the Madonna del Belvedere. The design is most satisfying, the colours gay and yet delicate in the manner of Gentile da Fabriano. The Virgin and Child sit enthroned in the centre, surrounded by angel musicians, while God the Father in a mist of angels holds a crown over her head. Framing the picture on either side, two bearded saints present the donors of the fresco.

At the end of the Via Savelli we come to the picturesque Via

231

Dante and the medieval Porta Romana. Just outside it is the thirteenth-century church of S. Agostino, which contains some more of the works of Ottaviano Nelli. The Madonna over the second altar on the right is his and so are all the paintings in the chancel. There is a Last Judgment over the chancel arch and on the walls of the choir twenty-six scenes from the life of St Augustine. Having been for centuries covered by whitewash, they are in good condition and have not been restored, but their uneven quality leads to the suspicion that not all of them come from the hand of the master himself. Interesting are the faces of the dead saint's mourners, which were no doubt portraits of fifteenth-century civic notables.

The patron saint of Gubbio is St Ubaldo. He was Bishop Ubaldo Baldassini, who miraculously saved the city when it was besieged by the Emperor Frederick Barbarossa in the twelfth century. His body lies in the basilica of S. Ubaldo on the top of Monte Ingino which overhangs the town (and his episcopal cap I found by the purest chance when exploring the ancient church of S. Urbano off the Appian Way just outside Rome). Every year on his feast day, 15th May, the famous Festival of the Ceri takes place, when one of the strangest races in the world is run in his honour. It is a race upon which no betting is possible, for the finishing order has not varied since the Middle Ages. The Ceri literally means the Candles, but some would derive the name from an ancient Umbrian festival in honour of Ceres, the Corn Goddess. They are three enormous wooden erections mounted on platforms and shaped rather like gigantic hour-glasses. (Year-glasses at the very least they would be.) They remind one a little of rude, wasp-waisted female idols and one wonders whether there may not be something in the Ceres theory after all. On top of the front one is an image of St Ubaldo, belonging to the masons; of the second one of St George, belonging to the merchants; and of the third one of St Antony, belonging to the peasants. Teams of strong men called *ceraioli* shoulder the platforms, dressed in white trousers and red scarves, with yellow shirts for St Ubaldo, blue shirts for St George and black shirts for St Antony.

At dawn trumpets awaken the captain who, sword in hand and attended by a second captain and a herald, is in charge of the proceedings. After a great luncheon presided over by the authorities, the *ceraioli* parade the town with the Ceri and at six o'clock the serious business begins with the blessing of the Ceri. The race itself starts from the Piazza Signoria, when the teams shoulder the platforms and race with the swaying Ceri through the ripid, dusty streets of the city and then by way of the even steeper serpentine path up the side of Monte

Ingino to the church of St Ubaldo on the summit. The record is said to be twelve minutes. As the Ceri always start in the same order and as there is no possibility of one overtaking the other on the narrow track, the result of the race is a foregone conclusion. First place to St Ubaldo; second to St George; third to St Antony.

Food and Wine in Tuscany and Umbria

The Tuscan, like the Bolognese or the Venetian, is one of the recognised gastronomic schools of Italy. That of Umbria, on the other hand, is less distinctive. It is a blend of the cuisines of Tuscany and Latium, so that the remarks on Tuscan cooking in general hold good for Umbria also. Among the *antipasti* of the two regions may be mentioned the ham of Volterra, celebrated for nearly five hundred years, the sausages and ham from the Casentino and the *mallegato* of Pisa, which is salami made from pig's blood mixed with lard, raisins and pine kernels. *Mazzafegati* ('kill-livers') are sweet liver-sausages from Umbria. Norcia has for centuries been so famous for its salami that in Umbria a salami merchant is called a *norcino*. Norcia is well known also for its black truffles, which are really grey-brown. In some other parts of Umbria the larger and more highly perfumed white truffle is common. But truffles are found in most of the hilly areas and once in San Gimignano I bought a dozen black truffles in a twist of brown paper from a man who swore he had gathered them the day before. Very good they were, too.

Regional specialities in the way of *paste* and *minestre* are *zuppa di fagioli alla fiorentina*, white beans stewed with oil, onions, garlic, tomato sauce and various herbs; *risotto alla fiorentina*, rice cooked in meat sauce with chicken giblets; *pappardelle alla lepre*, which are lasagne with a gravy made of hare stew and served with bacon, onions, butter and grated parmesan cheese, a speciality of Arezzo; *cannelloni ripieni alla toscana*, large macaroni stuffed with a mixture of meat, chicken's livers, eggs, truffles and parmesan. Pisa boasts of its frog soup (a delicacy I have only tasted so far in Hong Kong where the fried frog's fat is served in coconut milk) and its white bean soup of San Michele. Risotto and spaghetti are often served with truffles (*'ai tartufi'*) in Umbria.

Leghorn is the centre for sea-fish with its *triglie alla livornese*, red mullet with pepper and chopped tomato (*alla livornese* always involves tomatoes); *cacciucco*, also a speciality of Leghorn, is a fish soup cooked in oil with tomatoes, onions, pepper, garlic and a little red wine added; *arselle alla livornese* are mussels cooked in the shell in the same way as *cacciucco*. *Ceche* are elvers from the mouth of the Arno, cooked in oil and they are in season in January. The Pisans pride themselves on their *anguille in ginocchioni,* 'eels on their knees,' from the Arno. Trout are to be found in the Apennine streams and in the Casentino. Lake Trasimeno in Umbria yields all kinds of fresh-water fish, such as carp, pike and the great eels called *capitoni,* the traditional dish of Italians on Christmas Eve. Trout and eel are to be found in a number of Umbrian rivers, tench in Lake Piediluco and fresh-water prawns in the Clitunno.

The Tuscan cuisine specialises in meat, and the grilled beefsteak known as *bistecca alla fiorentina* is famous all over Italy. *Bistecca alla cacciatora* is cooked with garlic, onions, salt, pepper, tomato and red wine. *Agnello, pollo* and *quaglie alla cacciatora* are lamb, chicken and quail respectively done in the same way. *Pollo alla diavola* is devilled chicken, as its name implies. *Porchetta,* cold roast sucking pig stuffed with fragrant herbs, is another favourite in Umbria as in Latium and the Marches. Pork chops, *cotolette di maiale alla pisana,* are a Pisan delicacy. *Arrista* is loin of pork roasted with herbs on a spit or in an oven. *Cinghiale alla maremmana,* the richest and tenderest of all the pork dishes, is wild boar from the Maremma cooked with tomatoes and herbs and served with onions. *Arrosto d'agnello all' aretina* is leg of lamb soaked for some hours in oil and condiments and roasted on a spit. *Fegatelli alla fiorentina* consists of chopped pig's liver with fennel and other herbs.

Game is a great feature of the Tuscan cuisine and some of its specialities, besides the quail and wild boar mentioned above, include pheasant (*fagiano alla carovana*), jugged hare (*salmi di lepre*), stuffed partridge (*starna*), thrushes (*tordi*), on a spit and *salmi* of woodcock (*beccaccia*). The forest of Migliarino near Pisa is famous as a source of game of all kinds. The Umbrians eat a great many wood-pigeons (*palombe*) in March and October, when they pass through on the annual migrations. They either roast them on a spit or make them into a *salmi.* Try *palombacce alla todina.*

All the fruits of the temperate zone flourish in their due season. The Pisans boast in particular of the cherries of Palaia and of Lari, and the Aretines of the giant water melons of the Val di Chiana and the chestnuts and walnuts of the Casentino. White figs stuffed with almonds and nuts are exported from Amélia in Umbria.

Of cheeses we may single out the sheep's cheese or *pecorino* from the Casentino, whether fresh, when it is called *caciotta,* or ripened for grating like parmesan; the *brancolino,* cow's cheese like a soft paste from the

235

Lucchesìa; and the sheep's *crete* from Valdarno. The sweet fresh cheese called *ricotta* is much eaten in Umbria.

An astonishing number of these towns have their own specialities in the way of sweets and pastries. Among the best known is the *panforte* of Siena, made of flour, almonds, white cane sugar, orange and lemon peel, cinnamon and other spices. *Copate* and *ricciarelli* are other local specialities, as are the ice-creams called *baci di Siena*. The *schiacciate* of Pisa are pastries filled with fresh cheese mixed with sugar and cinnamon. There are the *bucellati* of Lucca; the *mandorlato* of San Gimignano; the *brigidini* of Lamporecchio; the *menta*, sugar-sticks flavoured with mint, of Viareggio; the *copate* of Siena; the *torta* of Pontasserchio. Many of these sweets are linked to some special season of the year, as the Pisan *schiacciate* to Easter, and the Perugian *torcolo, finocciata* and *ossi di morto* and the *pan peperato* of Terni to Christmas.

The wines of the two regions are famous far beyond the boundaries of Italy. In particular, the Chianti from the hills between Florence and Siena is recognisable the world over by the shape of its bottles. These are bulbous, with longish necks, and cannot be stood upright without the assistance of the plaited straw holders which provide them with a solid base. Astonishing as it may seem, these straw containers, of which hundreds of thousands must be used every year, are all made by hand. Once, in the red brick Gothic *castello* of Certaldo, where Boccaccio lived out his old age and died, I came on a large motor lorry containing thousands of these round-bottomed bottles, looking very naked and helpless, which it was delivering from door to door to the women who sat inside all day plaiting the straw petticoats with their deft fingers. It is a flourishing cottage industry in many of these little Tuscan towns.

Chianti is generally red, although there are a number of white Chiantis. There are also good white *vernaccias* such as that of San Gimignano and a number of sweet dessert wines made under such names as *passito*, *vinsanto* and *moscato* in different parts of Tuscany. Elba comes second only to the Chianti country for wine production, but I have found it more convenient to deal with its red and white wines in the chapter on the island. The glory of Umbria is the white Orvieto, which comes in two varieties, the dry (*secco*) and the sweet (*abboccato*). Orvieto was well known in all the officers' messes of South Italy twenty years ago, for according to the legend the grateful proprietor, Signor Bigi, presented a fabulous quantity to the British, who had saved his vineyards from destruction by the retreating Germans.

Hotels List

❧

Class of Hotel

L. Luxury Class **A.** First Class Hotel **B.** Second Class Hotel **C.** Third Class Hotel

ALTOPASCIO

C. I Cavalieri del Tau

AREZZO

B. Astoria   Europa
    Chiavi D'Oro   Graverini
    Continentale   Minerva

C. Autostazione   Etruria
    Da Cecco   San Marco

BAGNI DI LUCCA

C. La Corona

CAMPIGLIA MARITTIMA

C. Marconi   Rossi

CAPOLIVERI – (Elba)

B. Elba International   Della Lacona

C. Frank's   Le Acacie

CARRARA

B. Michelangelo

C. Da Roberto   San Marco

Hotels

CASTIGLIONE DELLA PESCAIA

A. Alleluiah   Riva Del Sole

B. David Poggiodoro   L'Approdo
Park Hotel Zibellino

C. Bristol   Miramare
Roma

CECINA

B. Stazione

C. Il Gabbiano   Il Settebello
La Smeralda   Massimo
Mediterraneo   Nelly
Stella Marina   Tornese

CHIUSI

C. Centrale   Longobardi
La Sfinge Etrusca

CORTONA

B. Villa Gugliemesca

C. Garibaldi   Portole
Italia

FORTE DEI MARMI

L. Augustus

A. Alcione   Raffaelli Park Hotel
President

B. Acapulco   Bijou
Astoria Garden

C. Carducci   Frisco
Elbano   Villa Cristina
Excelsior

LUCCA

B. Napoleon   Universe

C. Celido   Perduca
   Di Poggio   Piero Doro
   Ilaria   Rex
   La Luna

MASSA MARITTIMA

C. Duca Del Mare

MARCIANA – (Elba)

A. Del Golfo

B. Desiree   La Perla
   Fontalecco   Monna Lisa
   Hotel di Procchio

C. Brigantino   Delfino

MONTE ARGENTARIO – (Port 'Ercole)

A. Il Pellicano

B. Don Pedro

C. Stella Marina

MONTECATINI TERME

B. Columbia   Mediterraneo
   De La Ville   Minerva
   Ercolini & Savi   Salus
   Francia & Quirinale   San Marco
   Manzoni   Select-Petrolini

C. Adua   Brennero E Varsavia
   Ambrosiano   Bristol
   Bellandi   Buonamici
   Belvedere Vallini   Cavallotti
   Biondi   Continentale

239

Hotels

PIETRASANTA

A. Lombardi

B. Adrianna   Il Settebello
   Eden Park   Villa Ombrosa

C. Coluccini   Motel E-1
   Esperia   Orione
   Il Caravaggio   Villa I Tamerici

PIOMBINO

B. Centrale

C. Ariston   Esperia
   Aurora   Joli
   Baia Toscana   La Sosta
   Collode   Tuscania

POGGIBONSI

B. Alcide

C. Italia

PONTEDERA

B. La Rotunda

C. Armonia

PORTOFERRAIO – (Elba)

A. Hermitage

B. Adriana   Picchiaie Residence
   Darsena   Residence
   Garden   Touring
   Massimo

C. Ape Elbana   Villa Ottone
   Villa Fonteviva   Novel

240

PISA

A. Dei Cavalieri   Mediterraneo-Costa
    Grand Hotel Duomo

B. Ariston   Roma
    Arno   Royal Victoria
    Capitol   Terminus E. Plaza
    D'Azeglio   Touring
    La Pace   Villa Kinzica
    Nettuno

C. Bologna   Moderno
    Cecile   Pisa
    Fenice   Roseto

PISTOIA

B. Milano

C. Appennino   Patria
    Leon Bianco

SAN MINIATO

C. Miravalle

SIENA

A. Excelsior   Villa Scacciapensieri
    Park Hotel Marzocchi

B. Continental   Minerva
    Garden   Moderno

C. Cannon D'Oro   La Toscana
    Chiusarelli   Villa Terraia
    Italia

VIAREGGIO

A. Astor Hotel & Residence   Grand Hotel
    De Russie e Plaza   Palace

Hotels

C. La Pace   Nuovo Hotel Firenze
London   Tusismo
Luperi   Villa Ombrosa
Metropol

VOLTERRA

B. Nazionale

C. Etruria

APPENDIX IV

Useful Addresses

Tuscany and Umbria are comprised in the Consular District of Florence. The British Consulate is at Lungarno Corsini 2 (Tel. 284133 and 272594) and the U.S. Consulate at Lungarno Vespucci 38 (Tel. 298276).

Florence—Ente Provinciale di Turismo; Lungarno Mediceo 57.

Massa—Ente Provinciale di Turismo; Via Mazzini 14. A.C.I.; Automobile Club, Viale delle Nazioni.

Lucca—Ente Provinciale di Turismo; Piazza Guidoccioni 2. A.C.I.; Via Catalani 1.

Pistoia—Ente Provinciale di Turismo; Corso Gramsci 110. A.C.I.; Via Panciatichi 3.

Prato—Associazione Turistica Pratese, Via Cairoli 48. Automobile Club; Via S. Giovanni.

Pisa—Ente Provinciale di Turismo; Lungarno Mediceo 57. A.C.I.; Via S. Martino I.

Livorno—Ente Provinciale di Turismo; Piazza Cavour 6. A.C.I.; Via Verdi 32.

Grosseto—Ente Provinciale di Turismo; Viale Ximenes 21. A.C.I.; Via Bonghi 1.

Siena—Ente Provinciale di Turismo; Via di Città 35. A.C.I.; Viale Vittorio Venito 47.

Arezzo—Ente Provinciale di Turismo; Piazza Guido Monaco 1. A.C.I.; Via Roma 18.

Perugia—Ente Provinciale di Turismo; Corso Vannucci 5. A.C.I.; Via Mazzini.

Terni—Ente Provinciale di Turismo; Via Pacinotti 2. A.C.I.; Viale della Stazione.

Portoferraio—Ente per la Valorizzazione dell'Isola d'Elba, Piazza della Repubblica 22.

Assisi—Azienda Autonoma di Turismo; Piazza del Comune 12.

Chianciano—Azienda Autonoma di Cura; Via Varelle.

Useful Addresses

Gubbio—Azienda Autonoma di Soggiorno e Turismo; Piazza Oderisi 6.

Viareggio—Azienda Autonoma Riviera della Versilia; Viale Carducci 12.

Castiglioncello—Azienda Autonoma di Soggiorno e Turismo, Via Aurelia 959.

Bagni di Lucca—Azienda Autonoma di Cura, Viale Umberto 103.

Marina di Massa—Azienda di Cura e Soggiorno; Lungomare Vespucci 24.

Montecatini Terme—Azienda Autonoma di Cura; Viale Verdi.

Index

Index

Index

Index

Index

LEGHORN
7
Ardenso
• *Montenero*

Rosignano

Cecina R. *Cecina*

9 Termed
Bagnor

S. *Vincenzo*

Venturina

Populonia
Piombino *Follonica*
9

Elba
Portoferraio
8 *Procchio* *Porto Azzurro* *Castiglione*

I. di Capraia

S. Gim
Volt

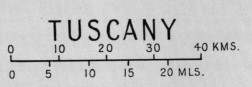

TUSCANY

0   10   20   30   40 KMS.

0   5   10   15   20 MLS.

Numbers in red refer to chapters
which describe the areas indicated

I. de Giglio